AF184258

A European Legal Framework for Nuclear Liability

Rethinking Current Approaches

Tobias Heldt

A European Legal Framework for Nuclear Liability

Rethinking Current Approaches

intersentia

METRO

Ius Commune Europaeum

Tobias Heldt

A European Legal Framework for Nuclear Liability. Rethinking Current Approaches

Intersentia Publishing Ltd.
Sheraton House | Castle Park
Cambridge | CB3 0AX | United Kingdom
Tel.: +44 1223 370 170 | Email: mail@intersentia.co.uk

ISBN 978-1-78068-355-3
D/2015/7849/136
NUR 825

© 2015 Intersentia
Cambridge – Antwerp – Portland
www.intersentia.com | www.intersentia.co.uk

Cover picture: Atucha Nuclear Power Plant (Argentina) – © Tobias Heldt, October 2014.

British Library Cataloguing in Publication Data. A catalogue record for this book is available from the British Library.

No part of this book may be reproduced in any form, by print, photocopy, microfilm or any other means, without written permission from the publisher.

Tobias Heldt

ACKNOWLEDGMENTS

When I started this PhD project in October 2011, the day of the finalisation of this book seemed to lie in the very distant future and I felt that I would have plenty of time to delve into the topic of nuclear liability and its different aspects and challenges. Looking back, I must say that the 4 years scheduled for this project went by extremely fast. Reasons for this can certainly be found in the set-up of this project that enabled me to meet and work with very interesting people within Europe and even around the entire world. I will therefore use the following paragraphs to thank those who enabled this journey and set the foundations for this book.

The research as presented in this book has been carried out at Maastricht University and the Belgian Nuclear Research Centre (SCK•CEN) and was also partially sponsored by GDF Suez S.A. (now Engie S.A.). Conducting this research, I also had the opportunity to visit and speak at plenty of conferences and workshops. The exchange and insights received and experiences made at these occasions were very valuable not only for my research but also for my personal development. I am therefore grateful to the organisations just mentioned that they have given me the opportunity to take this journey during the last 4 years.

I am also very thankful to the members of my reading committee, Gerrit van Maanen, Hubert Bocken, Tom Hartlief and Louis Visscher, for having taken the time to read my manuscript and provide additional food for thoughts on the topic of nuclear liability and the regulation of the nuclear sector in the European Union.

Being a cooperation between Maastricht University and SCK•CEN, this project gave me the unique opportunity to conduct research under the academic supervision of Michael Faure and the creative mentorship of Ludo Veuchelen. It is these two people to whom I want to express my biggest words of thanks. Michael's style of supervision allowed me to conduct my research very independently whilst he always provided guidance when it was needed. Meetings with him were always extremely constructive and there was not a single meeting that I did not leave with a clear focus and new energy and motivation to proceed. Michael, thank you for this and your patience and wit that have helped me to successfully complete this project!

As mentioned in the previous paragraph, the second person that deserves special attention and a separate word of thanks is Ludo Veuchelen. Being the father of this project it is indeed true that without him this project would not have existed. It is equally true, that without him this book would not look as it does now. With his experience and knowledge about the nuclear industry that he has gained during his professional career, he provided invaluable input during the time of my research and triggered me at numerous occasions to rethink approaches that I had chosen and to stay an out-of-the-box thinker. Next to this professional guidance, Ludo was also an important companion on a personal level. I always felt very welcome at his house in Binkom where we spent numerous evenings together enjoying a match of football, good music or the wonderful food of the wonderful Caroline. Ludo, I am sincerely grateful for your support and full acceptance and appreciation of me and my work!

I also want to thank a number of other people from the faculty that have supported me on all kinds of levels during my doctoral research. First and foremost this is of course the METRO team. Yleen Simonis, Chantal Kuypers, Elke Hundhausen, Marjo Mullers and Marina Jodogne were always of great assistance and offered friendly support whenever I had a question or needed help. I also want to express my gratitude towards Diana Schabregs and Licette Poll who never got tired of explaining to me all kinds of financial arrangements surrounding the 4 years of my doctoral research.

Lastly I also want to thank the 'non-academic' supporters of this project for giving me the strength and balance needed over the last years to finish this project successfully. As much as I enjoyed the international set-up of this project and to meet and discuss with different people at conferences, it has always been the quality time spent with good friends and family that gave me the energy to finish this book.

Tobias HELDT

CONTENTS

PART III.
THE WAY FORWARD

LIST OF FIGURES AND TABLES

ABBREVIATIONS

ABGB	Allgemeines Bürgerliches Gesetzbuch
ALARP	As Low As Reasonably Practicable
CDCIR	Community Documentation Centre on Industrial Risks
CJEU	Court of Justice of the European Union
CLC	Convention on Civil Liability for Oil Pollution Damage
CSC	Convention on Supplementary Compensation
CSR	Corporate Social Responsibility
ECH	European Chemicals Agency
EIA	Environmental Impact Assessment
ENSREG	European Nuclear Safety Regulators Group
EPZ	Elektriciteits Produktiemaatschappij Zuid-Nederland
EU	European Union
HPC	Hinkley Point C
IAEA	International Atomic Energy Agency
IBER	Insurance Block Exemption Regulation
ICJ	International Court of Justice
IPPC	Integrated Pollution Prevention and Control
MAPP	Major Accident Prevention Policy
MARPOL	International Convention for the Prevention of Pollution From Ships
MARS	Major Accident Reporting System
NEA	Nuclear Energy Agency
NGO	Non-Governmental Organisation
NPP	Nuclear Power Plant
OECD	Organisation for Economic Co-operation and Development
ONR	Office for Nuclear Regulation
OPA	Oil Pollution Act
SDR	Special Drawing Rights
SOLAS	International Convention for the Safety of Life at Sea
SOS	Sudden Oil Spills
TEU	Treaty on European Union
TFEU	Treaty on the Functioning of the European Union
UK	United Kingdom
US	United States

GENERAL INTRODUCTION

Background

On the 11th of March 2011 Japan was hit by an earthquake and a devastating tsunami which resulted in the biggest nuclear accident since Chernobyl. Four years after this accident happened, the entire extent of the negative consequences that this accident has had, and will have on humans and the environment is still not clear. What, however, became painfully clear is that existing regulatory regimes do not offer sufficient protection against nuclear accidents or for their mitigation. The unprecedented inappropriateness of the applicable liability limits is only one point on a long list of flaws. Naturally, the accident at Fukushima sent a shock wave throughout the entire world and nuclear power generation and its regulation has been high on the agenda. Historic events can have an influence on how legal rules are shaped and developed.[1] The Fukushima accident certainly qualifies as such an historic event and showed that due to the immense damage that can result from a nuclear accident, special rules are needed for the regulation of a sector that can cause such enormous losses.

In the years before the accident at Fukushima, the European Union was undergoing a nuclear renaissance. Since then, things have changed and the differences between Member States with regard to their attitudes towards nuclear energy production have become more and more apparent and a point of political discourse. With regard to nuclear energy production there is no common approach within the European Union. According to article 194 TFEU Member States are free to determine their energy policy which results in a split within the European Union between nuclear and non-nuclear countries

1 Van Dam 2009, p. 282.

Figure 1. Overview Nuclear Energy Countries in the EU 2008[2]

Whilst there are currently 131 nuclear power plants in operation in the European Union, some Member States, such as Germany and Belgium, have decided to phase out nuclear energy, contrary to others that still rely heavily on nuclear energy. Some Member States have decided to increase the capacity of their existing plants and some even have plans for the construction of new facilities.

Table 1. Overview NPPs in the EU[3]

Country	Reactors operable	Percentage of total electricity production	Reactors under construction (gross electric output in megawatts)	Reactors planned (gross electric output in megawatts)	Reactors proposed (gross electric output in megawatts)
Belgium	7	51	0	0	0
Bulgaria	2	31.6	0	1 (950)	0
Czech Republic	6	35.3	0	2 (2400)	1 (1200)

2 File taken from Wikimedia Commons; http://en.wikipedia.org/wiki/File:European_Union_map_Nuclear_Energy_Countries.png (last accessed on 21 August 2015).

3 Www.world-nuclear.org/info/Facts-and-Figures/World-Nuclear-Power-Reactors-and-Uranium-Requirements/ (last accessed on 21 August 2015).

Country	Reactors operable	Percentage of total electricity production	Reactors under construction (gross electric output in megawatts)	Reactors planned (gross electric output in megawatts)	Reactors proposed (gross electric output in megawatts)
Finland	4	32.6	1 (1700)	0	2 (2700)
France	58	74.8	1 (1720)	1 (1720)	1 (1100)
Germany	9	16.1	0	0	0
Hungary	4	45.9	0	2 (2400)	0
Italy	0	0	0	0	10 (17000)
Lithuania	0	0	0	1 (1350)	0
Netherlands	1	4.4	0	0	1 (1000)
Poland	0	0	0	6 (6000)	
Romania	2	19.4	0	2 (1310)	1 (655)
Slovakia	4	53.8	2 (942)	0	1 (1200)
Slovenia	1	53.8	0	0	1 (1000)
Spain	7	20.5	0	0	0
Sweden	10	38.1	0	0	0
United Kingdom	16	18.1		4 (6680)	7 (8920)
Total	131		4 (4362)	19 (22 810)	25 (34 775)

The different attitudes towards nuclear energy within the European Union and the potential of these differences to create transboundary problems is reinforced by the location of nuclear power plants within the European Union because such plants are often located close to border regions.[4] This leads to a situation in which non-nuclear countries can also be influenced by the externalities of nuclear energy production in nuclear countries. It is safe to say that the generation of nuclear energy is a prime example for transboundary externalities. This situation necessitates a robust and stable legal framework for nuclear liability within the European Union, to accommodate the different interests at stake.

For an effective regulation of the nuclear sector a holistic approach is needed, making use of different regulatory and legislative tools that are available. The required holistic approach has several dimensions. It should be holistic in the sense that it should focus both on *ex ante* as well as *ex post* incentives. These incentives should furthermore be combined, so as to allow the most benefit from the advantages of regulation as well as liability.[5] Regulation of the nuclear sector should make use of the entire toolkit that regulators and law-makers have at their disposal. A smart mix of reflexive regulation,

4 For an overview of the location of NPPs in Europe see http://news.bbc.co.uk/2/hi/europe/4713398.stm (last accessed on 21 August 2015).

5 See Wiener 2010, p. 537.

strong and enforceable legal obligations combined with increased participation of the public and access to justice can live up to this challenge.

It should also be holistic with regard to the actors involved in the legislative and regulatory process. For decisions to be legitimate, they have to be taken by elected representatives on the basis of full information. Also in the nuclear sector, scientific expertise cannot replace political decision making. Fundamental choices have to be taken at a political level and with democratic legitimacy. To be able to do this, transparency will be a prerequisite as will a functioning collaboration between politicians, the nuclear industry and society as a whole. As a Canadian judge recently put it, 'political decision makers must be in a position to understand whether they are being asked to take a leap of faith, and if so, how big a leap it is.'[6]

Lastly it should be holistic in a more figurative sense, namely based on solidarity between states in a homogeneous risk community. The European Union can arguably be regarded as such a community. If nuclear energy is to remain a part of the energy mix, countries that do rely on nuclear energy have to accept their responsibilities towards other countries, especially non-nuclear countries, given the transboundary risk that nuclear energy generation poses. This, however, will only be achieved if a major readjustment of the regulatory landscape takes place. The nuclear sector has to realise that the Euratom Treaty, claiming that nuclear energy is needed for the well-being and prosperity of European citizens, no longer provides the right forum for the regulation of a mature nuclear sector.

Research questions

In the light of the observations in the previous section, three main research questions can be specified.

Question 1: *Is the nuclear sector within the European Union currently regulated in a way that guarantees effective liability regimes for nuclear accidents?*

Question 2: *If question 1 has to be answered negatively, is the European legislator in a position to remedy these shortcomings by providing an improved European regime for nuclear liability?*

Question 3: What should a European regime for nuclear liability look like and how can the relevant stakeholders be convinced of its necessity?

To answer these main research questions, they will be divided into a number of sub-questions.

6 Judge Russel 2014 FC 463, para. 312, Ottawa, Ontario.

Part I will analyse from a theoretical perspective *according to which core paradigms ultra-hazardous activities should be regulated and the extent to which the oil, chemical and nuclear sectors are regulated in accordance with such paradigms* (Question 1a).

Part II will focus on the European dimension and answer Question 2a *concerning the extent to which lessons can be learned from general principles of European Law and experiences of national systems for the design of a European regime for nuclear liability.* It will also analyse Question 2b *whether there is a sufficient legal basis providing the opportunity for a better and more coherent regulation of the nuclear sector.* Finally, next to the issue of legal competences, this part will also address Question 2c *whether centralised or a decentralised regulation of nuclear safety and liability should be preferred within the European Union.*

Part III lastly will turn to Question 3a, analysing *according to which major principles nuclear liability should be regulated.* It will also assess *how a liability system can enhance its inclusiveness and provide for a mutually reinforcing role of ex ante regulation and ex post liability* (Question 3b). Finally, to answer question 3c analysis will be needed of *how the feasibility and implementation of a new European regime for nuclear liability as suggested in this thesis can be enhanced.*

Structure and brief overview

The first part will describe the regulation of nuclear catastrophes and other hazardous activities, thereby identifying the current status quo and the challenges it provides. The second part will then specifically focus on the European dimension of nuclear liability. Part three will discuss how the European Union could become more active in the regulation of its nuclear sector, departing from current international principles and taking responsibility as a forerunner in the area of nuclear safety and liability for nuclear accidents.

Part I

The first part will start by laying down the theoretical framework of the regulation of ultra-hazardous activities (Chapter 1). Different forms of regulation will be analysed, thereby delineating the most effective way to regulate ultra-hazardous activities. Within this analysis the role of safety standards will be critically assessed and it will be argued that a required feature for effective safety standards is that the process of creating such standards has to be as interactive as possible, also involving the general public. The underlying idea of this claim is that the general public should have a say on issues that may significantly affect their lives, as is the case with nuclear safety. This is nothing but the reformulation of Lord Chief Justice Hewart's well-known aphorism that justice not only has to be done but seen to be done.[7] The analysis of different types of regulations will

7 R v Sussex Justices, Ex parte McCarthy [1924].

be complemented by an economic analysis of how to set the right incentives both from an *ex ante* approach and an *ex post* approach to guarantee a high level of nuclear safety.

Building upon the theoretical framework as discussed in chapter 1, chapter 2 will analyse three risk sectors in the European Union to test their respective robustness and regulatory effectiveness. The inter-sectoral comparison will focus on the chemical sector (2.2), oil pollution (2.3) and the nuclear sector (2.4). The different sectors will be analysed to see how they are regulated in practice and whether core principles as identified in the first chapter are present in these different sectors.

Part II

Chapter 3 will offer a closer examination of the current situation within the European Union. It will firstly give a quick overview of the international Conventions that are in force at the moment (3.1) and mention the core principles of these Conventions (3.2). Next to this a comparative overview of the legal systems in France, Germany, the UK and Austria will be given (3.3.). These countries have been chosen because they have very specific characteristics. France is relying heavily on nuclear energy whilst Germany has decided on a phase out. UK was included in the analysis to describe also the legal system of a common law country in more depth and the case of Austria will provide an analysis of a liability regime of a non-nuclear state. The discussion in these parts will necessitate an analysis of the status and relevance of some fundamental principles of European law in the nuclear sector (3.4). The chapter will end with a call for a re-thinking of the regulation of the European nuclear sector (3.5).

Chapter 4 will examine the competences of the European Union in the area of a regime for nuclear liability from an institutional law point of view. This will also necessitate a discussion on the relationship between the Euratom Treaty and the TFEU (4.1.) and the complications that result from having two independent treaties that both could potentially deal with the matter of a liability regime for nuclear accidents. Possible legal bases in the Euratom Treaty as well as in the Treaty on the Functioning of the European Union will be analysed to find the most suitable legal basis to build a European regime for nuclear liability upon (4.2.).

The question of whether harmonisation at the European level is a desirable option from an economic point of view will be discussed in chapter 5. An economic analysis of federalism will be done (5.1 and 5.2) to analyse whether calls for harmonisation are justified from this perspective. Possible alternatives to harmonisation will be presented to see whether a harmonised liability regime would indeed be the optimal solution or whether other means such as for example an enhanced use of mutual recognition and increased collaboration between the Member States could be more desirable (5.3). The chapter will provide a discussion on the advantages and disadvantages of establishing a harmonised regime for nuclear liability and nuclear safety respectively within the European Union (5.4).

Part III

Chapter 6 will analyse the core features that a European regime for nuclear liability should be built upon. An economic analysis of liability regimes (6.2) will be followed by the question whether a European regime should follow the trend in international conventions on nuclear liability to channel liability exclusively through the operator, or whether alternative approaches should be followed (6.3). This discussion will also take into account the increased globalisation and focus on the complex group structures of companies and how far this has an influence on the question of which form of channelling should be preferred. Different ways of funding will be discussed (6.5) before the chapter ends with a proposal for a European regime for nuclear liability (6.7).

Chapter 7 will start with an analysis of how far a European regime would be compatible with the international nuclear liability conventions and how a European system could be integrated into the existing ones (7.2). Next to issues of legality and compatibility of a European regime, the feasibility thereof will also be analysed in the last chapter of this thesis (7.3). A number of tools will be discussed that could enhance the chances that the relevant stakeholders would accept the proposal as suggested in chapter 6.

Part I

The Regulation of Ultra-hazardous Activities

The aim of the first part of this thesis is to provide an overview of how ultra-hazardous activities, including the nuclear sector, are regulated in the European Union and to scrutinise whether the way it is done is satisfactory. After a primarily theoretical description of the regulation of ultra-hazardous activities (Chapter 1) attention will turn to the experience gained in the oil, chemical and finally the nuclear sectors (Chapter 2).

The theoretical discussion of the regulation of ultra-hazardous activities in Chapter 1 will identify some core principles according to which such activities should be regulated. The hypothesis is that *ex ante* incentives, set via regulation combined with liability that can be established ex *post*, can guarantee the highest preventive effect possible. To substantiate this claim an economic analysis of liability rules and different modes of regulation will be done to delineate the most appropriate regime for the regulation of ultra-hazardous activities. Examples from the nuclear sector will already give a first idea of the status of core principles of regulation such as transparency and public involvement in the nuclear sector.

Chapter 2 will serve as what can be termed a 'reality check'. It analyses whether the core principles which have been identified within the theoretical framework of chapter 1 can indeed be found in the way ultra-hazardous activities are presently regulated within the European Union. Different high risk sectors such as the oil, chemical and finally the nuclear sectors are compared to each other, analysing why certain sectors have been regulated more in accordance with principles of good regulation than others.

Chapter 1

THE REGULATION OF ULTRA-HAZARDOUS ACTIVITIES – THE THEORETICAL FRAMEWORK

1.1. Setting the scene

The regulation of risks has always been a crucial issue within a society. Successfully regulating risks allows a society to flourish and to be successful. This has become even more difficult in recent times given the increased inter-connectedness of risk.[8] Consequently, it is unsurprising that our society has been described as a 'world risk society'.[9] The regulation of ultra-hazardous activities is a particularly difficult issue since such risks 'transcend not only territorial boundaries but also temporal dimensions.'[10] A further crucial point to note is that when it comes to risky activities, the notion of what constitutes risky is not a universal one. Risk perceptions differ from country to country.[11] This chapter will discuss a theoretical framework for the regulation of ultra-hazardous activities. It should be noted here that the focus of this chapter is not economic but social regulation. The former is concerned with market power and the prevention of monopolies to ensure a certain degree of competition, whereas the latter deals with issues of a higher degree of generality such as safety and environmental protection.[12]

The main question of this chapter is to what extent a combination of *ex ante* regulation and *ex post* liability can guarantee the prevention of accidents. I will assess how far regulation itself can serve as an effective means of prevention and in what way and to what extent the use of liability rules can be used as a further tool to ensure a high level of prevention. Relevant sub-questions, which are answered in the course of this analysis, are how far regulation and liability rules can be used as supplements in the first place and what different means of regulation can be identified and which would be preferable for the nuclear sector. Attention will also be paid to the question of how to design a system in a way where the general public is also more involved and how the accountability of the different actors involved can be ensured together with an effective system of enforcement.

8 Wiener *et al.* 2011, p. 3.
9 Beck 1998.
10 Arcuri 2005, p. 3.
11 Pesendorfer 2011, p. 283.
12 Ogus 1994, p. 4.

1.2. Liability rules and regulation – Mutually exclusive or complementary?

For decades scholars have examined the use of regulation and liability rules and their relationship with each other. In his seminal article on the joint use of regulation and liability rules, Shavell discusses four criteria to assess the respective advantages and disadvantages of liability rules and regulation: Differential knowledge, the possible lack of resources of the injurer to pay for the committed harm, the possibility that the injurer will escape prosecution, and administrative costs.[13]

Concerning possible information asymmetries between private parties and the regulator, Shavell points out that the question of who possesses superior information about the risky activity and other factors involved, is crucial when choosing between liability rules or regulation.[14] Kolstad *et al.* also argue that when making this choice the degree to which the possible harm is known also plays an important role. According to them, new harms are more likely to be regulated *ex ante* whilst tort liability will be imposed for familiar harms.[15]

An advantage of regulation would be that it mitigates the problem of a judgment proof injurer. In the case of very high damages it is highly possible that the injurer, even after being held liable will be unable to pay for the harm committed. Of course a distinction has to be made between smaller and larger firms, given the different financial capacities.[16] In the corporate world limited liability, one of the core characteristics of corporate law, can aggravate this further. Mechanisms such as piercing the corporate veil have the potential to mitigate this problem. This is, however, a very exceptional tool and not common in corporate law.[17] Consequently the problem of the insolvency of the injurer pertains. Relying more on regulation circumvents this problem. Therefore, there is an inclination to favour regulation when the likelihood is high that the possible harm could be greater than the available assets.[18]

Regarding the third aspect established by Shavell, namely the impact of the probability of a lawsuit on the choice between liability rules and regulation, it should be noted that if the probability of such a suit is zero then regulation should be used alone.[19] Without law suits being actually brought, liability rules will not be effective.[20] In some instances it might also be possible that the threat of a possible suit is non-existent due to other circumstances. The harm that results from the hazardous activity in question might be widely dispersed and each individual victim does not always suffer enough harm to have

13 Shavell 1984a, p. 359–364.
14 *Ibid.*, p. 359.
15 Kolstad, Ulen and Johnson 1990, p. 900.
16 Tilindyte 2012, p. 12.
17 Armour *et al.* 2009, p. 138–140.
18 Shavell 1984a, p. 361; Innes 2004, p. 32.
19 Kolstad, Ulen and Johnson 1990, p. 900.
20 Shavell 1984a, p. 363.

the motivation to file charges.[21] Obstacles such as establishing a causal link between the activity and the harm caused aggravate this further.[22] These problems are of particular importance in the field of ultra-hazardous activities, because harm resulting from such activities can often materialise at a later stage.

With regard to the respective costs of the two means of controlling risky activities, Shavell points out that if a certain activity is regulated, this will always involve costs regardless of whether or not an accident occurs.[23] Liability rules would have the advantage that only the few bad actors in a society would incur costs.[24] However, as a downside of liability rules, Wittman points out that *ex post* liability can be more costly for the state because of the process of calculating the damages. Simply paying a fine to the state would obviously not involve these costs.

An interesting point which Shavell also raises is that if regulation is combined with liability rules, the regulatory standard can be decreased below the level that would have been optimal if regulation alone had been used.[25] This can be beneficial in terms of the flexibility that results from this. A regulatory standard may be set at a level which is too high to ensure sufficient deterrent effect. If deterrence is ensured by supplementing liability rules, a lower regulatory standard leaves more flexibility which can be beneficial in terms of more production.

In conclusion, in the case of ultra-hazardous activities regulation and liability rules should not be regarded as a matter of either or, but as a useful complement.[26] Both *ex ante* regulation and *ex post* liability present certain advantages and combining them seems to be the best option.[27] It is this flexibility and openness which makes Shavell's argument for the joint use of liability rules and regulation a very convincing one because he introduces enough nuances into the discussion to identify an optimal system in which liability rules and regulation can indeed complement each other yet no definitive choice between the two is required.[28] Having established this, the following sections discuss some specific features of liability rules and regulation respectively and how these tools can prevent accidents. Section 1.2.1 presents a general economic analysis of liability systems, in order to delineate the most appropriate liability rule which regulation should be combined with. In section 1.2.2 reference will be made to different modes of regulation, analysing the appropriateness of the respective regulatory tools for ultra-hazardous activities.

21 Faure 2007, p. 220.
22 Landes and Posner 1984.
23 Shavell 1984a, p. 364.
24 *Ibid.*, p. 368.
25 Shavell 1984b, p. 272; Kolstad, Ulen and Johnson 1990, p. 889.
26 Arcuri 2005, p. 152.
27 Shavell 1984a, p. 365.
28 Faure 2007, p. 218.

1.2.1. *Features of liability rules*

In academic literature consensus can be found, that in the case of unilateral accidents, meaning that only the injurer can influence the accident risk, not only strict liability but also a rule of negligence can ensure an efficient level of care.[29] However, when analysing the two systems in more depth, certain particularities can be identified which will show a superiority of a rule of strict liability for unilateral accidents.

1.2.1.1. Negligence

In a system that follows a rule of negligence, an injurer is held liable if he did not fulfil a level of due care set by the courts.[30] This means that in the case of an accident, a victim might have to bear the resulting damages because the injurer was taking due care.[31] This reveals a weakness of the rule of negligence from a compensatory point of view. Given the importance of the injurer's level of care, it can be said that the negligence rule is based on a behavioural standard.[32] This behavioural standard can be seen as a possible source of weakness for a liability system based on a rule of negligence. Judges may set the wrong standard of care in a negligence case[33] which might then lead to undesirable outcomes. This problem can be further aggravated by cognitive illusions, such as for example the hindsight bias.[34]

Another point of contention under a rule of negligence is that an act of negligence has to be proven and this presents an additional burden involving further costs.[35] This argument is of particular interest when speaking about the combination of liability rules and regulation, because it would not carry too much weight when dealing with a sector that is also strictly regulated, since in the case of not complying with regulation, proving negligence will not be very difficult.[36]

1.2.1.2. Strict liability

In contrast to a negligence-based rule, under a system of strict liability an injurer will always have to pay for damages resulting from an accident which he caused.[37] Given that strict liability will dictate the potential injurer's behaviour *ex ante*,[38] hindsight bias is no

29 Faure and van den Bergh 1987, p. 97; Faure and Skogh 1992, p. 507; Faure 1995, p. 23; Schaefer and Mueller-Langer 2009, p. 10.
30 Shavell 2004, p. 180.
31 Schaefer and Mueller-Langer 2009, p. 10.
32 Stavang 2010, p. 199.
33 Faure 2008, p. 88; Schaefer and Mueller-Langer 2009, p. 7.
34 Guthrie et *al*. 2001, p. 42–49.
35 Schaefer and Mueller-Langer 2009, p. 10.
36 Faure 1995, p. 27.
37 Shavell 2004, p. 179.
38 Stavang 2010, p. 199.

longer a problem if a rule of strict liability is followed.[39] This is only one great advantage of such a liability system. Another argument in favour of a rule of strict liability is that accidents resulting from ultra-hazardous activities can be seen as unilateral accidents and it has been pointed out that strict liability is indeed more efficient than negligence in such a setting.[40] This superiority can be explained by the potential of a rule of strict liability to ensure an optimal level of activity. Under a negligence rule, a potential injurer will be indifferent towards the frequency of activities which he engages in, because he will escape liability provided he exercises due care.[41] This is different under a system of strict liability. Since the injurer cannot escape liability, he will ensure that he adopts an efficient activity level.[42]

It is far from easy to choose between a system of negligence or strict liability.[43] However, it seems that in the field of liability for nuclear accidents an almost unequivocal preference for a rule of strict liability can be identified. This can be explained mainly by the advantages of a rule of strict liability with regard to the incorporation of an optimal activity level and its potential to control the potential injurer's behaviour.

Returning the discussion to the issue of possibly combining liability rules and regulation, clearly regulation should be combined with a rule of strict liability. Using liability rules as an *ex post* incentive and supplementing this with *ex ante* regulation can ensure the high preventive effect of the system. This leads to the next section which will analyse how ultra-hazardous activities should be regulated.

1.2.2. Features of regulation

Taking decisions is a natural part of the life of individuals in society and they are independent in choosing the option they favour most. Governments however are inclined to assume that individuals do not always take rational decisions which are for their best. Therefore governments often decide that certain things have to be regulated.[44] There are various means of regulations which regulators can use to achieve a certain goal. Generally, they can be distinguished from each other by reference to their degree of state intervention.[45] Before turning to these different tools of regulation and analysing their respective advantages and disadvantages, two subsets of regulation have to be discussed; the public interest theory and the private interest theory. Understanding these two approaches is necessary because they also affect how regulation should be designed in practice.

39 Korobkin and Ulen 2000, p. 1099.
40 *Ibid.*, p. 1098.
41 Schaefer and Mueller-Langer 2009, p. 9.
42 *Ibid.*, p. 12–13.
43 Faure 2008, p. 90.
44 Ogus and Zhang 2005 p. 129 + 133.
45 Ogus 1994 p. 5.

The public interest approach assumes that if regulation occurs, then the government is doing so in the general interest of society. The reason for such intervention has been described in law and economics literature as the need to prevent or cure market failure. Market failures that are generally identified entail information problems, externalities, the presence of public goods and market power.[46] For the regulation of ultra-hazardous activities, the first two are of main importance.

Concerning the problem of externalities it should be stressed that resources are wrongly allocated if the price of a product does not mirror the costs that the producer might impose upon third parties.[47] Engaging in ultra-hazardous activities such as operating a chemical factory or a nuclear plant runs this danger. Potential pollution will harm the environment and, therefore, intervention by the government in the form of regulation in the public interest is warranted. The issue of pollution, however, also highlights an inherent problem in such forms of regulation: Regulation is justified in the public interest but aspects such as environmental damage that materialise only at a later stage raise questions about the degree of necessary intervention and how this level can be defined.[48]

The second point of interest concerns the market failure of information deficits. Consumer choice is a pre-requisite for allocative efficiency. If consumers however cannot express their preferences this is problematic. To do so, two pre-requisites have to be fulfilled: the persons taking decisions must possess the necessary information, and on top of that they have to assess this information to reach rational decisions. If either of these two components is missing, regulatory intervention might be justified.[49] This is of paramount importance when it comes to ultra-hazardous activities. Consumers choose from products that have been produced by such activities and, especially in the case of more complex commodities, consumer choice will not be optimal if it is not regulated to a certain extent. Regulation can ensure that good products are more easily distinguished from bad products, thereby serving the public interest of overall better performance in the sector of ultra-hazardous activities, given the resulting economic pressure.

In contrast to the public interest approach, the private interest approach does not start from the premise of seeing regulation from the angle of what is good in the public interest but regards regulation as a product that is subject to the rules of supply and demand.[50] Since politicians want to be re-elected, they will tend to satisfy the preferences of interest groups. The former will thus supply the rules as demanded by the latter.[51] Olson identified criteria for interest groups to function effectively: They have to be small, well organised, share similar interests and the general public has to face high information costs to get to

46 Philipsen 2008, p. 94.
47 Ogus 1994, p. 35.
48 *Ibid.*
49 *Ibid.*, p. 38.
50 Faure 2007, p. 225.
51 Ogus 1994, p. 69.

know about the harmful effects of the rent-seeking behaviour.[52] These criteria are present in the sector of ultra-hazardous activities which makes this sector especially prone to the influence of lobbying groups. Due to this influence interest groups in favour of a certain sector can accept a certain degree of government intervention in the form of regulation without having to worry too much about its influence, because lobby groups can steer regulation according to the preferences of operators engaging in ultra-hazardous activities.[53] That this indeed takes place in practice is supported by the fact that some regulation can only be explained by reference to the industry interests that have been favoured by it.[54]

One aspect that might counter the problem of rent seeking behaviour is to focus more on transparency during the process of regulation.[55] Next to this procedural tool the combination of regulation with liability rules as discussed above could serve as a substantive tool to mitigate the influence of lobbying groups.[56] These aspects should be kept in mind when the different forms of regulation are analysed in the following sections.

1.2.2.1. Prescriptive regulation

In the field of environmental protection, there was a tendency starting in the early 1970's of the last century to rely heavily on prescriptive regulation.[57] In the literature this has also been referred to as command and control regulation. Baldwin has defined it as 'the exercise of influence by imposing standards backed by criminal sanctions.'[58] This definition captures the core feature of this mode of regulation very well: It occurs in a top-down manner. The essence of such regulation is a detailed set of requirements that have to be met. The regulator, via different possible tools of monitoring, will check compliance. Such monitoring and enforcement is crucial because otherwise this mode of regulation will not work. One of the biggest invoked advantages of prescriptive regulation, namely its certainty and clarity, stemming from the detailed regulatory standards that have to be adhered to, can only be guaranteed in the case of a watertight enforcement system.[59]

Next to the dependability of such standards, Gunningham and Sinclair further point to the potential of command and control regulation to protect societal values by prohibiting certain kinds of behaviours.[60] This can also be seen as an advantage of this kind of

52 Olson 1965.
53 Faure 2007, p. 227.
54 Ogus 1994, p. 75; The regulation of the nuclear sector will be analysed further below. See for public choice considerations especially section 2.5.3.
55 Faure 2007, p. 233.
56 *Ibid.*, p. 232.
57 Gunningham and Sinclair 1998, p. 38.
58 Baldwin 1997, p. 65.
59 Gunningham and Sinclair 1998, p. 41.
60 *Ibid.*, p. 42.

regulation. As a further advantage Latin mentions *inter alia* that prescriptive regulation would be better equipped to guarantee a level playing field, preventing differences between different geographical regions which might lead to some form of 'forum shopping'.[61] If this argument holds true, it could also have an important effect on the discussion of regulation of ultra-hazardous activities within the European Union, given its regional character.

Turning now to the disadvantages of prescriptive regulation that have been discussed in the literature, the issue of enforcement has to be discussed once more. As already pointed out above, a potential flaw of command and control regulation is that enforcement can arguably not always be guaranteed. Enforcement and compliance problems are aggravated further by the multitude of requirements and the high level of detail which is typical for prescriptive regulatory standards.[62] Further criticism that has been raised is that the prescriptive rules are not always sufficiently linked to the regulatory goals they want to achieve.[63] This opens the door for creative compliance, meaning that regulatees can come up with certain strategies to comply with the letter of the law, but the goal that the regulator actually wanted to achieve will still not be fulfilled.[64]

As another weakness of command and control regulation it has been argued that it is static and inflexible, not being able to adapt quickly to changes in the industry that is to be regulated.[65] This claim is related to a further criticism, namely that prescriptive regulation will not lead to dynamic efficiency. Providing firms with a mere checklist that has to be complied with does not encourage research into possibly more effective and efficient means to achieve a certain regulatory goal. Continuous improvement on the side of the regulatee is not an inherent feature of prescriptive regulation and there is no incentive to look for innovative new solutions.[66]

Before turning to the discussion of self-regulation as an alternative mode to command and control regulation, it will be useful to stress one point raised by Golay concerning prescriptive regulation and the consequences it has on the question of which of the actors involved bears the ultimate responsibility for safety. In the field of nuclear safety for example it is a core principle that the prime responsibility must rest with the licence holder.[67] However, in case of a list of very detailed rules it can be argued that the regulator takes up the ultimate responsibility and not the regulatee, because compliance with the 'check-list' provided by the regulator will be regarded as sufficient.[68]

[61] Latin 1985, p. 1271.
[62] May 2007, p. 13.
[63] *Ibid.*
[64] Baldwin 1997, p. 68.
[65] *Ibid.*, p. 67.
[66] Gunningham and Sinclair 1998, p. 45.
[67] Art. 6(1) Directive 2009/71/Euratom.
[68] Golay 2000, p. 221.

1.2.2.2. Self-regulation

Command and control regulation, as it has been discussed above, is the one extreme of different modes of regulation. At the other end of the spectrum there is self-regulation. Self-regulation itself can be further distinguished into different forms because they vary in the degree of governmental control that still plays a role.[69] However, this is further discussed in the section below, whilst the current section focuses on the advantages and disadvantages of self-regulation as discussed in the literature.

In his seminal article on the theoretical justifications of self-regulation, Miller discusses three arguments in favour of self-regulation: private parties possess better knowledge, self-regulation is more flexible, and costs of self-regulation are fully borne by the market.[70] With regard to the first argument it is argued that the industry will always possess more information about the activity that is to be regulated or can access this information with fewer costs than an external, governmental regulator.[71] The combination of the role of an expert and the role of the regulator will decrease costs and make self-regulation therewith more efficient.[72] Concerning the flexibility of self-regulation Miller argues that this flexibility will have a positive effect on innovation and will be capable of adapting to the rapid changes an industry might undergo.[73] This argument has been questioned by Philipsen who takes into account the private interest approach to regulation. He discusses that self-regulated entities might still prefer a certain standard to a newer possibly more efficient one if that allowed them to fight competition. The claim that costs would be fully borne by the industry cannot be unequivocally accepted either because it is still possible that costs that have to be borne by the industry would be passed on to the consumer, therewith resulting in an inefficient allocation of the costs between supplier and consumer. Philipsen therefore concludes that only the first argument can be regarded as valid.[74]

As the discussion above has shown, the main problem with self-regulation is that it is susceptible to abuse. The private interest approach to regulation, as discussed earlier in this chapter, has shown that rent seeking is a phenomenon that can occur to steer regulation in a way that is profitable for certain interest groups.[75] This can consequently lead to flawed command and control regulation if the regulatory standards are not set at an optimal level. The problem however is aggravated even further when regulation is completely left to the industry. This opens the gates for standards that are too low, because the industry will set them in a way that will be advantageous for itself but detrimental to

69 Philipsen 2003, p. 35.
70 Miller 1985, pp. 897 + 898.
71 *Ibid.*, p. 897.
72 Philipsen 2003, p. 38.
73 Miller 1985, 897.
74 Philipsen 2003, p. 39.
75 Ogus 1994, p. 69.

safety or environmental protection in general. This potential for abuse is the main disadvantage of self-regulation and means of mitigating it need to be found.

1.2.2.3. Hybrid forms of regulation

So far command and control regulation and self-regulation have been presented as two different modes of regulation and have been analysed in isolation from each other. The idea that these two ways to regulate had mostly been regarded as mutually exclusive was criticised by Sinclair who argued that this distinction would not enable anyone to profit from the full benefits which the two modes of regulation could generate.[76] This claim has found further support and hybrid forms of regulation have come more into the focus of attention and can also be identified within national regulatory regimes throughout Europe. Such forms are *inter alia* described as co-regulation or enforced self-regulation.[77] Rules for example could still be set by self-regulatory bodies, but the government will continue to play a role in oversight or approval of these standards.[78] These forms of regulation should be welcomed in the regulatory sphere because they allow the combination of the respective advantages of command and control regulation and self-regulation.

1.3. The role of safety standards

Having discussed different forms of regulation and their respective advantages and disadvantages, an important aspect that merits some further discussion is the role of safety standards in the regulation of ultra-hazardous activities. Such standards will always be of crucial importance since they will provide a certain benchmark according to which a sector will be regulated. The following sections will deal with the question of how such standards should be developed and what principles one should take into account when setting these standards.

1.3.1. The legitimacy of standard-setting bodies

Standards are rarely set in a democratic negotiated way. It is more common that expert bodies or agencies are setting standards that industry then has to comply with. Given the crucial importance of regulatory standards because they will be used as a benchmark for checking compliance of a certain aspect, bodies setting such standards have a significant influence. It is therefore important that these bodies have a certain legitimacy and are respected by the general public. In the area of environmental regulation such concerns are of particular importance because regulatory processes and the underlying debates have traditionally been very expert driven, neglecting the role of the general public affected by these decisions.[79]

76 Sinclair, 1997.
77 See Ayres and Braithwaite, 1992; Levi-Faur 2011.
78 Van den Bergh 2004.
79 Steele 2004, p. 160.

Taking the European perspective there are two more issues with regard to the role of standard-setting bodies. On the one hand such a discussion automatically leads to the issue of a battle of power between the European Union on the one hand, and national Member States on the other. The latter wanting to keep as much as possible under their control, whilst a regional body might be better placed to decide on the issue. On the other hand when speaking about European standard-setting bodies one also has to keep in mind the jurisprudence setting the limits for European agencies and their legitimacy. The *Meroni*[80] case law set limits concerning the delegation of powers in the European Union not allowing a delegation of powers to an agency if this would involve providing broad discretionary powers to such a body. These constraints have to be kept in mind when thinking about the most appropriate level and forum to set regulatory standards when regulating ultra-hazardous activities in the European Union.[81]

1.3.2. *Involving the public – Towards a participatory democracy*

With regard to safety standards, an important aspect that has to be discussed is that the process leading to such standards should be as interactive as possible. Engaging the general public in this process could have the potential to further increase the acceptability of such norms. The underlying idea of this claim is that the general public should have a say on issues that may significantly affect their lives. If we claim to live in a democracy in which fundamental rights will be guaranteed for every individual, then the logical consequence is that these individuals also have to participate in shaping the society they are living in. The following sections will first discuss justifications for a participatory approach before turning to possible barriers to such public involvement and how they can be tackled.

1.3.2.1. How much participation?

As a preliminary remark it is worth stressing what is meant by involvement of the public. Generally speaking there are two extremes: The level with the lowest degree of public participation entails mere communication of information in a top-down manner, the receiver not being able to react to the information received. The highest level implies a two-way information exchange which enables the participating public to engage in a dialogue with the policy maker, ultimately also having some decision authority.[82] As the title of this section already shows, what should be aimed for in the regulatory process of ultra-hazardous activities is a more meaningful involvement than mere top-down communication.

80 Case 9/56 *Meroni and Co., Industrie Metallurgiche S.p.A. v. High Authority of the European Coal and Steal Community* [1958] and Case 10/56 *Meroni & Co., Industrie Metallurgiche S.p.A. v. High Authority of the European Coal and Steal Community* [1958].

81 See also section 7.3.4.

82 Rowe and Frewer 2000, p. 6.

1.3.2.2. Theoretical justifications

Support for the claim raised above can also be found in literature. Arcuri states that when it comes to governing hazardous activities, one should also involve the citizens.[83] A very basic justification for this is that the groups that are affected by a regulatory decision should also have the right to participate in the underlying process.[84] From an institutional point of view it is important to mention that in a multi-level system such as the European Union, democratic legitimacy is always a point of concern. Public participation has the potential to increase democratic legitimacy.[85] Next to this, the quality of risk regulation could also be increased by involving stakeholders that are not experts. Taking an example from food safety, the BSE crisis for example has been highlighted in literature as an example where the assessment of risk was done too much in isolation from non-expert stakeholder groups.[86]

As already pointed out in section 1.3.1, risks originally had an exclusively expert-driven meaning. When talking about risks, scientist relied on statistics and the focus was on the technical dimension of risks. One can see, however, an evolution in the past that focuses more on the individual, and thereby on the necessarily private dimension of risk. Risk perceptions of people differ and this can no longer be ignored because the general public voices these concerns.[87]

Risk perception of course introduces an element of subjectivity. This is, however, not only the case with regard to the opinion of the general public. Experts can also make mistakes.[88] Therefore it is understandable that Slovic *et al.* hold that policy makers should not generally take decisions purely based on public opinion, but they equally stress that studying the attitude of people who are facing a certain risk and their approach to that risk can enrich the risk management process.[89] This also has to be seen together with the discussion by Wibisana who argues that public opinion is indeed not always irrational as it is sometimes claimed by proponents of more "technocratic approaches".[90] Thus the quality of regulation can also be enhanced by means of public participation.

Particularly in the nuclear sector the perception of risk is an important factor. The benefits associated with nuclear energy are relatively small as far as the public is concerned. The advantages that nuclear energy offers such as affordable and relatively clean energy are often disregarded by nuclear sceptics whilst the main focus lies on potential risks which are perceived to be too high to be accepted. Reassuring the general

83 Arcuri 2005, p. 238.
84 Heinelt 2002, p. 17.
85 Schmalz-Bruns 2002, p. 59.
86 Barker *et. al.* 2010, p. 767.
87 Steele 2004, p. 160+161.
88 Slovic *et al.* 1982, p. 88.
89 *Ibid.*, p. 89; Slovic 2000, p. 231.
90 Wibisana 2008, p. 251.

public of the safety of nuclear power plants, however, is a challenging task and not very likely to be successful because given the low amount of serious accidents it is difficult to demonstrate the safety of reactors empirically.[91] Involving the public to a bigger extent could be one approach to tackle this problem and enhance trust in the regulatory process.[92]

Building upon case studies on water supply and the Eco-Management and Audit Scheme in Germany, the United Kingdom and Greece, Getimis and Kafkalas identify both opportunities and also risks posed by participatory governance.[93] Amongst possible risks a crucial point raised by these authors is that public participation has to be designed in a way not to risk being subject to an "eye-wash effect", meaning that involving the public is only done as a marketing tool, but in fact decisions are taken without the involvement of other stakeholders.[94] Well-designed public participation on the other hand can lead to effectiveness gains and more innovative approaches.[95] When involving the public in the regulation of ultra-hazardous activities, the policy makers will have to take these factors into account, trying to profit from the identified advantages whilst reducing potential risks as much as possible.

The regulation of risks confronts democracy with a very fundamental challenge. If decisions on risks are taking by expert because the aim is to strive for rational decisions, this can be regarded as endangering a true and full commitment to deliberative policy making.[96] A balance needs to be stuck that allows rational decisions to be taken, as a prerequisite to be able to deal with and manage the risks a society is facing, whilst at the same time allowing for transparent methods of deliberation, thereby fostering democracy.[97] Such a regulatory process will also have positive effects on the trust of the public in the decision making process.[98]

1.3.2.3. Barriers to public participation

Having a system that involves the public during the regulatory process is however only the first step. Another issue is how to ensure that public participation indeed takes place. Several barriers can exist that prevent other stakeholders from actually engaging in participatory regulation. Braithwaite shows that contrary to what was expected, information technology did not increase public participation to a significant extent. It is consequently not technical barriers that prevent the public from engaging in public

91 Slovic 2000, p. 229–230.
92 Wibisana 2008, p. 258.
93 Getimis and Kafkalas 2002, p. 167–169.
94 *Ibid.*, p. 169.
95 Heinelt 2002, p. 17; Schmalz-Bruns 2002, p. 59; Getimis and Kafkalas 2002, p. 167–168.
96 Kahan *et al.* 2010, p. 183.
97 *Ibid.*, p. 210.
98 See Smith 2014.

participation, but rather motivational, cognitive and informational barriers.[99] This is a core challenge which has to be mastered when it comes to the regulation of ultra-hazardous activities, given the desirability of public participation as outlined above. An example how the problem of cognitive barriers could be mitigated can be found in the US. Stressing the importance of using plain language in new proposals to encourage the participation of the general public, Cass Sunstein, previous administrator of the White House Office of Information and Regulatory Affairs, encourages regulatory agencies to attach executive summaries to new proposals, thereby aiming at increasing public participation.[100] This trend should be followed. When regulating ultra-hazardous activities, the general public should be educated by the dissemination of information, enabling them to play a role in the regulatory process which actually has an added value.[101] Achieving this would also increase the public acceptability of such activities.

1.3.2.4. Designing effective tools for public participation

Public participation should indeed have an influence on the decisions that are later taken. However, criticism has been raised that the involvement of laymen also poses threats, given constraints on knowledge that individuals are facing in the consultation process. An assessment of Rowe and Frewer's framework for public participation leads to an innovative solution to this problem. Public opinion surveys for example are described as a good tool for the clarification of public opinions and values that underpin certain decisions. They face however the disadvantage of not having a real influence on the decision itself.[102] This could be counterbalanced by introducing a component of deferred influence. If opinion and assessment voiced during the consultation process are not taken into account but in a later dispute it can be established that if they had been taken into account the dispute would not have arisen, then not-taking them into account will be used to the detriment of the party not adhering to the comments made. This procedure could also mitigate the problem of allegedly insignificant input from the stakeholders consulted. It has been shown in literature that frequently those stakeholders who are consulted have very little to say that indeed matters to a decisive extent.[103] Furthermore, involving non-experts might also entail a danger because of their status of being only laymen. However, as it was shown in section 1.3.2.2, the perception of laymen also has its role to play in regulatory processes. Emotional or more intuitive responses to risks do not necessarily need to be irrational and can also have an important role to play in risk management.[104] Nevertheless an over reliance on public opinion arguably poses certain risks, especially in highly technical sectors such as ultra-hazardous activities. Providing for deferred influence would accommodate these concerns by allowing irrelevant input

99 Coglianese 2006, p. 964–967.
100 See www.albertoalemanno.eu/articles/towards-more-public-participation-in-european-policy-making (last accessed on 21 August 2015).
101 Rowe and Frewer 2000, p. 6.
102 *Ibid.*, p. 18–21.
103 Coglianese 2006, p. 959.
104 Slovic *et al.* 2004.

to be discarded whilst ensuring at the same time that input prematurely discarded can have a later influence and will therefore not over hastily be classified as insignificant.

1.3.3. Transparency, public participation and access to justice in environmental law – Theoretical considerations and available tools

Public involvement does play an especially important role when it comes to Environmental protection. Not surprisingly the Rio Declaration in the early 1990's identified access to information, public participation and access to justice as crucial elements when it comes to protecting the environment.[105] Given that many environmental problems are of a transboundary nature, due account also needs to be taken of the interest and interdependencies of neighbouring states with regard to projects and actions taken that can have an influence on the environment. Therefore tools enabling and facilitating an inclusive, participatory transboundary discourse are of crucial importance.[106] Participatory transboundary risk management reduces social and transaction costs because acceptance on both sides can be higher as a result. Without either consultation or some joint form of management each party goes for maximisation of profit at the cost of the other party, which is detrimental to the overall welfare.[107]

In the nuclear sector however, there used to be a certain reluctance concerning openness and a meaningful involvement of the public and this is arguably still the case today. It was only slowly that by legislative initiatives in the area of environmental law, public participation and transparency was also introduced into the nuclear sector. Within the European Union there are by now some well-established tools for public participation. The following sections will first give an overview of the tools available. After that an analysis will follow, highlighting certain problems and gaps that currently still pose threats to an effective transboundary environmental governance and a high level of environmental protection in the nuclear sector.

1.3.3.1. The Espoo Convention

The Espoo Convention[108] was adopted in 1991 and entered into force six years later in September 1997. It deals with transboundary environmental impact assessments and the obligation of neighbouring states to consult each other in the case of planned activities that are likely to cause a significant adverse transboundary effect.[109]

105 Principle 10 Rio Declaration, available at www.unep.org/Documents.Multilingual/Default.asp?documentid=78&articleid=1163 (last accessed on 21 August 2015).

106 Ebbesson 2011, p. 255.

107 Renn and Klinke 2001, p. 266.

108 For the text of the Convention see www.unece.org/fileadmin/DAM/env/eia/documents/legaltexts/Espoo_Convention_authentic_ENG.pdf (last accessed on 21 August 2015).

109 For a discussion of the role of the Espoo Convention to enhance transboundary environmental justice see Ebbesson 2011.

Laying down the general objective of the provisions of the Convention, article 2 of the Convention states that

'The Parties shall, either individually or jointly, take all appropriate and effective measures to prevent, reduce and control significant adverse transboundary environmental impact from proposed activities.'

Article 3 continues by specifying that:

'For a proposed activity listed in Appendix I that is likely to cause a significant adverse transboundary impact, the Party of origin shall, for the purposes of ensuring adequate and effective consultations under Article 5, notify any Party which it considers may be an affected Party as early as possible and no later than when informing its own public about that proposed activity.'

Article 5 states that:

'The Party of origin shall, after completion of the environmental impact assessment documentation, without undue delay enter into consultations with the affected Party concerning, inter alia, the potential transboundary impact of the proposed activity and measures to reduce or eliminate its impact.'

1.3.3.2. The Aarhus Convention

The Aarhus Convention[110] was adopted in June 1998 and was approved by the European Union in 2005.[111] Since the drafting of this Convention its importance has been increasing and has been described as having a significant impact on procedural rights in the field of environmental law.[112] Jendróska describes it as a 'milestone in the development of the environmental rights of the public'.[113] It basically entails three different pillars: access to information[114], public participation[115] and access to justice.[116]

Articles 4–5 of the Aarhus Convention deal with access to information. With regard to this right it can be said that the scope of it is very broad. According to article 4(1) in

110 For the text of the Convention see www.unece.org/fileadmin/DAM/env/pp/documents/cep43e.pdf (last accessed on 21 August 2015).
111 Council Decision 2005/370/EC of 17 February 2005 on the conclusion, on behalf of the European Community, of the Convention on access to information, public participation in decision-making and access to justice in environmental matters.
112 Wates 2005, p. 2.
113 Jendróska 2012, p. 73.
114 Articles 4–5 Aarhus Convention.
115 Articles 6–8 Aarhus Convention.
116 Article 9 Aarhus Convention.

conjunction with the definitions given in article 2, any person has the right to request environmental information without the need to state a specific interest. Environmental information is also defined in a very broad manner in article 2 of the Convention, so that a significant amount of data can fall under this heading. Articles 6–8 Aarhus Convention lay down the provisions concerning public participation and Article 9 of the Aarhus Convention concerns access to justice. The first two pillars of the Aarhus Convention have been transposed by Directive 2003/04/EC and Directive 2003/35/EC, the third pillar, however, has not been fully transposed so far.

1.3.3.2.1. The first two pillars – Access to information and public participation

Directive 2003/04/EC[117] implemented the first pillar of the Aarhus Convention, namely the access to environmental information. It states in its article 1 that

> *'The objectives of this Directive are:*
>
> *(a) to guarantee the right of access to environmental information held by or for public authorities and to set out the basic terms and conditions of, and practical arrangements for, its exercise; and*
> *(b) to ensure that, as a matter of course, environmental information is progressively made available and disseminated to the public in order to achieve the widest possible systematic availability and dissemination to the public of environmental information. To this end the use, in particular, of computer telecommunication and/or electronic technology, where available, shall be promoted.'*

Two crucial aspects of this Directive are thus environmental information and public authorities. Both these terms are very broadly defined in article 2 of the Directive. This broad definition is also supported by case law of the CJEU.[118] Given these definitions and their interpretations, the scope of the Directive can be regarded as sufficiently broad to effectively transpose the first pillar of the Aarhus Convention.[119]

117 Directive 2003/4/EC of the European Parliament and of the Council of 28 January 2003 on public access to environmental information and repealing Council Directive 90/313EEC.

118 Case C-321/96 *Mecklenburg* v. *Kreis Pinneberg* [1998]; Case C-266/09 *Stichting Natuur en Milieu and Others* v. *College voor de toelating van gewasbeschermingsmiddelen en biociden* [2010]; Case C-210/97 *Commission* v. *Germany* [1999].

119 See also Jans and Vedder 2010, p. 369–372.

The second pillar of the Aarhus Convention was implemented with regard to the obligations at Member State level by Directive 2003/35/EC.[120] The aim of this Directive was twofold. Article 1 states

The objective of this Directive is to contribute to the implementation of the obligations arising under the Århus Convention, in particular by:

(a) providing for public participation in respect of the drawing up of certain plans and programmes relating to the environment;
(b) improving the public participation and providing for provisions on access to justice within Council Directives 85/337/EEC and 96/61/EC.

As apparent from article 1 of Directive 2003/35/EC, the scope of the directive is not only limited to the second pillar of the Aarhus Convention. It also partially addresses the third pillar, namely access to justice. It does that, however, only with regard to the IPPC and the EIA Directive.

1.3.3.2.2. The third pillar – Access to justice in environmental matters

Whilst the first two pillars of the Aarhus Convention have been transposed by two Directives, this is not entirely the case for the third pillar. Already in 2003, the Commission proposed a Directive on access to justice in environmental matters.[121] This proposal, however, did not receive sufficient support from the Member States and has been termed by some legal authors as 'politically speaking, "dead" '.[122] Nevertheless, with regard to activities falling under the IPPC or EIA Directive, aspects of access to justice have been implemented in European Union law as mentioned above. Furthermore, the case law of the CJEU played an important role in the transposition of this third pillar of the Aarhus Convention as will be shown in section 1.3.4.

1.3.3.3. Environmental Impact Assessments

The Directive on Environmental Impact Assessments[123] from 1985 can certainly be described as the first major step within the European Union towards public participation in decision making. It was the first legal instrument that provided well-established requirements for public participation. It has to be noted at that point that this Directive

120 Directive 2003/35/EC of the European Parliament and of the Council of 26 May 2003 providing for public participation in respect of the drawing up of certain plans and programmes relating to the environment and amending with regard to public participation and access to justice Council Directives 85/337EEC and 96/61/EC.

121 COM (2003) 624 final.

122 Jans and Vedder 2012, p. 236.

123 Directive 85/337/EEC; the original Directive has been amended since its original introduction and the most recent codified version is now Directive 2011/92/EU on the assessment of the effects of certain public and private projects on the environment.

also applies to the nuclear sector, and is a first example of how more procedural rights strengthening the position of the public have been introduced into the nuclear sector by environmental law.

Article 1 of the Directive states:

> *'This Directive shall apply to the assessment of the environmental effects of those public and private projects which are likely to have significant effects on the environment.'*

Article 5 lays down obligations concerning the making available of necessary information:

> *'In the case of projects which, pursuant to Article 4, are to be made subject to an environmental impact assessment in accordance with this Article and Articles 6 to 10, Member States shall adopt the necessary measures to ensure that the developer supplies in an appropriate form the information specified in Annex IV.'*

Article 7 turns the attention to transboundary consultations:

> *'Where a Member State is aware that a project is likely to have significant effects on the environment in another Member State or where a Member State likely to be significantly affected so requests, the Member State in whose territory the project is intended to be carried out shall send to the affected Member State as soon as possible and no later than when informing its own public, inter alia:*
>
> *(a) a description of the project, together with any available information on its possible transboundary impact;*
> *(b) information on the nature of the decision which may be taken.'*

According to Article 8

> *'The results of consultations and the information gathered pursuant to Articles 5, 6 and 7 shall be taken into consideration in the development consent procedure.'*

With regard to the need to guarantee access to justice article 11 states:

> *'Member States shall ensure that, in accordance with the relevant national legal system, members of the public concerned:*
>
> *(a) having a sufficient interest, or alternatively;*
> *(b) maintaining the impairment of a right, where administrative procedural law of a Member State requires this as a precondition; have access to a review procedure before a court of law or another independent and impartial body established by law to challenge the substantive or procedural legality of decisions, acts or omissions subject to the public participation provisions of this Directive.'*

1.3.4. *Transparency, public participation and access to justice in environmental law – Some relevant case law*

According to article 19(1) TEU, 'Member States shall provide remedies sufficient to ensure effective legal protection in the fields covered by Union law.' In achieving this, member States have a certain autonomy and the European Union cannot dictate in detail how exactly for example a national court system has to work. This is known as the principle of procedural autonomy. In the area of access to justice, this principle has been influenced by case law of the CJEU. In the *Janecek*[124] case for example, the Court questioned restrictive national procedural requirements on standing and advocated a less restrictive approach. This development finds further support in other cases dealing with the access to justice requirements of the EIA Directive and the Aarhus Convention.

In the *Djurgarden*[125] case for example the Court ruled that requiring a minimum membership of 2000 members for an NGO to benefit from the access to justice provisions of the EIA directive could not be justified. It obliged the Member States to give a broad interpretation of access to justice, emphasising that additional national requirements

> '*must not be liable to nullify Community provisions which provide that parties who have a sufficient interest to challenge a project and those whose rights it impairs, which include environmental protection associations, are to be entitled to bring actions before the competent courts.*'[126]

Following the same spirit, in *Trianel*[127] the Court also ruled that German administrative procedural law restricting the standing of NGOs only to challenges against decisions that were in violation of legal rules that concern individual rights, as opposed to rights protecting the general public interest, was in violation of the right to access to justice as laid down in article 10a of Directive 83/337 as amended by Directive 2003/35. These two cases increase significantly the possibility of environmental organisations getting access to national courts.[128]

Another case which potentially can have very far reaching consequences in the area of access to justice in environmental matters is the *Slovak Bear*[129] case. Whilst the previously mentioned cases related to the access to justice provisions as laid down already in

124 Case C-237/07 *Dieter Janecek* v. *Freistaat Bayern* [2008].
125 Case C-263/08 *Djurgården-Lilla Värtans Miljöskyddsförening* v. *Stockholms kommun genom dess marknämnd* [2009].
126 Case C-263/08 para. 45.
127 Case C-115/09 *Bund für Umwelt und Naturschutz Deutschland, Landesverband Nordrhein-Westfalen eV* v. *Bezirksregierung Arnsberg* [2011].
128 Metro report on Possible initiatives on access to justice in environmental matters and their socio-economic implications, 2013, p. 11+12.
129 C-240/09 *Lesoochranárske zoskupenie VLK* v. *Ministerstvo životného prostredia Slovenskej republiky* [2011].

secondary legislation, the *Slovak Bear* case focussed on the question of the direct effect of article 9(3) Aarhus Convention. Whilst the Court denied this direct effect, it stated that the national court is under an obligation 'to interpret its national law in a way which, to the fullest extent possible, is consistent with the objectives laid down in Article 9(3) of the Aarhus Convention.'[130] If national courts are indeed under an obligation to interpret their national laws on access to justice in the light of and compliant with article 9(3) of the Aarhus Convention this can have far reaching consequences. Even in the absence of a directive implementing this article, such an approach could according to Jans and Vedder even extend to a situation in which the access to justice requirement as laid down in the Aarhus convention is applicable throughout the entire field of EU environmental law.[131]

1.3.5. *Transparency, public participation and access to justice in the nuclear sector*

As apparent from the discussion above, over recent years transparency, public participation and access to justice have been on the agenda of the European Union and significant progress has been achieved. Whilst the first two pillars of the Aarhus Convention were implemented by two Directives, the access to justice pillar has only been partially implemented by legislation. However, case law of the CJEU has strengthened the existing provisions and the recent *Slovak Bear* case might even be regarded as extending the access to justice requirement throughout the entire field of environmental law in the European Union through pro-active judicial interpretation.

The following sections will turn their attention towards the nuclear sector, to analyse how far these developments are also mirrored in that sector. Without making the claim of providing a representative picture with regard to the status of public participation and access to justice in the environmental area as a whole, the two examples will serve to illustrate some apparent shortcomings of the nuclear sector in this area.

1.3.5.1. An Taisce and Hinkley Point C

The following discussion focuses on the case law that deals with An Taisce's (National Trust for Ireland) challenge to the legality of the UK's decision to grant permission to build and operate Hinkley Point C. The High Court London found against An Taisce on 20th of December 2013 and refused leave for a Judicial Review. After a letter from the Espoo Compliance Committee An Taisce was granted leave to take the challenge to the Court of Appeal. This appeal, however, was not successful and denied by judgment rendered on the 1st of August 2014.

130 C-240/09, para. 50.
131 Jans and Vedder 2012, p. 236+237.

1.3.5.1.1. Decision of High Court London

The National Trust for Ireland challenged the legality of the development consent given by the Secretary of State for Energy and Climate Change because the Irish people had not been consulted, which was in violation of Article 7 EIA Directive. The UK had not consulted with the Irish public although the site of the nuclear plant is closer to the coast of Ireland than to Leeds.

An Taisce argued that by non-consultation of the Irish public article 7 of the Directive was violated because the defendant only considered 'impacts arising from the ordinary regulated operation of the nuclear power station and not "unlikely", but nevertheless possible, impacts from other scenarios'.[132] In other words, that issue boiled down to the question of how exactly to interpret the wording of article 7 of the EIA Directive on the likelihood of effects or more specifically the likelihood of a nuclear accident in the case at hand.

Whilst An Taisce was arguing for an extensive interpretation of the term likelihood, Justice Patterson followed a more restrictive, literal approach. She stated that:

> *'It is common ground that in the ordinary course of its operation there is no prospect of HPC being 'likely to have significant effects on the environment' of another EEA state. The claimant's case is premised on the basis of a severe accident occurring. Because the effect of such an event will be significant the claimant submits that a broad interpretation should be given to the word "likely" in Article 7 of the Directive and in Regulation 24.*
>
> *The defendant submits that the odd consequence of the claimant's position is that it would mean that 'likely' equals 'cannot be excluded' or, in other words, means unlikely. Further, in considering whether the prospect of unplanned releases can be excluded one would need to exclude the role of the statutory regulators. As a matter of law they are there to exclude accidents. The claimant submits that is the consequence of applying the Directive and European jurisprudence.*
>
> *In my judgement the claimant's approach is not consistent with the scheme or language of the Directive'*[133]

Justice Patterson argued that the term 'likely' cannot be interpreted in a same way as in the Habitats case law as exemplified by *Waddenzee*. She stated that:

> *'It has to be recalled that the purpose of the screening direction under the Habitats Directive is to invoke a substantive process and not a procedural one as in the EIA Directive. Further, Article 6 is highly targeted in looking to protect special areas of conservation (SAC). Article 6(2) injuncts member states to take appropriate steps to avoid the deterioration of habitats as well as*

132 Judgment of the High Court London, [2013] EWHC 4161, para. 4.
133 Ibid., para. 112–114.

> *disturbance of species for which the areas have been designated. Article 6(3) permits development to proceed, but only after an appropriate assessment has concluded that the plan or project will not adversely affect the integrity of the site concerned. That is why a 'no risk' approach is adopted.*
>
> *That leads to a difficulty in a simple reading over of the judgments in the Habitats Directive cases of Waddenzee, Solvay and Sweetman to those under the EIA Directive. They are all cases concerned to make decisions on the basis of the most complete, precise and definitive findings and conclusions capable of removing all scientific doubt as to the effect of the proposed works on the protected site concerned. That is a different approach to that which is required under the EIA Directive which is looking at the likely significant effects on the environment. One imposes a site-specific test whilst the other is a broader approach.'*[134]

As already mentioned above, in the end Patterson found against An Taisce and refused leave for a Judicial Review.

1.3.5.1.2. Role of Espoo Implementation Committee

On the 14th of March 2014, the Espoo Implementation Committee wrote a letter in which it criticised the approach taken by the UK government, pointing to guidance documents of the Espoo Convention which would justify a lower threshold for the obligation to consult with affected parties to be triggered. In the letter it was stated that 'notification is necessary unless a significant adverse transboundary impact can be excluded'. Therefore the Implementation Committee concluded that there 'was a profound suspicion of non-compliance'[135] of the UK. On the 27th of March 2014 then An Taisce was granted leave to challenge the decision of the London High Court.

1.3.5.1.3. Decision Court of Appeal London

In the appeal the main focus also was on the issue of how to interpret the term "likely". Justice Sullivan stated that 'whatever that meaning might be, in the context of the EIA Directive the word "likely" does not mean, as an English lawyer might suppose, more probable than not.'[136] When comparing the meaning of likelihood under the Habitats Directive with the meaning in the EIA directive, Sullivan pointed at the stricter level of protection that was an objective of the Habitats Directive. He stated:

> *'In order to achieve this very high level of protection for special areas of conservation an equally stringent approach is required at the screening stage when the competent authority is deciding whether an "appropriate assessment" is required: see paragraph 70 of the Opinion of Advocate General Kokott [2004] ECR 1-7405. It is for this reason that in a case falling within the Habitats Directive an 'appropriate assessment' must be carried out unless the risk of significant effects on*

134 Judgment of the High Court London, [2013] EWHC 4161, para. 120+121.
135 EIA/IC/INFO/12.
136 Judgment of the Appeal Court of London, [2014] EWCA Civ 1111, para. 11.

the site concerned can be 'excluded on the basis of objective information.' Reading the Waddenzee judgment as a whole, it is clear that significant effects can be excluded on the basis of objective evidence if 'no reasonable scientific doubt remains as to the absence of such effects.'

Standing back from a detailed analysis of the text of the two Directives, there is no obvious reason why such a strict approach should apply to the screening stage in the EIA Directive, which merely seeks to ensure that any likely significant effects on the environment are identified and properly taken into account in the decision making process. Even if significant environmental effects are identified, and are not merely likely, but are certain to occur, the EIA Directive does not require that approval for an EIA project within either Annex I or II of the EIA Directive must be refused in the absence of some overriding public interest.'[137]

This reasoning of the judge seems to suggest that since the EIA Directive is mostly concerned 'only' with participation and consultation, the threshold to invoke certain provisions is higher.[138] Thus, also Justice Sullivan followed a restrictive approach to the interpretation of 'likely' and denied the appeal by judgment rendered on the 1st of August 2014.

1.3.5.2. Borssele Nuclear Power Plant

Another example that demonstrates in what way instruments that enable public involvement are applied in the nuclear sector can be found in the Netherlands. In March 2013, the Ministry of Economic Affairs of the Dutch Government published a decision to allow the *Elektriciteits Produktiemaatschappij Zuid-Nederland* (EPZ) to operate the nuclear power plant in Borssele beyond 2013.[139] This year had been used in previous discussions as the date of shutdown of the plant when a license for an indefinite period had been granted in 1974. This date was used as a starting point in the Safety report that accompanied the initial licensing decision. The life time extension was not preceded by an Environmental Impact Assessment, because EPZ and the Ministry were both of the opinion that such a long term operation licence would not require an EIA.[140]

After the license had been published in March 2013, Greenpeace challenged the decision because it was of the opinion that a full EIA, covering all environmental aspects of the

137 Judgment of the Appeal Court of London, [2014] EWCA Civ 1111, para. 18+19.

138 The same reasoning is apparent in para. 120 Judgment of the High Court London, [2013] EWHC 4161 (*'It has to be recalled that the purpose of the screening direction under the Habitats Directive is to invoke a substantive process and not a procedural one as in the EIA Directive'*).

139 Kennisgeving Kernenergiewet: Definitieve vergunning 'Verlenging ontwerpbedrijfsduur KCB', available at www.unece.org/fileadmin/DAM/env/pp/compliance/C2014-104/Correspondence_with_communicant/fmCommC104_19.09.2014/1.e_2013-03-21_Kennisgeving_vergunning_LTO.pdf (last accessed on 21 August 2015).

140 Letter from Ministry to EPZ, 'm.e.r. – beoordelingsplicht Long Term Operation KCB', 13th of September 2011, available at www.unece.org/fileadmin/DAM/env/pp/compliance/C2014-104/Correspondence_with_communicant/fmCommC104_19.09.2014/1.f_2011-09-13_Letter_Minister_re_EIA_not_required.pdf (last accessed on 21 August 2015).

life time extension should have been done. In February 2014, however, the Dutch Council of State decided against Greenpeace and did not see the need for an EIA.[141] This decision has to be seen in the light of a report of the Implementation Committee of the Espoo Convention. In its 25th session, the Implementation Committee agreed that 'that the extension of the life-time of a nuclear power plant, even in absence of any works, was to be considered as a major change to an activity'.[142] Therefore, an EIA would be required in the case of a life time extension. The Council of State, however, did not see an obligation for national ministries to follow this interpretation.[143] After the decision of the Council of State had been published, Greenpeace decided to file a complaint with the Aarhus Compliance Committee. The outcome of this complaint is not yet clear because the parties involved are still in the process of exchanging documentation to come to a full understanding of the issue at stake.[144]

The example of the Borssele nuclear power plant shows a general problem in the area of environmental law. It highlights the reduced role that international initiatives and Committees play if their decisions are not formally binding. Taking into account the Espoo Implementation Committee's opinion would have been a chance to enable more public involvement and potentially a better scrutiny of environmental impacts of the longer operation of the Borssele nuclear power plant.

1.3.5.3. Analysis

For meaningful public involvement to be possible, the public of course needs to have access to relevant documents in the first place and have possibilities to engage in the decision making process. Access to justice after decisions are taken is also of crucial importance. Having discussed some available tools that deal with these issues in the previous sections, the question to be answered is whether there are sufficient provisions for public access to materials and courts and transboundary involvement. Keeping in mind the instruments and the applicable provisions, this question would need to be answered affirmatively. Another question, and arguably the more important one, however, is whether the existing legal instruments are satisfactory and enable indeed a meaningful public involvement. Aarhus and Espoo are sometimes seen as additional tools that could strengthen and go beyond European legislation. This was also to some extent the case in the challenge of An Taisce. Picking up this issue, Justice Patterson stated that 'the claimant argues that the wording of the Aarhus Convention and the Espoo Convention support its submissions. I do not agree. As set out, the consolidating

141 Uitspraak 201303313/1/A4, available at www.unece.org/fileadmin/DAM/env/pp/compliance/C2014-104/Correspondence_with_communicant/fmCommC104_19.09.2014/1.h_2014-02-14_Judgement_Raad_van_State_highlighted_NL.pdf (last accessed on 21 August 2015).

142 ECE/MP.EIA/IC/2012/4, p. 4.

143 Uitspraak 201303313/1/A4, para. 9 – 9.4.

144 The Complaint is registered as Netherlands ACCC/C//2014/104, documentation can be accessed at www.unece.org/environmental-policy/conventions/public-participation/aarhus-convention/tfwg/envppcc/envpppubcom/acccc2014104-netherlands.html (last accessed on 21 August 2015).

Directive takes into account both Conventions.'[145] This view, however, seems to underestimate the importance of international developments in the area of public participation and environmental democracy. Boyle for example points out that the practices in *MOX Plant* and *Pulp Mills* show that 'where activities with a known risk of potentially significant pollution are involved, the necessity of an EIA can be presumed, even if the actual risk is a small one.'[146]

As apparent from the examples above, we are facing a problem in nuclear law that although tools for access to information and access to justice are available, they do not really serve as adequate means to enhance environmental scrutiny, because the threshold to invoke them seems to be too high. This is particularly surprising given the far reaching interpretations of access to justice requirements in environmental law as given by the CJEU in recent case law.[147]

This is problematic because more procedural rights could counterbalance inadequate substantive laws in certain sectors in which environmental protection might not be safeguarded to a sufficient extent. If procedural rights, by reason of them being 'only' procedural, however need a higher threshold to be triggered, as is arguably suggested by the An Taisce judgments, they cannot play any meaningful role in environmental governance or environmental law in general.

These problems are put in an appropriate theoretical framework by Waite in an article from 2005 entitled *The Quest for Environmental Law Equilibrium*.[148] In that article Waite illustrates by a simple equation the interplay of environmental imperatives (A), environmental principles (B), substantive environmental law (C), access to justice/ powers of enforcement (D) and the behaviour of environmental actors (E). An equilibrium is reached when

$$A = B \times C \times D \times E$$

If we take a satisfactory level of environmental protection as the environmental imperative to be achieved and say a satisfactory level would be achieved at 1, then we would have an equilibrium if the other variables are also all 1. If however one of the factors is insufficiently developed, this would lead to an imbalance. The more factors there are below 1, the bigger the imbalance, and therefore the lower the level of environmental protection. Thus, weak substantive laws for environmental protection, as for example in the nuclear sector, will lead to an imbalance that could theoretically be brought back into balance by strengthening other variables, such as for example public participation. If, however, other factors are also under-developed, the imbalance is

145 Judgment of the High Court of London, [2013] EWHC 4161, para. 129.
146 Boyle 2011, p. 228.
147 See section 1.3.4.
148 Waite 2005.

aggravated further. This weighing of different variables can also be extended by other factors. Examples could be to lower the thresholds of causation or a more applicant friendly attitude in case an accident does indeed occur.

1.4. Summary

The aim of this chapter was to set up a theoretical framework for the regulation of ultra-hazardous activities. It started by discussing the relation between liability rules and regulation and their respective advantages. It was shown that in the area of ultra-hazardous activities a combination of regulation and liability rules should be the preferred option. Concerning liability rules the superiority of strict liability was shown for nuclear accidents. With regard to the different modes of regulation is was argued that regulatory standards should be of a hybrid nature, thereby striving for forms of regulation that incorporate the advantages of prescriptive regulation as well as more flexible styles of regulation. The third section of this chapter turned its attention to the issue of legitimacy and reflexiveness of the regulatory process. It was argued that a strong involvement of the public can lead to increased legitimacy and also has the potential to work as a counterweight and to correct possible shortcomings of the substantive rules. The findings as presented in this chapter will serve as loose guidelines for the cross-sectoral analysis in the following chapter, analysing the chemical, oil and nuclear sectors and the ways these sectors are regulated. Also at later points of this thesis the aspects discussed so far will serve as a reference point and will shape the discussion of a European Legal Framework for Nuclear Liability.

Chapter 2

THE REGULATION OF ULTRA-HAZARDOUS ACTIVITIES – EXPERIENCES FROM HIGH RISK SECTORS

2.1. Risk Regulation in the EU

The previous chapter provided a theoretical framework for the regulation of ultra-hazardous activities. The focus in the following chapter will be on a comparison between different high risk sectors in light of the discussion from chapter 1. This comparison will serve to illustrate differences between these sectors with regard to their adherence to core principles of the regulation of ultra-hazardous activities as discussed above. Before turning to this comparison, the following paragraphs will first sketch the way that risk in general is regulated within the European Union. This is done because general trends and some changes in risk regulation are discussed, and these can serve as an additional benchmark according to which the specific sectors that will be discussed in the following sections can be tested. Do all these sectors follow this trend or are there differences and how can these differences be explained? This analysis will also build upon some examples from the US especially in comparison to the EU. The scope of this section, however, does not extend to a discussion of divergences or convergences between US and EU law in the area of risk regulation. Nevertheless some comparisons with the US regime are interesting to illustrate developments in this field of law and to examine how far the respective regions were responsive towards catastrophes that happened during the last decades.

It can be said that some time ago, between the years 1960 until approximately the 1980s, risk regulation of environmental and health concerns within the European Union was not as strict as it was in the US.[149] Risk aversion was higher amongst American regulators and they were especially influenced by public perceptions if people perceived risks to be intolerable.[150] Reviewing relevant case law from US courts during that time, Vogel observes that the approach in the US has been a precautionary one. This was also supported by Applegate, concluding that the precautionary principle plays an important role in American environmental law.[151] Vogel apparently criticises this approach when

149 See Vogel 2001.
150 *Ibid.*, p. 2.
151 Applegate 2000, p. 438.

he claims that 'much American regulatory policy, especially between the mid-1960s through the mid-1980s, was characterised by the triumph of "passion" over "sound science".'

With regard to institutional design the regulatory system prevalent in the US during this time can be described as an adversarial approach. This means that regulatory processes were more legalistic and formal and not only open to NGOs but also subject to important influence by them.[152] This can be explained by reference to a greater mistrust towards industry and government officials. This mistrust had not been present in the 1970s and 1980s in Europe. Here the picture was completely different. In a survey from 1979 for example, the close collaboration between the regulator and the industry was only perceived to be improper by 4% of the British respondents. Public trust into regulators was high and prevalent throughout Europe.[153] This was also mirrored in the institutional design of the regulatory systems within Europe which, contrary to the US, followed mainly a consensual style of regulation. This model is characterised by a close working together of industry and the regulators where regulatory decisions were made in a rather closed way, not open to the public and therefore somewhat elitist in nature.[154] A closed circle of interest groups was regarded as representing society at larger and further involvement of the public was rare and it was also not expected to take a more active role.

As just discussed, the main difference between the US and Europe was that in the United States there was more mistrust towards the regulator than was the case in Europe. This however changed in the 1980s and 1990s. It has to be noted at this point that in the area of environmental regulation the European Union did not have any competences until the Single European Act came into force in 1987.[155] The centralisation of regulation at the European level led to greater mistrust towards the regulators. This is to a certain extent already understandable *per se,* because decisions are taken at levels that are further away from the people that are affected by them, but this mistrust has furthermore been aggravated by a number of regulatory failures that occurred in Europe towards the end of the 20th and beginning of the 21st century in Europe such as the crisis concerning Bovine Spongiform Encephalopathy or the scandal involving dioxin in chickens in Belgium. These scandals led to claims that the consensual style of regulation was inappropriate and that a new system was needed.[156]

The birth of a new model of regulation was most probably the result of the combined effects of the new competences of the European Union and the above mentioned regulatory failures. With regard to its core features it can be characterised as aiming to be more inclusive instead of exclusive, thereby enabling and facilitating the participation of a broader group of stakeholders. Furthermore it emphasises the importance of

152 Löfstedt and Vogel 2001, p. 399 and Vogel 2001, p. 2.
153 Löfstedt *et al.* 2011, p. 410.
154 *Ibid.*, p. 409.
155 Löfstedt and Vogel 2001, p. 402.
156 Löfstedt *et al.*2011, p. 410.

transparency and openness and requires regulators to be accountable for their actions. It also decreases the role of science because an increase in public participation and the desire to consult with a broader group of actors concerned leads to a situation in which scientists continue to play a different role under this new model, namely that of being merely one of many stakeholders.[157]

2.2. The Chemical Sector

Historically, industrial accidents have always been part of continuing industrialisation. In the 20th century however these accidents became strikingly more frequent, calling for an approach to regulate ultra-hazardous activities in an effective way.[158] With regard to the chemical sector Bengtsson identifies three advantages coming along with a transnational regulation of chemicals: It can provide a level playing field between the different states involved, it thereby has the potential to stimulate trade in chemicals and very importantly it has positive effects on health.[159]

The essential thing when it comes to the regulation of chemicals is that whilst being fully aware of the fact that chemicals can cause harm and the use of chemicals entails certain dangers, one has to aim for striking a balance between the risk the use of chemicals bears and the advantages coming along with their use.[160] The following sections will describe how in the case of the European Union chemicals have been regulated and are regulated today.

2.2.1. *The Seveso Directives*

The Seveso Directives were the response of the European Union to the Seveso accident in 1976 which showed the need for effective regulation in the chemical sector and the possibly fatal consequences of a lack thereof.[161] The following section will give a brief overview of this accident before turning to the resulting legislative initiatives at the level of the European Union in the sections thereafter.

2.2.1.1. The Seveso accident

The accident occurred on the 10th of July 1976 in Italy. The plant at which the accident occurred was a small chemical manufacturing plant. Due to increased pressure in a vessel, caused by an exothermal reaction, a safety valve broke and approximately 3000 kg of chemicals were released into the air.[162] It is reasonable to say that amongst the causes

157 *Ibid.*, p. 410.
158 Arcuri 2005, p. 203.
159 Bengtsson 2010, p. 184.
160 Chapman 2007, p. 59.
161 Arcuri 2005, p. 203.
162 For a detailed description of the accident see Sambeth 1983.

of the accident a low level of safety precautions together with unskilled staff who had not been properly trained and informed about the risks of the activities they were engaging in, greatly contributed to the accident.[163]

2.2.1.2. Seveso I

It took six years after the accident until the first Seveso Directive[164] was adopted in the European Union. Although the title of the Directive refers to industrial activities in general, the scope of application actually limits the Directive to chemical installations as is apparent from the Annexes. Article 2 substantiates this by excluding for example nuclear and military installations and also the manufacture and storage of explosives as well as mining operations from the scope of application.

Article 1 of the Directive established the general objective of the Directive as being 'the prevention of major accidents which might result from certain industrial activities and [...] the limitation of their consequences for man and the environment.' It consequently has a twofold purpose, not only the prevention of accidents, but also the protection of health and the environment. The latter is interesting because the Community gained formal competences in the environmental field only with the Single European Act in 1987. Nevertheless Seveso I can be regarded as one of the first legislative instruments also aiming at the protection of the environment.

The Directive sets a very general obligation for Member States to 'adopt the provisions necessary to ensure that [...] the manufacturer is obliged to take all the measures necessary to prevent major accidents and to limit their consequences for man and the environment.'[165] As is apparent from this wording, it left a lot of discretion and independence to the Member States about how to implement this obligation in national law. It does not as such set standards according to which measures taken can be evaluated. This may be explained by the general spirit of the Directive. As Arcuri points out, the most innovative feature of the Directive is its emphasis on the importance of information and the exchange thereof.[166] Multiple provisions can be found in Seveso I which aim at facilitating the dissemination of information and education of the staff. Article 4 for example established the obligation that staff need to be trained to possess the necessary knowledge needed for performing the activities. This is an important internal dimension of dissemination of information. Concerning the external dimensions the Directive deals with three different kinds of information flows: The one between the operator and the national competent authority, between operator and people that would be affected by an accident and finally the exchange of information between Member States. Concerning the relationship between operator and the competent authority the Directives institute a

163 Arcuri 2005, p. 205+206.
164 Directive 82/501/EEC on the major-accident hazards of certain industrial activities.
165 Article 3 Directive 82/501/EEC.
166 Arcuri 2005, p. 209.

system in which the operator has to stay in contact with the authority to enable the latter to control the appropriateness of the former's behaviour.[167] Article 8 obliges the Member States to keep persons likely to be affected by an accident informed about the industrial activity and its implications for safety. The establishment of a European register documenting accidents that did occur[168] facilitates the exchange between Member States as mandated in articles 8 and 18.

2.2.1.3. Seveso II and III

In December 1996, the second Seveso Directive[169] was adopted which replaced the first one. It extended the scope of application and introduced a link between the dangerous activity and land-use planning. According to article 12 it has to be ensured that the siting of new establishments for example is controlled so as to minimise the consequences of an accident as far as possible via appropriate land-use policies. Emergency preparedness was also further stimulated by article 11, requiring the operator to come up with an internal emergency plan.

Article 7 of the Seveso II Directive introduced an important new requirement. It obliged the operator to come up with a Major Accident Prevention Policy (MAPP). In this document the operator has to lay down clear commitments towards prevention and control of major accidents. Its introduction into the Seveso II Directive was a result of the realisation that a holistic approach to accident prevention, including internal management systems is necessary to guarantee the highest level of protection against industrial accidents.[170]

Another feature of the Seveso II Directive that is worth mentioning is the establishment of the Major Accident Reporting System (MARS) and the Community Documentation Centre on Industrial Risks (CDCIR). The former is a register entailing information concerning accidents provided by Member States. The latter is a database comprising information on prevention and lessons learned from past accidents.[171]

It should be noted that in 2003 in the light of several industrial accidents, such as a cyanide spill in Baia Mara, the firework accident at Enschede or the explosion at a fertiliser tank in Toulouse, the Directive was amended by Directive 2003/105/EC[172] to extend its scope. Referring explicitly to these accidents the preamble justifies an extension to storage and processing activities in mining, storage of pyrotechnic and explosive

167 Articles 4–7 and 10 Directive 82/501/EEC.
168 *Ibid.*, Article 12.
169 Council Directive 96/82/EC on the control of major-accident hazards involving dangerous substances.
170 Wettig *et al.*, p. 22.
171 *Ibid.*, p. 26.
172 Directive 2003/105/EC amending Council Directive 96/82/EC on the control of major-accident hazards involving dangerous substances.

substances and the storage of ammonium nitrate and ammonium nitrate-based fertilisers.

Recently a third Seveso Directive[173] was adopted. This Directive continues the development of the first two Seveso Directives by granting more access rights to citizens to access information about the activities and resulting risks from a nearby located company. It further lays down provisions on public participation and access to justice. It also tackles the issue of enforcement by introducing stricter standards for inspections. The requirement of a MAPP is now put into article 8 stating:

> *'Member States shall require the operator to draw up a document in writing setting out the major-accident prevention policy (MAPP) and to ensure that it is properly implemented. The MAPP shall be designed to ensure a high level of protection of human health and the environment. It shall be proportionate to the major-accidents hazards. It shall include the operator's overall aims and principles of action, the role and responsibility of management, as well as the commitment towards continuously improving the control of major accident hazards, and ensuring a high level of protection'*

Generally it can be said that the Seveso Directives are not ambitious enough to strive for a complete harmonisation of safety measures throughout the Member States, but to provide a certain unified regulatory framework.[174] Their focus on information is well suited for the regulation of ultra-hazardous activities because such activities involve a multitude of actors who are either affected by the industrial activity, or who affect it themselves. The information asymmetries that result from such a complex set up can only be tackled by an approach that puts a lot of emphasis on dissemination of information.[175]

2.2.2. *The REACH Regulation*

The REACH Regulation[176] deals with the Registration, Evaluation, Authorisation and Restriction of Chemical substances. This regulation represents an enormous effort for a comprehensive regulation of chemical substances. This is also mirrored in the size of the regulation. With over 800 pages in total the Regulation is together with its Annexes more than twice as big in size than for example the Treaty on European Union and the Treaty on the Functioning of the European Union together. Due to this volume, a general

173 Directive 2012/18/EU on the control of major-accident hazards involving dangerous substances, amending and subsequently repealing Council Directive 96/82/EC.

174 Arcuri 2005, p. 222.

175 *Ibid.*, p. 225.

176 Regulation (EC) No 1907/2006 concerning the Registration, Evaluation, Authorisation and Restriction of Chemicals (REACH), establishing a European Chemicals Agency, amending Directive 1999/45/EC and repealing Council Regulation (EEC) No 793/93 and Commission Regulation (EC) No 1488/94 as well as Council Directive 76/769/EEC and Commission Directives 91/155/EEC, 93/67/EEC, 93/105/EC and 2000/21/EC.

description of the structure of the Regulation, will be given, before turning to a more detailed discussion thereof.

The Regulation is separated into 15 titles: General Issues, Registration of Substances, Data Sharing and Avoidance of Unnecessary Testing, Information in the Supply Chain, Downstream Users, Evaluation, Authorisation, Restrictions on the Manufacturing, Placing on the Market and Use of Certain Dangerous Substances and Preparations, Fees and Charges, Agency, Classification and labelling Inventory, Information, Competent Authorities, Enforcement, Transitional and Final Provisions, Annexes I-XVII. Already this mere listing of the different titles of the Regulation shows the ambitious and comprehensive nature of the Regulation. The following paragraphs will describe how this ambition has been realised in the Regulation, firstly by highlighting some particularities of the decision making process under the REACH and by introducing some institutions created by the Regulation before turning to registration, evaluation, authorisation and restriction of chemical substances, which can be seen as key components of REACH, aiming at improving the management of chemical risks to health and the environment.[177]

2.2.2.1. European Chemicals Agency

As one of the key actors newly created by REACH one has to firstly mention the European Chemicals Agency (ECHA). This agency is located in Helsinki and can rightly be described as 'the driving force among regulatory authorities in implementing the EU's ground-breaking chemicals legislation for the benefit of human health and the environment'.[178] Within ECHA an important role is played by the Member State Committee which is composed of representatives from the Member States. Bronckers and van Gerven point out that ECHA has a bit of a strange character because its powers depend on several circumstances making it possible that it can both be seen as an independent body with decision making power but also as playing in certain circumstances only a minor role being under the strict supervision of the Member States.[179]

In the literature this ambiguity has been identified. Heyvaert for example states that 'REACH significantly dis-empowers the Member States as risk regulator.'[180] This statement however has to be nuanced by the fact that in certain instances Member States 'retain considerable influence in the decision-making.' The escalation procedure for example which is foreseen under REACH for certain disagreements between the parties involved in the decision making process effectively dis-empowers the ECHA.[181]

177 Bronckers and van Gerven 2009, p. 1829.
178 Http://echa.europa.eu/about-us (last accessed on 21 August 2015).
179 Bronckers and van Gerven 2009, p. 1827.
180 Heyvaert 2010, p. 224.
181 Bronckers and van Gerven 2009, p. 1828.

2.2.2.2. Registration

As a core principle, article 5 lays down the 'no data no market rule'. This article states that unless chemical substances have properly been registered they cannot be marketed in the European Union. The registration is required if a threshold of one tonne per year is met. REACH introduces a distinction between new chemicals and already existing ones, terming the former 'phase in' substances and the latter 'non-phase in' substances. The regulation established a transitory regime for phase in substances to accommodate them in the newly established system.[182] In case companies do not comply with these registration requirements and market chemical substances in violation of the regulation, article 126 provides member States with the obligation to ensure appropriate penalties are available under national law for infringements of the requirements.

2.2.2.3. Evaluation

Title VI of the Regulation deals with the process of evaluation. It comprises both dossier evaluation[183] and substance evaluation.[184] According to article 40, dossier evaluation entails an obligation on ECHA to examine any testing proposals mentioned in the registration. This phase serves to analyse the chemical substances further and to enhance the knowledge about the risks coming along with the substance. It also checks whether the proposed tests are appropriate for the substance at stake.[185] The second element of dossier evaluation is a more formal one because it boils down to an examination of whether the registration complies with the required conditions.[186] If the Agency finds that the registration is not compliant with the Regulation, it can issue a decision to this end, requiring the Member State to remedy the shortcomings.[187] This is an important aspect of the evaluation phase because it gives the procedure a certain dialectic feature.

Concerning substance evaluation, the ECHA mainly plays a co-ordinating role. It is the competent authorities in the respective Member States that are in charge of the substance evaluation itself.[188] Whilst under the dossier evaluation it is the ECHA that prepares a draft decision, it is in this case the competent authority in the Member State that plays this role. The final decision however lies with the ECHA as long as ECHA does not receive a proposal for amendment which would lead to the installation of the escalation procedure, taking away the final decision from ECHA.[189]

182 See Article 23 and 28 Regulation (EC) No 1907/2006.
183 Chapter 1 of Title VI Regulation (EC) No 1907/2006.
184 *Ibid.*, Chapter 2.
185 Bronckers and van Gerven 2009, p. 1832.
186 Article 41(1) Regulation (EC) No 1907/2006.
187 *Ibid.*, Article 41(3).
188 Article 45 Regulation (EC) No 1907/2006.
189 Bronckers and van Gerven 2009, p. 1833.

2.2.2.4. Authorisation and restriction

The main aim of the authorisation regime is to control substances of very high concern and to strive for substituting these substances with alternatives.[190] Articles 56 and 58 prohibit the placing on the market of such substances unless authorisation is granted. Authorisation can only be granted by the Commission.[191] To gain such an authorisation, an individual company would have to apply at the ECHA, presenting a chemical safety report explaining the risk that might be caused by the chemical substances.[192] Based on this report ECHA will prepare an opinion which the Commission will use to decide whether to grant the authorisation or not.

Another feature of REACH is that it is possible in the case where a substance poses unacceptable risks, to adopt a community wide restriction for the manufacture, use or putting on the market of such substances.[193] It is again the Commission which decides on that, and the Agency plays a preparatory role by preparing a proposal for restrictions upon request by the Commission.[194] The substance subject to restriction may only be used in such a way as compliant with the restriction. Thus whilst the authorisation procedure represents an all or nothing approach, possible restrictions can lead to a more nuanced outcome.

2.3. The oil sector

2.3.1. International Conventions

Since the European regime also relies on some International Conventions, some legislative instruments have to be quickly introduced in this section. In the international regime one can mainly distinguish between two different types of instruments in the area of oil pollution. There are instruments designed to prevent accidents from happening and there are also instruments focussing on the compensation of accidents and possible victims that suffered from such an accident.[195] With regard to the preventive feature the main conventions are the International Convention for the Safety of Life at Sea (SOLAS) from 1974 and the International Convention for the Prevention of Pollution From Ships (MARPOL) from 1973. With regard to legislative instruments dealing with the ex post component the International Convention on Civil Liability for Oil Pollution Damage (CLC) from 1969 and the International Convention on the establishment of an International Fund for Compensation for Oil Pollution Damage (Fund Convention) from 1971 have to be mentioned as the first international instruments that dealt with the

190 Article 55 Regulation (EC) No 1907/2006.
191 *Ibid.*, Article 60.
192 *Ibid.*, Article 62.
193 *Ibid.*, Article 68.
194 *Ibid.*, Article 69(1).
195 Faure and Wang 2004, p. 55.

issue of liability and compensation for oil pollution. These two conventions were the answer to the Torrey Canyon incident in 1967 which necessitated a legal framework for the liability and compensation of oil pollution.[196] These conventions were in the following years amended and led to the CLC 1992 and the Fund Convention 1992. One of the main changes was an increase in liability amounts under the new conventions. Only a few years after this legal regime had entered into force it was, however, again revised in the light of new incidents at the end of the 1990's. The Erika incident led to an increase of the compensation levels that were available under the 1992 Conventions.[197] The Prestige accident in 2002 necessitated another review of the compensation amounts. The 2003 Supplementary Fund Protocol introduced another tier of compensation for the Contracting States to the 1992 Conventions. This Protocol entered into force on the 3rd March of 2005 and increased the compensation amount to 750 million Special Drawing rights (SDR). SDR is a currency value defined by the International Monetary Fund by reference to a basket of several major currencies taking into account the market exchange rates.[198]

2.3.2. *European regime*

2.3.2.1. Maritime safety

In general it can be stated that the approach of the Commission was to stay within the International regimes, and further action was not really on the agenda. After the Erika disaster however it was shown that the international Conventions have their deficiencies and the Commission took a more active role.[199] As a direct response to the accident, the Commission issued two Communications. The Communication on the Safety of Seaborne Oil Trading[200] in March 2000 led inter alia to stricter rules for classification societies whilst the Communication on a Second Set of Measures on Maritime Safety[201] in December 2000 led to the creation a new agency to improve maritime safety, namely the European Maritime Safety Agency.[202]

196 Liability and Compensation for Ship Source Oil Pollution, p. 9.

197 UNCTAD/DTL/TLB/2011/4, p. 11.

198 For more information see www.imf.org/external/np/fin/data/rms_sdrv.aspx (last accessed on 21 August 2015); Given that some international conventions refer to SDR and keeping in mind that the exchange rate of SDR to EUR is not fixed, throughout this thesis references to SDR will also be made. In the interest of a better comparison, however, reference to the equivalent amounts of EUR is also made when appropriate.

199 Faure and Wang 2004, p. 56.

200 Communication from the Commission to the European Parliament and the Council on the Safety of the Seaborne Oil Trading, 21 March 2000.

201 Communication from the Commission to the European parliament and the Council on a Second Set of Measures on Maritime Safety following the sinking of the Oil Tanker Erika, 6 December 2000.

202 Regulation (EC) No 1406/2002 establishing a European Maritime Safety Agency.

2.3.2.2. Liability and compensation

The majority of EU Member States are parties to both the international CLC[203] and the Fund Convention.[204] As it became apparent after the Erika disaster that the international regimes were not adequate especially in terms of having sufficient funds for compensation, the Commission proposed to create a European Supplementary fund which would have a higher ceiling than in the international regime so as to be able to compensate victims of oil spills.[205] The Commission had in mind to increase the amount to € 1 billion. As already mentioned above, this European initiative led in 2003 to a protocol to the Fund Convention, increasing the available amount, coming close to the € 1 billion under the suggested European Fund.[206] This development shows how the European Commission actively influenced the international regime and in the end successfully 'lobbied' for raising the amounts of compensation

2.4. The nuclear sector

Fukushima has once more shown the devastating consequences of a nuclear accident. Nuclear safety and robust regulation of the nuclear sector to ensure the safe use of nuclear energy are at the forefront more than ever. Despite loud calls for better and stricter regulation in the nuclear sector, one can say that this sector is still lagging behind in terms of risk regulation.[207] The following sections will develop this point further and describe how the nuclear sector is currently regulated.

2.4.1. Euratom Treaty

The starting point for any discussion on the regulation of the nuclear sector has to be the Euratom Treaty because it is the founding Treaty of The European Nuclear Community and forms therewith part of EU primary law which makes it the highest ranking source. Despite being of such a fundamental nature, the Euratom Treaty does not seem to have brought much added value in the area of nuclear safety. In the late 1980s, Woodliffe criticised the Euratom Treaty for not having taken as pro-active a role in the nuclear sector as may have been desirable. He points out that even after decades of being in force, it has still left the main responsibilities with the respective Member States.[208]

[203] Belgium, Cyprus, Denmark, Estonia, Finland, France, Germany, Greece, Iceland, Ireland, Italy, Latvia, Luxembourg, Malta, Netherlands, Poland, Portugal, Slovenia, Spain, Sweden, and the UK.

[204] Belgium, Cyprus, Denmark, Estonia, Finland, France, Germany, Greece, Iceland, Ireland, Italy, Malta, Netherlands, Poland, Portugal, Slovenia, Spain, Sweden and the UK.

[205] See Communication from the Commission to the European parliament and the Council on a Second Set of Measures on Maritime Safety following the sinking of the Oil Tanker Erika, 6 December 2000.

[206] Faure and Wang 2004, p. 61.

[207] See also Veuchelen 2009.

[208] Woodliffe 1989, p. 101.

Article 2(b) of the Euratom Treaty states that it is the goal of the European Community to 'establish uniform safety standards to protect the health of workers and the general public and ensure that they are applied'. Article 30 furthermore establishes that

> *'basic standards shall be laid down within the Community for the protection of the health of workers and the general public against the dangers arising from ionizing radiations. The expression "basic standards" means:*
>
> *a) maximum permissible doses compatible with adequate safety;*
> *b) maximum permissible levels of exposure and contamination;*
> *c) the fundamental principles governing the health surveillance of workers.'*

As is apparent from these two provisions, the Treaty lays down a very broad and general framework and does not give precise guidance on what level of nuclear safety is desirable, neither does it entail any concrete obligations. This is as such not very surprising since a Treaty often serves only for laying down basic principles and not detailed rules. It is however important to analyse the extent to which these requirements, as laid down in the Treaty, have been implemented in practice.

2.4.2. *Convention on Nuclear Safety*

When discussing nuclear safety in the European Union one of the first main instruments deserving of attention is an international one, namely the Convention on Nuclear Safety which was adopted in 1994. Its objective is 'to achieve and maintain a high level of nuclear safety worldwide through the enhancement of national measures and international co-operation'.[209] The Convention is mainly based upon the IAEA safety standards.[210] The provisions in the Convention do not establish conditions strict enough to achieve its actual objectives because it still leaves a large degree of freedom to the Contracting Parties, and its value is further decreased by its enforcement mechanism. Contracting Parties have to submit reports on their efforts to implement the provisions of the Convention. These reports are subject to review by the other Contracting Parties, which

209 Article 1 Convention on Nuclear Safety.

210 The standards are laid down in the form of the following ten principles: 1. The prime responsibility for safety must rest with the person or organisation responsible for facilities and activities that give rise to radiation risks. 2. An effective legal and governmental framework for safety, including an independent regulatory body, must be established and sustained. 3. Effective leadership and management for safety must be established and sustained in organisations concerned with, and facilities and activities that give rise to, radiation risks. 4. Facilities and activities that give rise to radiation risks must yield an overall benefit. 5. Protection must be optimised to provide the highest level of safety that can reasonably be achieved. 6. Measures for controlling radiation risks must ensure that no individual bears an unacceptable risk of harm. 7. People and the environment, present and future, must be protected against radiation risks. 8. All practical efforts must be made to prevent and mitigate nuclear or radiation accidents. 9. Arrangements must be made for emergency preparation and response to nuclear or radiation incidents. 10. Protective actions to reduce existing or unregulated radiation risks must be justified and optimised.

takes place at regular meetings as foreseen in Article 20. Thus the Convention has established only a system of peer review. The worst thing that could happen would be that one Contracting Party might be criticised for its lack of implementation. No consequences would follow from this except peer pressure. Due to this lack of enforcement, the Convention has rightly been described as merely an incentive instrument.[211]

2.4.3. *Case 29/99*[212]

As outlined in the previous section, the Convention on Nuclear Safety cannot be regarded as an instrument that has contributed much to the improvement and harmonisation of safety standards for nuclear installations throughout the European Union. Nevertheless, it could be said that it has played a decisive role in the area of nuclear safety in the European Union due to a judgment of the CJEU which was triggered by the accession of the European Union to the Convention on Nuclear Safety.

The case in question resulted from the Council Decision approving the accession of Euratom to the Nuclear Safety Convention. It dealt with an issue of competences, more precisely the extent to which the Community possesses competences in the field of nuclear safety. Before this case it was commonly held that Article 30 of the Euratom Treaty only gave competences to Community institutions in the fields of radiation protection and waste management.[213] In Case 29/99 however the Court established that 'it is not appropriate, in order to define the Community's competences, to draw an artificial distinction between the protection of the health of the general public and the safety of sources of ionising radiation.'[214] The Court continued by stating that

> *'even though the Euratom Treaty does not grant the Community competence to authorise the construction or operation of nuclear installations, under article 30 to 32 of the Euratom Treaty the Community possesses legislative competence to establish, for the purpose of health protection, an authorisation system which must be applied by the Member states.'*

This judgment clearly makes the Community institutions competent in the field of nuclear safety and the powers described by the Court even exceed the measures that have been taken in this area so far. The formulation of the Court is even more remarkable in the light of the opinion of Advocate General Jacobs in this case.[215] He followed a narrower interpretation but the Court in contrast deemed it necessary to include the siting, design and construction of nuclear installations as well.[216]

211 Stanic 2010, p. 148.
212 C-29/99 *Commission of the European Communities* v. *Council of the European Union* [2002].
213 Stanic 2010, p. 151.
214 C-29/99, para. 82.
215 Opinion of Mr. Advocate General Jacobs C-29/99 *Commission of the European Communities v Council of the European Union.*
216 See also: Cenevska 2009, p. 483.

2.4.4. *The Nuclear Safety Directive(s)*

2.4.4.1. The 2009 Safety Directive

There has been enormous resistance from the Member States to harmonise nuclear safety standards. This is to a certain part understandable, because issues of national sovereignty have always been an obstacle toward harmonisation. This is of course of even greater importance in such a sensitive field as nuclear energy or more generally energy policies, and how Member States choose to use their resources.[217] During the negotiation process the European Nuclear Safety Regulators Group (ENSREG) was created.[218] The installation of ENSREG has been hailed by the industry and people involved in establishing it as an important step towards co-operation and increased nuclear safety. From an objective viewpoint however it is arguably no more than a further tool to delay far-reaching changes in nuclear safety. ENSREG established ten principles that should serve as a framework for possible legislation in the field of nuclear safety.[219] Amongst these principles two are of particular importance, namely the third and the fifth one. The third principle states that all changes or legislative measures to be taken shall not change the regulatory approach of the nuclear sector in the Member states and emphasises the importance of upholding flexibility. The fifth principle prevents the Commission from expanding its power in regulatory decision making and also rules out the establishment of new bodies in the regulatory landscape. These two principles already show the reactive attitude of the ENSREG and suggest that a fundamental overhaul was not to be expected from the Directive. This is also supported by the text of the Directive[220] as it was eventually formulated.

Article 4(1) states that 'Member States shall establish and maintain a national legislative, regulatory and organisational framework for nuclear safety'. Article 5(2) establishes an obligation upon the Member States to 'ensure that the competent regulatory authority is

217 Note that also in the TFEU the newly introduced article 194 on Energy does not lay down a Community wide energy policy but leaves this with the Member States.

218 Commission Decision 2007/530 Euratom of 17 July 2007 on establishing the European High Level Group on Nuclear Safety and Waste Management.

219 Report of the European Nuclear Safety Regulators Group, July 2009, p. 22.
The principles are: 1. Maintain and seek to continuously improve nuclear safety and its regulation, and add value. 2. Just as every Member State has the right to decide to use nuclear power or not, so every Member State has the right to impose more stringent nuclear safety requirements than those commonly applied. 3. Allow flexibility and not fundamentally change a Member State's national nuclear regulatory approach. 4. Seek to enhance, not reduce, the power, roles, responsibilities or capability of the national nuclear regulatory body. 5. Do not expand the role of the Commission in regulatory decision-making or activities or introduce other bodies. 6. Do not divert resources away from national nuclear regulatory responsibilities or international nuclear safety cooperation. 7. Be compliant with the principles/obligations of the Convention on Nuclear Safety. 8. Any proposals should be non-discriminatory towards those who use or do not use nuclear power. 9. Seek to improve the transparency of nuclear safety and its regulation. 10. Be clear on the roles and responsibilities of any organisations involved.

220 Council Directive 2009/71/Euratom establishing a Community framework for the nuclear safety of nuclear installations.

functionally separate from any other body [...] in order to ensure effective independence'. Article 6(1) and (2) require that 'Member States shall ensure that the prime responsibility [...] rests with the licence holder' and 'that [...] licence holders [...] regularly assess and verify and continuously improve, as far as reasonably achievable, the nuclear safety or their nuclear installations'. These articles resemble very much the Safety Convention and the IAEA standards and do little to enhance the status quo of nuclear safety.

2.4.4.2. The proposal for a revised Safety Directive

At the end of 2013 the Commission published a proposal for a revised Safety Directive.[221] Although not many of the suggested changes were eventually incorporated into the final amendments, some aspects of the proposal will be discussed in the following sections to provide a better insight into the developments of safety regulation in the nuclear sector.

Article 3

Article 3 of the 2009 Safety Directive gives a number of definitions. The following concepts are defined: nuclear installation, nuclear safety, competent regulatory authority, licence and licence holder. The draft proposal for a new Directive adds some definitions to this, amongst which the following are worthy to be mentioned because they clarify important concepts, thereby enhancing the status of the former rather vague principles:

> *'"practically eliminating" means that it is physically impossible or it can be considered extremely unlikely with a high degree of confidence for a condition to occur;*
>
> *"reasonably achievable" means that, in addition to meeting the requirements of good practice in engineering, further safety or risk reduction measures for the design, commissioning, operation or decommissioning of a nuclear installation should be sought and that these measures should be implemented unless it can be demonstrated that they are grossly disproportionate with regard to the safety benefit they would Confer;*
>
> *"periodic safety review" means a systematic reassessment of the safety of an existing installation carried out at regular intervals to deal with the cumulative effects of ageing, modifications, operating experience, technical developments and siting aspects and aimed at ensuring a high level of safety throughout the service life of the installation'.*

Such definitions provide an added value in the sense that broad principles are explained in more detail which increases their practical use and enforceability. The suggested changes would have been a step away from the current reliance on vague terms which are left without much guidance with regard to how they should be put in practice.[222]

221 COM(2013) 343 final.
222 See Liermann and Veuchelen 2006.

Article 8

The current article 8 of the 2009 Nuclear Safety Directives obliges

> *'Member States [to] ensure that information in relation to the regulation of nuclear safety is made available to the workers and the general public. This obligation includes ensuring that the competent regulatory authority informs the public in the fields of its competence. Information shall be made available to the public in accordance with national legislation and international obligations, provided that this does not jeopardise other interests such as, inter alia, security, recognized in national legislation or international obligations.'*

The proposal goes further than this by introducing article 8(3) which states that:

> *'Member States shall ensure that the public shall be given early and effective opportunities to participate in the licensing process of nuclear installations, in accordance with relevant Union and national legislation and international obligations.'*

The draft proposal clearly strengthens public participation. Whilst the 2009 Directive merely puts into place a sort of one stream information, the draft proposal foresees the true involvement of the public. This adds some responsiveness to the regulation of the nuclear sector and combines a 'purposive orientation with an emphasis on participation in the law-making processes'.[223]

Article 8 under the draft proposal entails a second section which introduces a further important change:

> *'Member States shall ensure that the national framework requires that nuclear installations are designed, sited, constructed, commissioned, operated and decommissioned with the objective of avoiding potential radioactive releases by:*
>
> *(a) practically eliminating the occurrence of all accident sequences which would lead to early or large releases.'*

This is a very strict standard if we recall the definition of "practically eliminating" given by the proposal. Stricter standards are crucial to allow the nuclear sector to benefit from hybrid forms of regulation and more flexible rules whilst not compromising nuclear safety in the European Union.[224]

223 Teubner 1983, p. 246.
224 Haines 2009, p. 33.

A new article 8e(2) strengthens the peer review process in the European Union:

'Member States, with the support of the competent regulatory authorities, shall periodically arrange, and at least every six years, a system of topical peer reviews and agree on a time-frame and the modalities for implementation. For this purpose Member States shall:

a) jointly and in close coordination with the Commission select one or more specific topics related to the nuclear safety of nuclear installations. Should Member States fail to jointly select at least a topic within the time frame specified in this paragraph, the Commission shall select the topics to be the subject of the peer reviews; b) based on these topics, perform in close collaboration with licence holders, national assessments and publish the results; c) jointly define a methodology, arrange and carry out a peer review of the results of the national assessments referred to in point (b), to which the Commission is invited to participate; d) publish the results of the peer reviews referred to in point (c).'

Article 8e(3) continues:

'Each Member State subject to the peer review referred to in paragraph 2 shall arrange for the planning and mode of implementation on its territory of relevant technical recommendations resulting from the peer-review process and shall inform the Commission thereof.'

Finally Article 8e(4) gives more powers to the Commission in the peer review process:

'Should the Commission identify substantial deviations or delays in the implementation of the technical recommendations resulting from the peer review process, the Commission shall invite the competent regulatory authorities of Member States not concerned to organise and carry out a verification mission to get a full picture of the situation and inform the Member State concerned about possible measures to remedy any identified shortcomings.'

The provisions dealing with the peer review process lay down a shorter time frame and aim at more dialogue between the parties involved. The rules according to which the reviews have to take place are put down in detail and enforcement is strengthened by the possibility of a verification mission mandated by the Commission.

Article 9a

The proposal introduces a new article 9a dealing with penalties. It states

'The Member States shall lay down the rules on penalties applicable to infringements of the national provisions adopted pursuant to this Directive and shall take all measures necessary to ensure that they are implemented. The penalties provided for must be effective, proportionate and dissuasive.'

It is of course up to the Member States to indeed come up with penalties, but introducing this article is clearly an improvement because it introduces also the *ex post* component that if regulation of nuclear safety fails, penalties have to be in place as a back-up. Further, if penalties are not deemed to be effective, proportionate and dissuasive it could open the door for infringement proceedings.

2.4.4.3. The 2014 amendment

In July 2014, the Council eventually adopted a final version of a directive that would amend the 2009 Nuclear Safety directive.[225] Focussing on the changes suggested in the draft proposal as discussed above, the following changes have to be highlighted. With regard to article 3 it has to be said that whilst some definitions will indeed be added, none of the definitions that were discussed above were kept in the final amendments. Thus the amendment does not take the opportunity to clarify broad concepts such as 'reasonably achievable' as originally foreseen in the draft proposal. Also the stricter standard that would have been introduced by the definition of "practically eliminating" has not made it into the final version.

Transparency and public involvement are indeed strengthened in the 2014 amendments. The wording and structure is different compared to article 8 of the draft proposal, but it is safe to speak of an enhancement of these rights under the 2014 amendments. With regard to section 2 of the article, however, it has to be admitted that the more ambitious standard of 'practically eliminating the occurrence of all accident sequences which would lead to early or large releases' has unfortunately been replaced by a softer provision, requiring 'that nuclear installations are designed, sited, constructed, commissioned, operated and decommissioned with the objective of preventing accidents'.[226] Concerning article 8e it can be observed that apparently the role foreseen for the Commission by the draft proposal went too far for Member States, and this led to less power for the Commission during the process of peer reviews.[227] Lastly it has to be mentioned that Article 9a dealing with penalties did not make it into the final version of the new Directive either.

2.4.5. Liability and compensation

The Member States of the European Union rely on international conventions in the field of liability and compensation for nuclear accidents.[228] Generally it can be said that there are two main systems, namely the one established under the auspices of the NEA of the

225 Council Directive 2014/87/Euratom amending Directive 2009/71/Euratom establishing a Community framework for the nuclear safety of nuclear installations.

226 Compare article 8(a) as foreseen in the Draft Proposal COM(2013) 343 final with the final article 8(a) of the Council Directive 2014/87/EURATOM.

227 Compare article 8(e) as foreseen in the Draft Proposal COM(2013) 343 final with the final article 8(e) of the Council Directive 2014/87/EURATOM.

228 For an overview of the International Conventions in more detail see Section 3.1 and 3.2.

OECD with the 1960 Paris and 1963 Brussels Conventions and its following amendments and protocols, and the one in the framework of the IAEA, with the 1963 Vienna Convention as amended in the following years by the 1997 Protocol.[229, 230]

Article 7 of the Paris Convention lays down that the maximum liability shall be 15 million Special Drawing Rights (hereinafter SDR) but each state can under certain circumstances increase or lower these amounts provided that the amount is never less than 5 million SDR. The 1963 Brussels Convention supplementing the 1960 Paris Convention increased the amount to 300 million SDR.[231] This amount is financed through three layers: up to at least 5 million SDR shall be provided by insurance, the difference between this amount and 175 million SDR shall be financed by public funds from the installation state and the third layer up to 300 million SDR shall be provided out of collective public funds.[232] What is apparent from these observations is that there is a big reliance in public funding. This situation is not different under the 2004 Protocol to amend the Paris Convention[233] which was adopted to react to the needs for higher amounts of liability that had become apparent arter the Chernobyl accident.[234] The minimum liability under the protocol is increased to € 700 million[235] This protocol however has not yet come into force.[236]

The 1963 Vienna Convention allows the installation state to limit the liability to not less than 5 million USD.[237] In 1997 a protocol to amend the 1963 Vienna Convention was adopted and increased liability to 300 million SDR.[238] It allows the installation state to decrease the amount of liability of the nuclear operator under certain circumstances if the state guarantees that in the case of an accident public funds will be made available.[239]

229 Protocol to Amend the Vienna Convention on Civil Liability for Nuclear Damage, 29th of September 1997, available at: www.iaea.org/Publications/Documents/Infcircs/1998/infcirc566.pdf (last accessed on 21 August 2015).

230 Belgium, Denmark, Finland, France, the Netherlands, Germany, Sweden, Italy, the UK, Spain and Slovenia are parties to the Paris/Brussels regime whilst Portugal and Greece are only parties to the Paris Convention. Bulgaria, the Czech Republic, Estonia, Lithuania, Hungary, Poland, Slovakia, Latvia and Romania are parties to the 1963 Vienna regime. Latvia and Romania have also signed the Protocol from 1997 to amend the Vienna Convention, the Czech Republic, Lithuania, Hungary and Poland have signed it.

231 Article 3(1) Convention of 31st January 1963 Supplementary to the Paris Convention.

232 *Ibid.*, art. 3(2) sec. (1)-(3).

233 Protocol to Amend the Convention on Third Party liability in the Field of Nulcear Energy of 29 July 1960, as amended by the Additional Protocol of 28 January 1964 and by the Protocol of 16 November 1982, 12th of February 2004, available at: www.oecd-nea.org/law/paris_convention.pdf (last accessed on 21 August 2015).

234 Www.oecd-nea.org/law/paris-convention-protocol.html (last accessed on 21 August 2015).

235 Art. I(H)a.

236 For the latest status of ratifications or accessions see www.oecd-nea.org/law/paris-convention-ratification.html (last accessed on 21 August 2015).

237 Article V(1) Vienna Convention.

238 Article 7 Protocol to Amend the Vienna Convention on Civil Liability for Nuclear Damage.

239 *Ibid.*, article 7(2).

2.5. Comparative analysis

Having provided the main features of the regulatory landscapes in the chemical, oil and nuclear sectors respectively, the following sections will focus on the differences between these sectors. With regard to the regulatory regimes attention will be paid to the question of what sort of regulation is at stake (2.5.1). Also the responsiveness of the respective sectors to catastrophes in terms of adapting the regulatory regime to new needs under new circumstances will be analysed in that section. Turning to the issue of liability and compensation section 2.5.2 will discuss how far the financial limits, if any, in the different sectors are appropriate. Finally, the chapter will end with a short discussion of some public choice considerations that will provide some explanations for the differences between the different sectors (2.5.3).

2.5.1. Regulation at stake

The Chemical sector is regulated mainly by European legislation. Core instruments such as the Seveso Directives and the REACH regulation originated from Brussels and it can be said that the EU was a driving force. The sector tried to adapt the legislation according to the new needs as apparent from accidents that questioned the appropriateness of the existing regimes. The constant revision and amendments of the Seveso Directives after accidents such as, for example, the Baia Mare or the Enschede accident, show an adequate level of responsiveness and the required flexibility.

The Seveso Directives with their focus on information distribution and dialogue between the different actors involved can also be regarded as being more in line with an adversarial style of regulation. This is also confirmed by the stronger provisions on public participation and access to justice in Seveso III. Next to this, the REACH regulation, by introducing the European Chemical Agency and processes that are characterised by more interaction between Commission, Member States and ECHA can also be seen as supporting a dialectic style of regulation.

The Oil sector relies both on international and European instruments. The European Union however plays a strong role in setting the regulatory agenda in this sector. Keeping in mind the establishment of the European Maritime Safety Agency for example the importance of European initiatives becomes apparent. And also in the areas dominated by international conventions the European Union has had a strong influence on the legal regime as it was shown for example by the role that the European Commission played in lobbying for the increased compensation amounts under the 2003 Supplementary Fund Protocol.

The legal framework for oil pollution has constantly been adapted and can be regarded as very responsive. Actually every major accident in the last decades has led to amendments and revisions of the existing Conventions. The 1992 Conventions for example entered into force in May 1996, but in the light of the Erika incident in 1999 the compensation amounts were changed and increased by 50% in 1999. The new amounts came into force in November 2003. Meanwhile, however, the Prestige incident had already led to new changes, leading to the 2003 Supplementary Fund Protocol which entered into force in March 2005. Looking at these developments it can be said that every few years the oil sector was prepared to change the legal regime if needed.

With regard to the nuclear sector, the currently applicable legal instruments are to a certain extent at odds with the core features of the chemical and the oil sector. The regulations at stake are very influenced by international conventions or international agencies. The European Union cannot be seen as the main driver of changes in the nuclear sector. This is for example in clear contrast to the oil sector where the European Commission has taken a more active role in lobbying for example for higher compensation amounts. Generally it has to be said that the nuclear sector seems to be less adaptive to new challenges than the other sectors. Amendments in response to catastrophes take more time or in certain situations are not even suggested. The Fukushima accident for example has not led so far to serious attempts to increase the compensation amounts available. Thus, the nuclear sector can be described as not very responsive. Teubner describes responsiveness as the ability to adapt to changing social circumstances, including the different interested parties in a continuous process of change.[240] The oil sector for example has to be qualified as being more in line with this criterion, given the constant changes that took place in reaction to changing circumstances as described above. A possible reason for that is that in the oil sector one can witness a more dialectic negotiation process of conventions and applicable rules. Given that during the negotiations of the applicable legal frameworks the interests of the oil industry, shipping companies and coastal states are involved, a more balanced outcome is understandable.[241] Next to this, Wang also points out that in the area of oil pollution there was more political pressure to adapt the existing regimes to changing circumstances in the light of accidents that heavily affected some coastal states.[242] In the nuclear sector however, an apparent lack of well-functioning counter-vailing powers prevents the striking of a balance between different interests at stake.[243] Thus there is a risk that industry interests prevail whilst interests of other stakeholders are not taken into serious consideration.

Furthermore, we still see a more consensual style of regulation in the nuclear sector, having in mind the importance attached to for example ENSREG and not very strong provisions on public participation. Under the proposal for a revised Safety Directive, the development from a consensual towards a more adversarial approach became apparent. This change was for example mirrored in the new title of article 8 which would have been 'Transparency' which is a core aspect of good regulation[244] and also of an adversarial regulatory style. The final version that was adopted as the 2014 amendments to the

240 Teubner 1983, p. 247+248; see also Braithwaite 2006.
241 Wang 2007, p. 238.
242 Wang 2011, p. 185+186.
243 Becker 1983; Becker 1989.
244 Black and Jacobzone 2009, p. 51.

Nuclear Safety Directive did also incorporate these changes. It remains to be seen whether these changes will indeed lead to a strengthening of a meaningful public participation in the nuclear sector which would be desirable given the current lack thereof as discussed in the previous chapter.[245]

2.5.2. *Compensation limits and financial coverage*

With regard to the compensation limits in the different sectors the following observations have to be made. In the chemical sector there is no international or regional instrument limiting possible compensation claims in amount. This is different both in the oil and the nuclear sectors where the liability of the operator is capped. These two sectors deserve consequently some further attention.

Having already said that in both sectors liability is capped, the attention now will turn to the question of how much money is available in the two sectors. With regard to the oil sector it should be observed that the most compensation is currently available in states that are parties to the 1992 CLC and the 1992 Fund Convention and the 2003 Supplementary Protocol. Under these instruments the compensation is limited to approximately € 950 million.[246] Looking at incidents that have happened in the oil sector, this amount, which is the result of constant amendments and revision of the compensation amounts in the light of accidents seems to be sufficient. The Erika accident for example cause damage of around € 400 million, the Prestige accident almost exceeded this damage by 100% with € 785 million in damages.[247] Both these amounts are below the currently available liability limits. This takes away some criticism against the limitation of liability in the oil sector because indeed the limits are regarded as sufficient to cope with the majority of accidents in that sector.[248] If the limitation is set at appropriate levels and accident costs do not surpass these limits, at least the compensatory function is still given. Another interesting aspect of the oil sector is that national courts have also been very pro-active in trying to mitigate possible negative consequences of some of the principles of the conventions in the oil sector. In the Erica case for example national courts in France tried to circumvent the requirements of the international conventions.[249]

In the nuclear sector this looks rather different. The 2004 Paris Protocol allows liability to be limited to a total of € 1.5 billion. This represents the highest amount that is currently foreseen amongst the international instruments. The Protocol was introduced in reaction to the Chernobyl accident in 1986. Not only did it take almost 20 years after the accident to come up with the protocol, the possibility to limit liability already at

245 See section 1.3.5.
246 The Supplementary Fund Protocol increased the available compensation to 750 SDR.
247 See Faure and Wang 2008, p. 594.
248 *Ibid.*, p. 602.
249 See Kopela 2011.

such comparably low amounts is inappropriate as demonstrated by the accident in Fukushima. 18 months after the accident, more than € 10 billion had already been paid in compensation.[250] In May 2015, this amount had more than tripled.[251] A study from the end of 2014 estimated the entire cost related with the Fukushima accident at almost € 100 billion.[252] Further it has to be recalled that the Paris Protocol is not even in force yet. The highest limits that are currently available would be a combination of the revised Vienna Convention and the Convention on Supplementary Compensation (CSC) which came into force in April 2015. The former allows a limit of € 378 million and the CSC provide additional funds of € 756 million. Combined this would be approximately € 1.13 billion. At the moment, thus, liability limits are in the majority of cases much too low, although there are exceptions in some domestic laws that go beyond the requirements of the Conventions in force, most notably for example Germany with unlimited liability.[253]

2.5.3. *Public choice considerations*

The discussion of the different regulations at stake and the differences with regard to the efficiency of regulation in different sectors, raise the question of how such differences can be explained. As apparent from the above discussion, the oil and the chemical sector are regulated more strictly and also more along the lines of better regulation philosophy than the nuclear sector. Public choice considerations will serve to shed some light on the flaws that are being facing with regard to the regulation of nuclear safety in the European Union. It has already been pointed out in a previous section, that ultra-hazardous activities and the regulation thereof are susceptible to rent-seeking behaviour.[254] Olson's framework to assess the potential success of rent-seeking behaviour has to be recalled at this point once more. Groups will especially be successful if they are small, homogeneous in their interests, well organised, and have an information advantage over the general public for which it must be costly to obtain sufficient information about the harmful effects of the influence by interest groups.[255]

As discussed in the previous chapter, contrary to such a private interest approach that focuses on the influence of interest groups on regulation, the public interest approach assumes that if regulation occurs, then the government is doing so in the general interest of society. This has also been described by Buchanan, observing that in the 19th and 20th centuries the common opinion was that government would act as a profit maximising entity for the benefit of all citizens. Governments would not be left entirely without

250 Japan's Compensation System for Nuclear Damage, OECD 2012, p. 3.

251 For the most recent status of paid compensation see http://translate.googleusercontent.com/translate_c?anno=2&depth=1&hl=nl&rurl=translate.google.com&sl=en&tl=nl&u=www.tepco.co.jp/en/comp/index-e.html&usg=ALkJrhgo2XS-xKB_SBLLOCA73c4MMOpNJQ (last accessed on 21 August 2015).

252 Http://rt.com/news/183052-japan-fukushima-costs-study/ (last accessed on 21 August 2015).

253 See section 3.3.5.2.

254 See section 1.2.2.

255 Olson 1965.

control but regular elections would suffice to work as a sufficient control mechanism to steer government behaviour.[256]

In an introductory essay on the theory of public choice, Buchanan, whilst fittingly referring to the term of politics without romance, describes a change in that view, leading to a different perception of government. Politicians and other state actors are not regarded anymore as different than any other actors in society and political decisions are regarded as the outcome of different influences from the actors involved. The people involved in this process can have very different objectives and outcomes need not necessarily be efficient.[257] As a logical follow up the question that then arises is why there is not more resistance against lobbyism that protects the interests of the nuclear industry. One explanation can possibly be found in one of Olson's criteria for successful rent-seeking, namely insufficient information with the general public to know about the harmful consequences of such behaviour. Another possible answer would be a reference to 'the rationally ignorant voter'. The group that would have to organise itself to work effectively against regulation that is in favour of the nuclear sector is very large. Taking action in a coordinated way is therefore complicated and for an individual the interest to strive for changes that will benefit society as a whole is not strong enough, which leads to a collective action problem.[258] In the nuclear sector there seems to be a lack of an effective countervailing power as described by Becker.[259] Industry interests can therefore be furthered to the detriment of the environment and potential victims of nuclear accidents. This is different in other high risk sectors. With regard to the oil sector for example, there apparently is a better balance between interest groups involved in the process of drafting legislation. Wang therefore describes the international legislative framework applicable to the oil sector as the result of competing interest groups.[260]

The observations discussed in this section can offer some explanations for the relatively lenient regulation in the nuclear sector, both with regard to safety requirements and compensation and liability limits. Public choice theory can shed some light on the question of why safety regulation in the nuclear sector has developed differently than in other high risk sectors such as the chemical or the oil sectors. Rent-seeking as described by Olson apparently does take place. Certain provisions in the legislative framework of the nuclear sector indeed might only be explainable through successful lobbying attempts and the furtherance of industry interests.[261]

256 Buchanan 1984, p. 15.
257 *Ibid.*, p. 20.
258 Svendsen 1998, p. 29+30.
259 Becker 1983; Becker 1989; For a deeper analysis of the effect of competing interest groups and how public choice literature can also help to readjust the balance of powers within the nuclear sector see chapter 7.
260 Wang 2011, p. 347.
261 Ogus 1994, p. 75.

Part II

The Regulation of Nuclear Accidents – The European Dimension

The previous part of this thesis has focussed on the theoretical background of the regulation of ultra-hazardous activities, and has identified major differences in the regulation of such activities if compared by sector. The following part will turn the focus of this thesis exclusively to the nuclear sector and provide an analysis of the European dimension of the problem of nuclear liability. Chapter 3 will discuss the currently applicable liability systems, mainly based on international conventions. Core principles of these international conventions will be presented. The principles of the currently applicable regimes will then be compared to some national systems to identify possible shortcomings of the current regimes but also good practices which should be adopted by an EU system. For the national comparison a choice was made for Austria, Germany, France and the United Kingdom.

Chapter 4 will then make the bridge to the European Union by analysing possible legislative bases for a future European liability system for nuclear accidents. The main focus will be on legal bases coming from the Lisbon Treaty. This departs from currently prevailing approaches. On occasions where nuclear liability is currently discussed in the European Union, the focus is still almost exclusively on the Euratom Treaty. It will be questioned whether this is still the appropriate forum for this issue, keeping in mind the outdated nature of the Euratom Treaty and the need in the European Union to remove the nuclear sector from its artificial isolation and to regulate the nuclear sector under a Treaty that is more in line with recent core paradigms of risk regulation and environmental protection.

Chapter 5 will approach the question of whether there are economic justifications for the harmonisation in the area of nuclear liability. Should the nuclear sector be regulated in a centralised or a decentralised manner? A discussion of harmonisation versus regulatory competition will analyse how far arguments such as the risk for a race to the bottom, the need for economies of scale or transboundary externalities can be used to justify further harmonisation in the nuclear sector

Chapter 3

THE CURRENT SITUATION WITHIN THE EUROPEAN UNION

3.1. Overview of the International Conventions

Generally it can be said that there are two main systems, namely the one established under the auspices of the NEA of the OECD with the 1960 Paris and 1963 Brussels Conventions and its following amendments and protocols, and the one in the framework of the IAEA, with the 1963 Vienna Convention as amended in the following years by the 1997 Protocol.[262]

3.1.1. One Union, two main systems

With regard to the membership to the different conventions the following split represents the unsatisfactory situation within the European Union: Belgium, Denmark, Finland, France, the Netherlands, Germany, Sweden, Italy, the UK, Spain and Slovenia are parties to the Paris/Brussels regime whilst Portugal and Greece are only parties to the Paris Convention. Bulgaria, the Czech Republic, Estonia, Lithuania, Hungary, Poland, Slovakia, Latvia and Romania are parties to the 1963 Vienna regime. Latvia and Romania have also signed the Protocol from 1997 to amend the Vienna Convention, the Czech Republic, Lithuania, Hungary and Poland have signed it.[263]

3.1.2. Joint Protocol

The NEA regime and the IAEA regime were linked to each other by the Joint Protocol from 1988.[264] It bridges the two main Conventions in the field of nuclear liability by laying down rules to make sure that in the case of a nuclear accident only one of the

262 Protocol to Amend the Vienna Convention on Civil Liability for Nuclear Damage, 29th of September 1997, available at: www.iaea.org/Publications/Documents/Infcircs/1998/infcirc566.pdf (last accessed on 21 August 2015).

263 Handrlica 2010, p. 8–9.

264 Joint Protocol Relating to the Application of the Vienna Convention and the Paris Convention, 21st of September 1988, available at: www.iaea.org/Publications/Documents/Infcircs/Others/inf402.shtml (last accessed on 21 August 2015).

Conventions will apply.[265] Its conclusion was a consequence of the Chernobyl accident and was praised as a step towards a comprehensive nuclear liability regime.[266]

3.1.3. *Convention on Supplementary Compensation*

The current system is complicated further by the Convention on Supplementary Compensation for Nuclear Damage[267] which was signed as an autonomous convention in 1988. The underlying aim was the creation of a global liability regime and to increase the available funds for compensation.[268] Joining the CSC in January 2015, Japan triggered its entry into force in April 2015. Amongst the Member States of the European Union, however, only Romania has ratified this Convention and the Czech Republic, Italy and Lithuania have signed it.[269] It is noteworthy that Japan triggered its entry into force in April 2015.

As one of its core features, and to achieve higher amounts of compensation, it establishes a tier of compensation which is funded by all parties.[270] This additional layer of compensation of the CSC introduces an idea of mutual risk sharing between nuclear operators. Pelzer points out that this has its flaws because it is incomprehensible why European taxpayers should finance nuclear power plants overseas.[271] Whilst one cannot but agree with this, it is possible to draw different conclusions from this then Pelzer does. The answer to this must be a European solution because only on a regional scale can one speak, if at all, from a risk society with mutual solidarity.[272]

3.1.4. *Resulting liability regimes*

In addition to the observations above, it has to be recalled that Austria, Luxembourg, Ireland, Cyprus and Malta are not party to any of these conventions. The liability regimes that currently exist in the European Union are summed up in the following overview:

265 Handrlica 2010, p. 4.

266 Von Busekist 2006.

267 Convention on Supplementary Compensation for Nuclear Damage, 12th of September 1997, available at: www.iaea.org/Publications/Documents/Infcircs/1998/infcirc567.pdf (last accessed on 21 August 2015).

268 *Ibid.* Preamble.

269 Https://www.iaea.org/sites/default/files/supcomp_status_1.pdf (last accessed on 21 August 2015).

270 Article III Convention on Supplementary Compensation.

271 Pelzer 2008, p. 279.

272 See also section 3.5 and later chapters of this thesis.

Table 2. Overview of the different regimes in the European Union[273]

International Regime		Member States	
Paris regime (NEA)	*Paris (1960) and Brussels (1963)*	Belgium, Denmark, Finland, France, the Netherlands, Germany, Sweden, Italy, the UK, Spain, Slovenia	
		Ratified *Joint Protocol (1988)*	Signed *Joint Protocol (1988)*
		Denmark, Finland, the Netherlands, Germany, Sweden, Italy, the UK, Spain, Slovenia	Belgium, France, the UK
	Paris (1960) only	Portugal, Greece	
	Paris (2004)	none	
Vienna Regime (IAEA)	*Vienna (1963)*	Bulgaria, the Czech Republic, Estonia, Lithuania, Hungary, Poland, Slovakia, Latvia, Romania, Croatia	
		Joint Protocol (1988)	All
	Vienna (1997)	Ratified *Vienna (1997)*	Signed *Vienna (1997)*
		Latvia, Romania	The Czech Republic, Lithuania, Hungary, Poland
Convention on Supplementary Compensation for Nuclear Damage (1997)		Ratified	Signed
		Romania	Lithuania, the Czech Republic, Italy
Nothing		Austria, Luxembourg, Ireland, Cyprus, Malta	

273 Handrlica 2010, p. 1–18.

3.2. Core principles of the international conventions

Four core characteristics can be identified which are common to both the 1960 Paris Convention as well as the 1963 Vienna Convention. The liability of the nuclear operator is strict[274] which means that no fault is required. Liability is channelled exclusively to the nuclear operator[275] meaning that victims will have to make their claims against the nuclear operators and they cannot go after other persons involved as for example suppliers or designers. The liability of the operator of a nuclear installation is limited[276] and the conventions require compulsory insurance.[277] In the following sections there will be a brief introduction to these principles, whilst a more critical and deeper analysis will follow at a later stage of this thesis.[278]

3.2.1. Strict liability of the nuclear operator

As already discussed earlier in this thesis[279], strict liability is the most appropriate rule for unilateral accidents such as the ones that might result from the operation of a nuclear power plant. This is also the prevailing opinion amongst nuclear experts.[280] Therefore it is not surprising that the international conventions also follow such a rule and a further analysis will not be provided at this point.

3.2.2. Legal channelling

One of the most remarkable features of the international regimes is that fact that liability is exclusively channelled to the operator of a nuclear installation. It is that special because one can say that it is a principle that has been tailored specifically for nuclear activities. The reason behind this principle was the wish to protect suppliers in the early days of the nuclear industry.[281] Another aspect that has been brought forward in the literature to justify the notion of legal channelling is that it facilitates the bringing of claims for victims and it was argued that it would be detrimental to the compensation of victims if one departed from this core principle.[282] Even proponents of legal channelling have conceded, however, that the simplification for victims is only the second reason for its introduction, with protection of suppliers remaining the first and actual one.[283]

274 Article 3 Paris Convention; article IV(1) Vienna Convention.
275 Article 6(a) Paris Convention; article II(5) Vienna Convention.
276 Article 7 Paris Convention; Article V Vienna Convention.
277 Article 10 Paris Convention; Article VII Vienna Convention.
278 See Chapter 6, in particular sections 6.2 – 6.6.
279 See Chapter 1.
280 See for example Pelzer 1999, p. 426.
281 See Vanden Borre 2007.
282 Kohlemainen 1999, p. 459.
283 Pelzer 1999, p. 428.

3.2.3. *Amounts and limitation of liability*

Article 7 of the Paris Convention lays down that the maximum liability shall be 15 million Special Drawing Rights (hereinafter SDR) but each state can under certain circumstances increase or lower these amounts provided that the amount is never less than 5 million SDR. The 1963 Brussels Convention supplementing the 1960 Paris Convention increased the amount to 300 million SDR.[284] This amount is financed through three layers: up to at least 5 million SDR will be provided by insurance, the difference between this amount and 175 million SDR will be financed by public funds from the installation state and the third layer up to 300 million SDR will be provided out of collective public funds.[285]

What is apparent from these observations is that there is a big reliance on public funding. This situation is not different under the 2004 Protocol to amend the Paris Convention[286] which was adopted to react to the needs for higher amounts of liability that had become apparent by the Chernobyl accident.[287] The minimum liability under the protocol was increased to € 700 million[288] This protocol however has not come into force yet.[289]

The 1963 Vienna Convention allows the installation state to limit the liability to not less than 5 million USD.[290] In 1997 a protocol to amend the 1963 Vienna Convention was adopted and increased the liability to 300 SDR.[291] It allows the installation state to decrease the amount of liability of the nuclear operator under certain circumstances if the state guarantees that in case of an accident public funds will be made available.[292]

It has to be noted at this point that the conventions as amended in the meanwhile do provide for the possibility of introducing unlimited liability.[293] However, states do not really make use of this opportunity. The limitation of liability has several negative effects. On the one hand, the Fukushima accident has shown that in case of a nuclear accident the current liability limits are not even close to the actual cost of damage. This also means that victims cannot be satisfactorily compensated. Furthermore one can speak of

284 Article 3(1) Convention of 31st January 1963 Supplementary to the Paris Convention.

285 *Ibid.*, art. 3(2) sec. (1)-(3).

286 Protocol to Amend the Convention on Third Party liability in the Field of Nuclear Energy of 29 July 1960, as amended by the Additional Protocol of 28 January 1964 and by the Protocol of 16 November 1982, 12th of February 2004, available at: www.oecd-nea.org/law/paris_convention.pdf (last accessed on 21 August 2015).

287 Www.oecd-nea.org/law/paris-convention-protocol.html (last accessed on 21 August 2015).

288 Art. I(H)a.

289 For the latest status of ratifications or accessions see www.oecd-nea.org/law/paris-convention-ratification.html (last accessed on 21 August 2015).

290 Article V(1) Vienna Convention.

291 Article 7 Protocol to Amend the Vienna Convention on Civil Liability for Nuclear Damage.

292 *Ibid.*, Article 7(2).

293 Carroll 2008, p. 93.

an inherent subsidy to the nuclear industry by the limitation of liability which can also raise concerns from an EU state aid perspective.[294]

3.2.4. Compulsory insurance and the principle of congruence

The limited liability amounts as discussed in the previous section have also to be seen together with issues of insurability. An underlying principle of the international conventions is also the principle of congruence between liability and coverage. That means that liability can only be as high as coverage can be guaranteed. When discussing higher limits under the revised conventions and protocols, issues of insurability have been brought forward against too high amounts. Looking at the limits, even as proposed in the instruments that are not yet in force, one has to observe, however, that the limits have not reached a point above which they would not be insurable anymore. In other sectors much higher amounts are apparently available and specific national solutions also show that higher coverage amounts would be possible. Raising the principle of congruence as a defence against higher limits seems not entirely justified, having in mind insurance capacities and other solutions for higher coverage already in existence in some states. It further has to be pointed out that the requirement to take out compulsory insurance can also be decoupled from questions of liability, circumventing the problem of insurability.[295]

3.3. The European dimension – A comparative overview

The following sections will sketch the main issues of the nuclear sector in four different member States of the European Union. Focussing not only on the key points of nuclear liability, but also trying to draw some lessons from a more general approach to the regulation of the nuclear sector, which can enable a certain learning effect for a future European liability regime. Which aspects can already be identified in Member States that are worth keeping and which ones have to be revisited?

3.3.1. Austria

The Federal Law on Civil liability for damages caused by radioactivity was adopted in October 1998 and presents a different approach to the issue of nuclear liability compared to the international liability conventions, because the goal of this law is to regulate nuclear liability more in line with general rules of tort law and not anymore in a

294 Faure and Fiore 2009; See also Chapter 6.

295 This approach can also be found in the more recent liability conventions. Under the Paris Protocol from 2004 for example, section I.K states: 'Article 10 shall be replaced by the following text: [...] Where the liability of the operator is not limited in amount, the Contracting Party within whose territory the nuclear installation of the liable operator is situated shall establish a limit upon the financial security of the operator liable, provided that any limit so established shall not be less than the amount referred to in Article 7(*a*) or 7(*b*).

specialised and isolated way.[296] Austria is an especially interesting example because it represents a non-nuclear country which understandably 'decided to completely break away from the approach toward nuclear liability taken by the Paris and Vienna Convention.'[297] Nuclear energy production is constitutionally forbidden in Austria.

3.3.2. *Germany*

An interesting aspect of German nuclear law that should be mentioned at this point is the dynamic character of the regulation of nuclear safety as laid down in the German Atomic law. In the German Atomgesetz from 1960 article 7(2)3 requires that precautions must be taken in accordance with the state of science and technology against the hazards arising from the operation of a nuclear plant. The dynamic interpretation of this article was supported by the BGH in the Kalkar I decision. The Wyhl decision increased the standard even further by introducing an obligation that risks that are not scientifically proven but merely represent a potential concern (*Besorgnispotential*), have also to be taken into account. This indeed represent a very dynamic approach to nuclear safety and gives some shape to concepts such as continuous improvement of nuclear safety. A European regime could also benefit from such an approach.[298]

3.3.3. *France*

France relies heavily on nuclear energy. More than 70% of the generated energy is nuclear energy. Concerning the regulatory framework in France, the Act on Transparency and Security in the Nuclear Field[299] deserves specific attention. It is a much elaborated piece of legislation, providing the institutional set up of the nuclear sector. In its article 2 it states that the participatory principle and the polluter pays principle are core principles that have to be respected in the nuclear sector.

Title II of the Act established the Nuclear Safety Authority and lays down its relationship towards the public and the parliament, thereby creating a relationship of accountability of the different actors involved.[300] Title III lays down in quite some detail the rights of the public to information on nuclear safety and procedures to guarantee compliance with this right. Concerning Title IV of the act the most remarkable point is that its chapter IV also pays attention to the issue of penal sanctions.[301] The use of penal sanctions

296 See Explanatory Memorandum, p. 8, available at www.parlament.gv.at/PAKT/VHG/XX/I/I_01357/fname_140246.pdf (last accessed on 21 August 2015).

297 Hinteregger 2008, p. 28.

298 The proposal for a new Safety Directive seems to go indeed into this direction. It remains to be seen how this proposal will develop.

299 Act No. 2006-686 of 13 June 2006 on Transparency and Security in the Nuclear Field, English version available at: www.french-nuclear-safety.fr/index.php/content/download/22273/123572/file/loiTSN-uk.pdf (last accessed on 21 August 2015).

300 See article 7 Act No. 2006-686.

301 See articles 46 ff Act No. 2006-686.

to guarantee a high level of nuclear safety is in the current debate not always given enough attention, and the French approach has to be applauded for this. The holistic approach of the French Act on Transparency and Security in the Nuclear Field makes it an important source of inspiration for the regulation of the nuclear sector in a harmonised liability regime within the European Union.

3.3.4. United Kingdom

The United Kingdom was the first country that produced nuclear energy commercially. Since 1956 it has been relying on nuclear energy in its energy mix. Currently the share of nuclear energy is around 18% of the total energy production in the United Kingdom.[302] Concerning the regulatory framework three main acts are of importance, namely the Nuclear Installation Act from 1965, the Health and Safety at Work Act from 1974 and the Energy Act 2013. The United Kingdom had to witness already at the very beginning of their nuclear energy production history a nuclear accident with the Windscale fire in 1957. As a lesson learned from this accident the Nuclear Installations Inspectorate was established to ensure independent regulation of the nuclear sector. Originally the nuclear regulator of the UK was part of the Health and Safety Executive. Recently the institutional set up has changed. The Energy Act 2013 established the ONR as a statutory public corporation. This new legal status is foreseen to strengthen the independence and effectiveness of the regulator.[303]

An interesting aspect of the regulatory regime in the United Kingdom is that the Health and Safety at Work Act from 1974 incorporated the principles of 'as low as reasonably practicable' (ALARP). ALARP entails an optimisation duty to reduce risks as much as reasonably practicable. This principle can also be found in similar formulation in European legislation.[304] Contrary to the situation in the European Union, however, in the UK this principle has been put into practice and guidance explains what exactly is meant by it.[305] As an example for this one can refer to a publication by the Health and Safety Executive from 1992 entitled 'The Tolerability of Risk from Nuclear Power Stations'. In this document ALARP is explained by means of a cost benefit analysis, stating that further safety investments are required up to the point where further expenditure would be grossly disproportionate to the risk'.[306] It is desirable that a European regime should benefit from such national experiences because it allows taking out the best of national practices and incorporating them into a European regime.[307] It

302 A guide to Nuclear Regulation in the UK, ONR, 2014.

303 A strategy paper of ONR is available at www.onr.org.uk/consultations/2014/strategy/onr-strategy-2015–2020.pdf (last accessed on 21 August 2015).; see also: www.world-nuclear-news.org/E-ONRs-new-role-comes-at-crucial-time-for-UK-industry-16011501.html (last accessed on 21 August 2015).

304 See section 2.4.4.

305 Veuchelen 2009, p. 222+223.

306 The Tolerability of Risk from Nuclear Power Stations, HSE, 1992, p. 10.

307 Veuchelen 2009, p. 223.

is interesting to see that the proposal for an amended Safety Directive[308] actually did that, by suggesting the introduction *inter alia of* a definition of reasonably achievable in the amended Nuclear Safety Directive. Article 1 of the proposal provides the following definition:

> *'reasonably achievable means that, in addition to meeting the requirements of good practice in engineering, further safety or risk reduction measures for the design, commissioning, operation or decommissioning of a nuclear installation should be sought and that these measures should be implemented unless it can be demonstrated that they are grossly disproportionate with regard to the safety benefit they would confer'*

The proposal thus followed the test of gross disproportion to provide more guidance to the term of ALARA. In the final version of the amended Directive, however, this definition was not included eventually.[309]

3.3.5. *Comparative summary of the status of the core principles of the international conventions in the national regimes*

3.3.5.1. Types of damage covered

The Austrian act on liability includes damages to persons and property which is, according to article 11, to 'be governed by the provisions of the ABGB (*Allgemeines Bürgerliches Gesetzbuch*). The duty to compensate property damage also includes the cost of eliminating the radiation danger presented by such property'. The reference to the ABGB shows the intention of the drafters of the act that it should not become a closed and independent system for damages resulting from radioactivity, but rather be seen as specific rules that should be accommodated in the broader legal system.[310] This is a specific feature of the Austrian Act because it positions it clearly amongst other rules of the legal system, thereby abolishing the very specific *lex generalis* character that the nuclear sector often benefits from.

The article continues by stating:

> *'If the damage to physical property also creates serious harm to the environment and if the person liable is unable or unwilling to restore it to its former condition, then the person who suffered damage shall also be entitled to recover compensation for costs of re-instatement, even if such costs exceed the value of the property damaged. The injured party can request these costs in advance, but must return the excess of costs over value if he does not restore the damaged property to its former condition within a reasonable time.*

308 COM(2013) 343 final.

309 See Council Directive 2014/87/Euratom of 8 July 2014.

310 See Explanatory Memorandum, p. 8.available at www.parlament.gv.at/PAKT/VHG/XX/I/I_01357/fname_140246.pdf (last accessed on 21 August 2015).

The duty to compensate includes the costs of reasonable preventive measures adopted in order to avoid an imminent threat of emission of ionising radiation from a nuclear installation, nuclear material or a radionuclide (rescue expenses). Such costs shall be recoverable by the person who actually incurs them.'

The scope of compensable damage has been significantly broadened by this article compared to the older Austrian law. Also in comparison to currently applicable international regimes it is an improvement in terms of environmental protection.

This cannot be said about Germany and France, in line with the international conventions covering personal damage and damage to property. The environment is not protected *per se*. This is also the case in the UK. The Nuclear installation Act only foresees damage to persons or property as compensable damage.[311] The UK provides an interesting example concerning the definition of personal injury. Defining the scope of this type of damage it was made clear in case law that damage to the person has to be 'proved personal injury and not the risk of future personal injury'.[312] It has also been established that stress and anxiety cannot be regarded as damage to a person either.[313]

3.3.5.2. Limitations of liability and amounts

In Austria liability of the nuclear operator is unlimited. Next to Austria there is only Germany, Switzerland and Japan that also follow a rule of unlimited liability. Concerning the insurance, obligation article 6(2) established an obligation of at least 406 Million € per incident. This amount goes beyond limits which are still applicable in the international regimes.

In Germany Article 31 of the German Atomic Act established unlimited liability:

'The liability of the operator of a nuclear installation under the Paris Convention in conjunction with section 25, paragraphs (1), (2) and (4), and also under the Paris Convention and the Joint Protocol in conjunction with section 25, paragraphs (1), (2) and (4), shall be unlimited.'

As already observed above, liability is of course never truly unlimited. In Germany however the currently available amounts go far beyond the obligations under the international conventions. Total coverage in Germany amounts to 2.5 Billion €. Every reactor is insured up to 255,645 Million €. And the remaining 2.244 Billion € are covered by a voluntary pooling agreement between the 4 operators in Germany.[314]

311 Article 7 Nuclear Installations Act 1965.

312 Thomas and Heffron 2012, p. 12.

313 *Ibid.*

314 Www.bee-ev.de/_downloads/presse/2011/110511_DKVG-Praesentation-PK.pdf (last accessed on 21 August 2015).

In clear contrast to these two countries with unlimited liability, France currently limits the liability of the operator at below 91.5 Million €. This is one of the lowest limits within the European Union which is especially surprising given the strong reliance of France on nuclear energy. It has to be noted however that France is prepared to increase the limit once the Paris Protocol from 2007 enters into force. The latter also holds true for the UK where the liability of the operator is currently limited at 140 Million £.[315]

3.3.5.3. Channelling

The Austrian Act states in its article 16:

> *'Provisions under the ABGB and other laws governing damages of a broader scope or liability of persons other than those provided for under this Federal Act shall remain unaffected hereby. Persons having suffered damage may bring such claims directly in the courts.'*

It has thereby also abolished the international core principle of channelling. Victims remain free to claim compensation for damages against the operator or against other persons. As a basis for this claim general provisions of tort law can also be used. The Explanatory Memorandum shows that it was the conviction of the drafters of the Act that the principle of legal channelling is outdated and had therefore to be replaced.[316]

In Germany article 25(1) of the German Atomic Energy Act states:

> *'If damage is caused by a nuclear incident originating from a nuclear installation, the provisions of this Act, in addition to the provisions of the Paris Convention, shall apply to the liability of the operator of such nuclear installation. Irrespective of its binding character under international law, the Paris Convention and the Joint Protocol shall apply as national law in the Federal Republic of Germany [...].'*

As apparent from this article, in Germany liability is also channelled towards the operator. However, Rehbinder points out that Germany has reserved itself the right to apply general rules of tort law against other persons than the operator.[317] Thereby the German Act departs as well from the general principle of legal channelling as laid down in the international conventions.

France on the other hand adheres to legal channelling, thereby restricting possible rights of recourse of the operator to other parties. The same holds true for the liability law in the United Kingdom which also adheres to legal channelling.[318]

315 Article 16 Nuclear Installations Act 1965; 140 Million £ are roughly 195.5 Million €.

316 See Explanatory Memorandum, p. 28. available at www.parlament.gv.at/PAKT/VHG/XX/I/I_01357/fname_140246.pdf (last accessed on 21 August 2015).

317 Rehbinder 2010, p. 422.

318 Article 12(1)b Nuclear Installations Act 1965.

3.4. General principles of EU environmental law and nuclear liability

The following sections will focus on two fundamental principles of EU Environmental law, namely the Precautionary and the Polluter Pays Principle. And analysis of their function and status and of possible consequences of their application will serve a twofold purpose. On the one hand, this analysis will be used as a benchmark against which the currently applicable regimes, based upon the international conventions, will be measured. This will show if and to what extent the international regimes are in line with these two principles of EU law. On the other hand the analysis will serve to reveal some more general aspects of these two principles that could inspire also the rethinking of the current principles of nuclear liability and that should be taken into account when designing a European solution later on in his thesis.

3.4.1. The Precautionary Principle

When dealing with the regulation of nuclear energy, discussing the Precautionary Principle and its reach and implications is inevitable. This principle is especially appealing in the area of ultra-hazardous activities. Given that accidents in these sectors mostly result in large scale catastrophes, a precautionary approach seems desirable. A precautionary approach, however, should not be confused with an application of the Precautionary principle *stricto sensu*. It is unfortunate that this differentiation is not always made. De Sadeleer uses the terms Precautionary Principle and precautionary approach as synonyms.[319] Sands and Peel also do not seem to see differences between these two terms with regard to their meaning and content.[320] With regard to its application in the nuclear sector, however, an analysis can benefit from a distinction between the Precautionary Principle and a precautionary approach. The following two sections will focus on this distinction. After that will come an analysis of what role an emphasis on precaution can play with regard to the decision-making processes. It has to be noted that the following sections will depict some aspects of the Precautionary Principle and its influence on the regulation of the nuclear sector. This analysis does not, however, intend to give an exhaustive overview of the different interpretations of the Precautionary Principle. It rather limits itself to picking up some aspects that are of relevance for the discussion at stake.[321]

3.4.1.1. The Precautionary Principle *stricto sensu*

The Precautionary Principle has been severely attacked in literature. Pesendorfer for example claims that this principle is not backed by science but by more general values,

319 De Sadeleer 2002, p. 92.

320 Sands and Peel 2012, p. 218.

321 For a more comprehensive analysis of the origins of the Precautionary Principle and its different interpretations both from a legal and an economic perspective see for example Wibisana 2008 and Haritz 2011.

thereby entailing an element of arbitrariness.[322] Majone points out that following the Precautionary Principle can lead to situations in which regulators will not consider the average cases anymore in their calculations, but rather base their consideration of the worst scenario that could happen.[323]

In its Communication on the Precautionary Principle the Commission emphasises that 'the precautionary principle is relevant only in the event of a potential risk, even if this risk cannot be fully demonstrated or quantified or its effects determined because of the insufficiency or inclusive nature of the scientific data.'[324] How the Precautionary Principle can empower the Commission to take decisions aiming at the protection of public health was already clearly reflected in the BSE crisis. Confirming the Commission's decision to ban the export of beef during that crisis, the Court of Justice of the European Union stated that

> *'at the time when the contested decision was adopted, there was great uncertainty as to the risks posed by live animals, bovine meat and derived products. Where there is uncertainty as to the existence or extent of risks to human health, the institutions may take protective measures without having to await the reality and seriousness of those risks become fully apparent.'*[325]

As apparent from this judgment and the Commission's Communication on the Precautionary Principle, a pre-requisite for the principle to apply is scientific uncertainty. It is this condition that makes an application of the Precautionary Principle in its strict sense questionable in the nuclear sector, given that whilst nuclear activities undoubtedly create dangers and it is not certain whether an accident will happen, this is rather an issue of probability than scientific uncertainty. Risks stemming from radiation are fairly well researched and it is hardly conceivable to argue that we are facing a situation of scientific uncertainty with regard to the question whether radiation can have negative consequences. Invoking the Precautionary Principle as a tool to stop nuclear activities for example, seems to be pushing the limits of this Principle too far. This view is supported by case law from the European Court of Human Rights, clarifying that the Precautionary Principle does not imply an obligation to shut down any industrial plants due to the mere fact that the operation of such plants implies certain risks.[326]

Building upon German theory, de Sadeleer distinguishes three different types of risks, namely certain risks (dangers), uncertain risks and residual risks. Whilst the first category present the most severe ones, namely unacceptable risks, the last category of residual risks represents the risks that society would have to tolerate. Residual risks are

322 Pesendorfer 2011, p. 287–289.
323 Majone 2011, p. 302.
324 COM(2000) 1 final, p. 13.
325 Case T-76/96 R, *The National Farmers' Union and Others* v. *Commission of the European Communities* [1996].
326 De Sadeleer 2002, p. 102+103, see also ECtHR, Balmer-Schafroth and Others v. Switzerland, 67\1996\686\876, 1997.

therefore also not subject to further regulatory measures. The precautionary principle thus would not apply to these risks either. It would only be the category of uncertain risks, to which the precautionary principle can be applied. Requiring a zero risk approach based on the Precautionary Principle, however, cannot be required of public authorities.[327]

According to Waite the application of the Precautionary Principle has to be seen as a compromise between the importance of innovation and development on the one hand, and the inherent uncertainty of science on the other hand.[328] When dealing with ultra-hazardous activities such as nuclear energy generation, a balance consequently has to be struck between an extensive (over)application of the Precautionary Principle and an up-front dismissal of this principle. Furthermore, in some situations the Precautionary Principle is not applicable, because not all conditions needed for its application are fully given. How the principle in a qualified form can still be of significant relevance in the nuclear sector will be discussed in the following sections.

3.4.1.2. A precautionary approach

Whilst the preceding section argued that the Precautionary Principle *stricto sensu* is not applicable to the issue of nuclear safety or a liability regime for nuclear accidents and therefore does not pose a major issue in the assessment of the current liability regimes or in the design of a future European system for the liability of nuclear accidents, the need for a precautionary approach in this sector is beyond doubt.

In the communication on the Precautionary Principle the Commission makes clear that it entails that public health concerns should be given an important status and that such concerns should take precedence over economic considerations.[329] This requirement could be implemented in the area of nuclear power generation by a precautionary approach. It implies a stricter level of scrutiny and requires nuclear operators to minimise the risks that power plants pose to public health as far as possible.[330] It also requires a certain degree of care and foresight when being faced with activities that could pose a risk to the environment.[331] Such an approach also implies an increased burden that is put on an operator not to cause damage to the environment. If damage nevertheless occurs, one effect of an application of the Precautionary Principle could, according to de Sadeleer, be to facilitate the establishment of liability because the operator is not only required to assess the operation of a power plant according to the knowledge he possesses, but also with the knowledge that he should have had.[332]

327 De Sadeleer 2002, p. 156–158.
328 Waite 2005, p. 57.
329 COM (2000) 1 final, p. 20.
330 De Sadeleer 2002, p. 129.
331 Sands and Peel 2012, p. 222.
332 De Sadeleer 2002, p. 213.

The previous aspect focuses on how an application of the Precautionary Principle can lead to liability. This aspect is also extensively discussed by Haritz. Using climate change liability as an example, she shows how the Precautionary Principle could tackle a number of obstacles in liability claims in that sector. It could facilitate the establishment of liability by a number of tools, including for example a higher required standard of care, adjustments in the burden of proof, and limiting available defences.[333] If uncertainties surrounding a potential liability claim discourage victims from bringing a suit, this can also lead to under-deterrence and excessive risk taking on the side of the potential tortfeasor. By removing some of these uncertainties, an application of the Precautionary principle that facilitates the establishment of liability can mitigate these effects.[334] It can thereby re-inforce both the preventive and the compensative function of liability law and has the potential to influence the behaviour of the tortfeasor.[335]

Next to the issue of how the Precautionary Principle can help to accommodate a number of uncertainties in a liability claim, it can also serve as a guidance in setting regulatory standards when being faced with ultra-hazardous activities that are characterised on the one hand by a low-probability that an accident will happen but on the other hand by dramatic consequences if such an accident occurred. Wibisana points out that for such activities the Precautionary principle can justify stricter, more precautionary regulation by focussing on quasi-option value.[336] Precautionary regulation enables a regulator to prevent irreversible harm by allowing 'the decision-maker to err on the side of under-development rather than over-development.'[337] This is of particular relevance for the example of nuclear power generation, given the irreversible nature of the damage that can result from a nuclear accident.

Whilst throughout the previous paragraphs indeed the term Precautionary Principle was used, it is apparent from the discussion above that the different tools and approaches to liability and regulatory processes that were presented are again an indirect rather than a direct application of the Precautionary Principle and could also be qualified as elements of a precautionary approach.

3.4.1.3. The Precautionary Principle and its role on decision-making

The Precautionary Principle can on the one hand be regarded as disempowering experts leading to a decreased role of scientific expertise in the decision-making process, given the realisation that science is not the solution to everything anymore in the face of uncertainty. This development would arguably have a democratising effect because decisions would again be taken more by political bodies instead of by technical experts.[338]

333 See Haritz 2011, p. 293–337.
334 *Ibid.*, p. 284.
335 *Ibid.*, p. 380+382.
336 Wibisana 2008, p. 209+210.
337 *Ibid.*, p. 531.
338 De Sadeleer 2002, p. 175–179.

On the other hand one could also argue that reliance on technical expertise is stronger under the Precautionary Principle because a core aspect of it is the continuous reassessment of scientific evidence to justify precautionary decisions taken and change them if necessary.[339] Choosing one of these two extremes of the spectrum would, however, be too simplistic. A better and more nuanced approach describes the Precautionary Principle as a tool that can bring political actors, scientists and the general public closer together in the decision making process. Realising the uncertainty that is at stake in certain areas and accepting that science cannot give an answer to everything, allows a reinforced role for the general public, emphasising the multi-dimensional nature of risk.[340] The Precautionary Principle can provide an impetus to enhance deliberative regulatory processes, thereby also functioning as a means to achieve better governance and striving for more openness.[341]

Another important aspect of precautionary regulation is the conviction that one should not be secretive about the lack of certainty. If there are doubts, these should be voiced, involving once more also the general public to allow them to have an influence and also to take a well-informed decision.[342] Precautionary regulation and governance in that sense then does not mean creating regulatory impasses and blocking innovation and certain technologies; it rather empowers decision makers and society to take transparent decisions. It thereby increases the legitimacy of the decision makers on the one hand, whilst enhancing inclusiveness on the other hand at the same time.[343] Regulatory decisions then can still involve risks, but it will be risks that society has agreed that it is willing to take.

3.4.2. The Polluter Pays Principle

The Polluter pays principle is a key principle of Community law, the importance of which has also been confirmed in the Court's case law.[344] The importance of the principle is also mirrored in its introduction into the TFEU. Article 191(2) states 'that environmental damage should, as a priority, be rectified at source and that the polluter should pay.' The scope of this principle is increased by article 7 of the TFEU which could be termed an all-encompassing policy linking clause: 'The Union shall ensure consistency between its policies and activities, taking all of its objectives into account and in accordance with the principle of conferral of powers.' Article 7 TFEU is also applicable to Euratom in accordance with article 106a of the Euratom Treaty. Thus the Polluter Pays Principle is also applicable to the nuclear sector.

339 *Ibid.*, p. 179.
340 *Ibid.*, p. 190–195.
341 Wibisana 2011, p. 189+190; see also Wibisana 2008, p. 536.; Haritz 2011, p. 276.
342 Steele 2004, p. 193+194.
343 *Ibid.*, p. 197.
344 See e.g. Case C-188/07 *Commune de Mesquer v Total France SA and Total International Ltd* [2008].

3.4.2.1. The Polluter Pays Principle and Euratom

The Polluter Pays Principle was already mentioned in 1975 in a Council recommendation dealing with cost allocation and action by public authorities on environmental matters[345] which also applies to Euratom.[346] The definition of a polluter which is given in this recommendation is quite interesting. According to section 3 'a polluter is someone who directly or indirectly damages the environment or who creates conditions leading to such damage.' This recommendation is still today of crucial importance in the shaping and understanding of the polluter pays principle within the European Union. Whilst formally the recommendation has to be classified as soft law, this does not mean that it is void of any legal effects.[347] The CJEU increasingly attaches importance to soft law instruments in its judgments which shows that the clear cut distinction between binding and non-binding instruments cannot be upheld anymore.[348] The teleological approach of the CJEU has in the past and will undoubtedly in the future be guided also by soft law instruments as persuasive evidence.

The importance and potential reach of soft law instruments are also mirrored in other fields of EU law, such as for example the case law on direct effect and harmonious interpretation of national law in the light of EU law. In *Grimaldi*[349] the Court ruled that soft law has also to be taken into account when national law is interpreted in the light of European law and instruments. Soft law can further create legitimate expectations which it has to respect. In this regard it has to be emphasised that the form of the instrument at stake does not influence the legitimate expectations. This can be illustrated by way of analogy with communications published in the area of competition law. The *de minimis* notice for example, although not formally binding on the CJEU and national authorities, does create legitimate expectations which the Commission has to respect.[350] Another example from this field would be the guidelines of the Commission on the setting of fines. Despite the formal classification of such guidelines as soft law, the Court has consistently ruled that such rules of conduct can nevertheless produce legal effects.[351] This same reasoning certainly applies to the recommendation invoked above and the definitions and guidance given by Council Recommendation 75/436/Euratom, ECSC,

345 Council Recommendation 75/436/Euratom, ECSC, EEC on cost allocation and action by public authorities on environmental matters.

346 In the area of decommissioning the more recent Recommendation 2006/851/Euratom on the management of financial resources for the decommissioning of nuclear installations, spent fuel and radioactive waste confirms the applicability of the Polluter Pays Principle to the nuclear sector.

347 De Sadeleer 2002, p. 28.

348 Case C-176/96 *Jyri Lehtonen and Castors Canada Dry Namur – Braine ASBL* v. *Fédération royale belge des societies de basket-ball ASBL* [2000]; Case C-322/88 Salvatore Grimaldi v. Fonds des maladies professionnelles [1989].

349 Case C-322/88.

350 Ritter and Braun 2005, p. 276.

351 See e.g. Joined Cases C-189/02 P, C-202/02 P, C-205/02 P to C-208/02 P and C-213/02 P *Dansk Rorindustri and Others* v. *Commission of the European Communities* [2005].

EEC on cost allocation and action by public authorities on environmental matters are of legal relevance in the nuclear sector.

3.4.2.2. Application and consequences of the Polluter Pays Principle

With regard to the question of who actually has to pay and the identification of the actual polluter this can sometimes be difficult if different actors arguably contributed to the pollution. Council Recommendation 75/436/Euratom, ECSC, EEC refers to 'the point at which the number of economic operators is least and control is easiest'.[352] De Sadeleer points out that this could also mean that the person who actually caused the pollution might not have to pay, but the person who had a decisive influence on enabling the pollution such as for example the producer of a product and not the user thereof.[353] Another approach described by de Sadeleer is to determine the actor that has the most control over the polluting activity. This approach leads him to the conclusion that the principle of channelling of liability, as foreseen for example in the oil and nuclear liability conventions, is in line with the Polluter Pays Principle.[354] This interpretation can arguably be challenged. Recalling the focus on the actor that has the most control one could also argue that not the nuclear operator, but suppliers and designers would be in the best position because without the technology the operator would not have been able to pollute. This is similar to the analogy that de Sadeleers draws that the responsible person can also be the producer of a product. As shown above, however, one of the core principles of the international conventions is legal channelling, which effectively closes the route of legal claims against designers and nuclear suppliers. Not taking into account the entire supply chain could then be regarded as raising concerns with regard to the Polluter Pays principle, also in the light of the broad definition of a polluter in Council Recommendation 75/436. However, legal doctrine does not seem to support this argument. Sands and Peel, for example, also give the nuclear liability conventions and its principle of legal channelling as an example for an early application of the Polluter Pays Principle.[355]

Besides the question of who actually can be qualified as a polluter according to the principle, in legal doctrine a multitude of interpretations and effects of the Polluter Pays Principle are described. The principle has for example been used as a justification for the increased use of strict liability in liability regimes dealing with environmental matters.[356] De Sadeleer refers *inter alia* to the 1993 Lugano Convention on Civil Liability for Damage Resulting from Activities Dangerous to the Environment, the Commission Green Paper on environmental liability and some national experiences to confirm this. Referring also explicitly to the first nuclear liability conventions he shows that this trend is not one that came into existence only recently.[357]

352 Council Recommendation 75/436/Euratom, ECSC, EEC, para. 3.
353 De Sadeleer 2002, p. 42.
354 *Ibid.*, p. 55.
355 Sands and Peel 2012, p. 229.
356 De Sadeleer 2002, p. 30.
357 *Ibid.*, p. 50+51.

The Polluter Pays Principle can also have an influence on the scope of damage that is recoverable or that needs to be remedied. Given that it is the essence of this principle to prevent the general public at large having to bear certain costs, it justifies also the reparation of damage to parts of the environment that are not private property but *res communes*.[358] This aspect is of particular relevance in the nuclear sector, given that a large part of damages from a nuclear accident could very well be environmental damage.[359] Coupled with civil liability the Polluter Pays Principle can also strengthen the role of victims of environmental pollution by obliging polluters not only to restore the environment but also to compensate victims affected by accidents.[360]

The Polluter Pays Principle clearly has a preventive function. If polluters were allowed to reap the profits of their activities whilst the costs would be covered by the state, this would not give incentives for enterprises to internalise negative externalities such as pollution, and would enable companies to keep their prices artificially competitive.[361] This would also lead to a situation in which society ultimately would be responsible for the costs to fight pollution. Such policies should be avoided and the protection of the environment should not be financed by state subsidies[362] In this regard it also has to be mentioned that limiting the amount of liability for accidents is questionable in the light of the Polluter Pays principle. Some authors therefore conclude that liability conventions that do allow for a liability limit are not in full compliance with the Polluter Pays Principle.[363]

3.5. The need for a new system

As apparent from the analysis above, the Polluter Pays Principle and the Precautionary Principle, or a precautionary approach respectively, have different facets and can have several consequences for the regulation of the nuclear sector. With regard to the Precautionary Principle it was argued that it is not applicable to the issue of nuclear liability in its strict sense. However, a precautionary approach is certainly required in the nuclear sector and it requires stricter scrutiny of the nuclear sector and can facilitate the establishment of liability, given that operators would be under an obligation to take more hypothetical aspects into account.

The Polluter Pays Principle can be seen as an additional factor contributing to the trend towards strict liability for hazardous activities. In that regard the nuclear liability conventions are no exception because they also follow a rule of strict liability. As discussed, other consequences of the Polluter Pays Principle can be a broader definition

358 *Ibid.*, p. 53.
359 For a discussion on personal injury versus environmental damage and the compensability thereof see section 4.3.1.
360 De Sadeleer 2002, p. 37.
361 *Ibid.*, p. 36.
362 Jans and Vedder 2012, p. 50.
363 De Sadeleer 2002, p. 59.

of recoverable damages, also protecting the environment *per se*. Looking at them from this angle, the international conventions reveal certain flaws.[364] It was also shown that the Polluter Pays Principle, according to some authors, requires unlimited liability. Following this argument most of the currently existing liability regimes do raise problems of non-compliance with the Polluter Pays Principle because the limitation of liability is a core principle of almost all nuclear liability regimes.

Furthermore, the discussion in the earlier parts of this chapter has shown that the current system is extremely patchy. The multitude of conventions and supplementing protocols which have not been widely ratified leads to a system of multiple co-existing regimes. The legal complexity that results from this is a flaw of the currently existing liability regimes. Another important aspect has to be mentioned and this turns attention towards the issue of guaranteeing a robust legal framework for nuclear energy: There are two general objectives of the regulation of nuclear accidents, namely prevention of the accident and compensation of the victims.[365] In academic literature it has been observed that the current system leads to under-deterrence[366] which demonstrates its unsuitability to guarantee a high preventive effect. With regard to its compensatory aspect several studies have already pointed at the fact that under the current regime the coverage is not high enough.[367] Consequently it is doubtful whether the way in which nuclear liability is currently regulated in the international conventions is entirely in line with the two goals of the regulation of nuclear accidents.

The currently applicable regime is the result of a strong nuclear lobby and clearly serving the interests of the nuclear industry. The rationale of some core principles has been the promotion of a then young nuclear industry.[368] Although the revision processes of the international conventions would have been an opportunity to depart from this situation and adapt the liability regimes to a mature nuclear industry, this approach has not been followed and nuclear liability is still regulated along promotional core principles. A European initiative could position the European Union as a front runner in the area of nuclear liability. The following chapter will therefore analyse the competences that the European Union possesses in this area.

364 See section 4.3.1.
365 Faure 1995, p. 22.
366 *Ibid.*
367 Faure and Skogh 1992, p. 499.
368 Pelzer 2008, p. 274.

Chapter 4

RE-EXAMINING THE COMPETENCES OF THE EUROPEAN UNION

4.1. Euratom Treaty *versus* TFEU

Going back to the origins of the European Union it has to be recalled that before the European Union, as we know it today, things were a bit different. From the late 1950's onwards, there were three separate communities: The European Coal and Steel Community (ECSC), the European Economic Community (EEC) and the European Atomic Energy Community (Euratom). Two of the three Communities were thus focused on the field of energy, but lived a relatively separate life from each other. In this section the focus will be on the Euratom Treaty and the TFEU and core differences between these two treaties will be discussed. A more general understanding of the two treaties and their origins is relevant to fully grasp the conflicts at stake which will be picked up again when discussing different possible legal bases for a European nuclear liability regime.

The European Union as it is known today has undergone many institutional reforms. It was only with the coming into force of the Maastricht Treaty in 1993 that the European Union was created. Two amending treaties changed the nature of the Union, further, culminating in the Lisbon Treaty which abolished the pillar structure introduced by the Maastricht Treaty and led to the currently known European Union. The Lisbon Treaty however left Euratom untouched and it continued as a separate community, leading to a situation that next to the TEU there remain two fundamental Treaties in the European Union: The Euratom Treaty and the TFEU. It is remarkable how differently Euratom developed compared to the EEC. Whilst the latter was continuously developed and adapted according to new needs and calls for further integration, Euratom and its founding Treaty did not undergo major reforms and Euratom is still founded on the older rationale of its founding fathers that nuclear energy is worthy of being promoted and necessary for high standards of living.[369] The TFEU as it stands now on the other hand has been benefiting from the constant evolution of the earlier Treaties, adapting it

[369] Article 1 of the Treaty establishing the European Atomic Energy Community:
'It shall be the task of the Community to contribute to the *raising of the standard of living* in the Member States and to the *development of relations with the other countries* by creating the conditions necessary for the *speedy establishment and growth of nuclear industries.*'

according to the needs of political and economic unification, but also taking other goals into account. This can be explained by the fact that the TFEU has a clear very attractive goal, namely the internal market. This objective is a long lasting one. The Euratom Treaty on the other hand has been written to create and foster an industry in its early stages leading to a situation that the Euratom Treaty does not reflect economic reality any more. The creation of Euratom has also to be seen together with the circumstances that existed at that time on the energy market. Due to the Suez crisis, oil was scarce and Europe was faced with the challenge to increase its independence concerning energy supplies. Nuclear energy promised to be the solution to this problem.[370] Consequently the TFEU can be described as market oriented, whilst the Euratom Treaty has to be regarded as 'dirigiste and promotional'[371] and was not established to create a level playing field. It is, however, difficult to accept this promotional nature for ever. Once an industry has matured, which is certainly the case for the nuclear sector, core paradigms have to be reconsidered and changed if necessary. This however has not happened for the core provisions of the Euratom Treaty. This was recently brought up again by a joint declaration of Germany, Ireland, Hungary, Austria and Sweden stating that 'the core provisions of the Treaty establishing the European Atomic Energy Community have not been substantially amended since it came into force and they need to be brought up to date', thereby calling for a revision of the Euratom Treaty.[372] Such a revision however has not taken place and the discussion about the relationship between the Euratom Treaty and the TFEU also has to be seen against this background.

4.1.1. Lex specialis derogat lex generalis

When discussing the relationship between the Euratom Treaty and the TFEU, the natural starting point is article 106a(3) of the Euratom Treaty which states that 'the provisions of the Treaty on the European Union and of the Treaty on the Functioning of the European Union shall not derogate from the provisions of this Treaty.' This is a codification of the well founded principle of *lex specialis derogat lex generalis*, the Euratom Treaty in this case being of course the more specialised legislation. It leads to the following conclusions: First of all it has to be observed that in order for this principle to lead to a conflict between the two Treaties which would be solved by giving the Euratom Treaty priority over the TFEU, provisions from the latter would need to deviate from the former. If they do not, both Treaties can apply. As a second observation it can be maintained that in case the Euratom Treaty does not lay down provisions in a certain area that is to be regulated, the TFEU can apply unless the problem at stake is contrary to the objective of the Euratom Treaty or if it reaches into the sphere of exclusive competences of the Euratom Treaty, such as for example radiation protection or nuclear safety. Thirdly, application of the TFEU is excluded if a certain matter has been addressed exhaustively by the Euratom

370 Cusack 2003, p. 118–119.

371 *Ibid.*, p. 125.

372 Declaration 54 of the Declarations Annexed to the Final Act of the Intergovernmental Conference which adopted the Treaty of Lisbon, OJ C 326/337, 2007.

Treaty.[373] As already apparent from these three consequences of article 106a(3), the delineation of competences between the two Treaties is everything but straightforward. It has been pointed out in the literature that the current situation leads to inconsistencies between the treaties. This is also the result of the fact that certain principles which are taken for granted in the European Union do not apply to Euratom. This necessitates that the TFEU supplements the Euratom Treaty in certain fields.[374] The complexity of the (inter)relationship between the Euratom Treaty on the one hand and the TFEU on the other hand will be illustrated in the next section by the example of environmental protection and more particularly how environmental protection is currently addressed in the nuclear sector. There will also be discussion about how the complicated relationship between the Euratom Treaty and the TFEU has the potential to undermine environmental protection in the EU.

4.1.2. Environmental protection

Keeping in mind the potentially disastrous effects that nuclear accidents can have on the environment, environmental protection should be one of the main concerns of nuclear law. However this does not seem to be the case as will be discussed in the next sections. Current flaws will be identified first from a broader perspective, analysing nuclear law and the role it plays in environmental law, before turning then to the question of to what extent the Euratom Treaty enhances environmental protection in the European Union.

4.1.2.1. Environmental law and nuclear law – Allies or enemies?

Concerning the relationship between nuclear law and environmental law, Emmerechts points out that the latter applies both in a direct and indirect way to the former. By direct application he refers to international environmental law that is applicable to the nuclear sector and the indirect application he describes as the process that environmental law principles are more and more introduced into international nuclear law.[375] Concerning international law that is also applicable to the nuclear sector, principle 21 of the Stockholm Declaration[376] is of paramount importance. It states that

> *"States have, in accordance with the Charter of the United Nations and the principles of international law, the sovereign right to exploit their own resources pursuant to their own environmental policies, and the responsibility to ensure that activities within their jurisdiction or control do not cause damage to the environment of other States or of areas beyond the limits of national jurisdiction."*

373 See Montjoie 2012, p. 473.
374 True 2003, p. 684.
375 Emmerechts 2010, p. 123.
376 Declaration of the United Nations Conference on the Human Environment, June 1972, available at: www.unep.org/Documents.Multilingual/Default.asp?documentid=97&articleid=1503 (last accessed on 21 August 2015).

The importance of this principle has also been confirmed by the ICJ, stating in its Advisory Opinion *Legality of the Threat or Use of Nuclear Weapons*[377] that it is 'part of the corpus of international law relating to the environment.'[378] Despite the strong status of this principle, nuclear law does not seem to be entirely in line with it. Emmerechts points out that nuclear activities are still excluded from a lot of international and regional instruments in the field of environmental law.[379] He explains this exclusion by the fact that nuclear law is specifically regulated in other international conventions, which pre-empts the necessity to include it in environmental law instruments. This however is a wrong perception of the situation at stake. The international instruments that specifically focus on nuclear law are not in line with core paradigms of environmental protection, and therefore do not guarantee a sufficient level of environmental protection. It can be said that currently, rather than promoting environmental law, nuclear law indeed obstructs the progress achieved by environmental law.

4.1.2.2. Environmental protection under the Euratom Treaty

Looking at the preamble of the Euratom Treaty and its main goals, environmental protection does not seem to fit in there and seems not to be a competence that was originally foreseen by the founding fathers of the Treaty. This absence however has to be seen in the special light of a lack of revision of the Euratom Treaty since its coming into force in 1957. Has environmental protection over the time become an objective of the Euratom Treaty? Sticking to the wording of the Treaty such a conclusion cannot be justified. Environmental protection is not mentioned in the Treaty, and only some small references to the environment can be identified as for example in article 37 of the Euratom Treaty dealing with the disposal of radioactive waste which states that

> *'Each Member State shall provide the Commission with such general data relating to any plan for the disposal of radioactive waste in whatever forms will make it possible to determine whether the implementation of such plan is liable to result in the radioactive contamination of the water, soil or airspace of another Member State.*

This leads to the *prima facie* conclusion that the Euratom does not possess competences in the area of environmental protection, leading to the situation that there would be room for the TFEU to apply in this field. The latter clearly has environmental protection as one of its competences and could arguably legislate in this area even to remedy effects of radiation if this did not fall under the exclusive competence of Euratom.[380] In 1988 however the Court of Justice of the European Union in *Land de Sarre*[381] ruled that article 37 indeed does confer 'upon the Commission powers of some considerable scope

377 *Legality of the Threat or Use of Nuclear Weapons*, ICJ reports 1996, p. 226.
378 *Ibid.*, para. 30.
379 Emmerechts 2010, p. 127.
380 Montjoie 2012, p. 474.
381 Case 187/87 *Saarland and Others* v. *Minister for Industry, Post and Telecommunications and Tourism and Others* [1988].

in order to protect population and the environment against the risks of nuclear contamination'.[382] The Court thus gave Euratom some competences in the field of environmental protection; however they seem to be limited. These limited competences of Euratom result in problems concerning the delineation of competences between the two Treaties.[383] If we look at secondary legislation stemming from the Euratom Treaty or the TFEU, the complexity of the issue becomes apparent further. Certain TFEU Directives take the nuclear sector into account[384], others explicitly exclude it.[385] Directives which are based on the Euratom Treaty do not explicitly refer to environmental protection. The Directive on the management of spent fuel and radioactive waste[386] or the Nuclear Safety Directive[387] for example only mentions environmental protection in a rather indirect and incidental way in the respective preambles. The latter in its article 3(2) even defines nuclear safety without reference to environmental protection.

At this point it has to be mentioned that the split between the Euratom Treaty and the TFEU potentially weakens environmental protection in the European Union. In the Temelin case[388] for example the CJEU was convinced that the Euratom Treaty and the framework in place is strong enough to function as a safeguard for nuclear safety, thereby not accepting environmental concerns brought forward by the claimant. Whilst the operator of the power plant could rely on benefits derived from the TFEU, the applicant was barred from invoking stricter conditions because this would have gone further than the requirements established under the Euratom Treaty.[389] This is at odds with earlier case law in which the Court held that the Euratom regime only sets a minimum framework which would not prevent Member States from providing more protection, going beyond the level of protection afforded under the Euratom Treaty.[390] Against this background, the Temelin case raises some concerns with regard to the balancing and accommodation of interests and obligations arising from the TFEU on the one side and the Euratom Treaty on the other. There is a risk of inconsistencies leading to potential gaps in the regulatory system as a result of an unclear division of competences and an unclear relationship between the two Treaties. It remains to be seen whether a European nuclear liability regime has the potential to remedy this shortcoming.

382 Case 187/87, para. 11.

383 Montjoie 2012, p. 475.

384 See for example Directive 2008/56/EC establishing a framework for Community action in the field of marine environmental policy.

385 See for example Directive 2004/35/EC on environmental liability with regard to the prevention and remedying of environmental damage.

386 Council Directive 2011/70/Euratom establishing a Community framework for the responsible and safe management of spent fuel and radioactive waste.

387 Council Directive 2009/71/Euratom establishing a Community framework for the nuclear safety of nuclear installations.

388 Case C-115/08 *Land Oberösterreich* v. *CEZ* [2009].

389 Wolf 2011, p. 1647+1648.

390 Case C-376/90 *Commission* v. *Belgium* [1992], para. 18+19.

4.1.3. *The role of the European Parliament*

The democratic legitimacy of the European Union has always been a major concern both to proponents of further integration and to those against the creation of a European Union in which more powers are delegated to the European Commission and thereby taken away from national parliaments. The role of the European Parliament has continuously been strengthened throughout the last decades. Whilst in earlier years the European Parliament had merely a consultative role, it has been put by now on an equal footing with the other European institutions which is demonstrated the most significantly by its role in the decision making procedure. Under the ordinary legislative procedure in the framework of the TFEU, the European Parliament has an important role to play and can veto European legislation.

The powers of the European Parliament under the Euratom Treaty, however, are quite different. As mentioned above, the Euratom Treaty has not been very much affected by the institutional reforms of the last decades. Nevertheless the European Parliament has been very active in its attempts to achieve more influence on nuclear matters.[391] The Parliament has taken, despite its rather limited role from a legal angle, a very active role. Already in the 1970's it has been very active in the field of nuclear energy.[392] In some cases it challenged its rather limited role. Probably the most far reaching attempt to strengthen its position in the nuclear sector is to be found in its demand for the annulment of Regulation 3954/87.[393] This regulation was adopted pursuant to article 31 of the Euratom Treaty which only foresees a consultative role for the European Parliament. The latter however argued that the Regulation should have been adopted under the legal basis for the Internal Market, which is now art. 114 TFEU. This article would have given the European Parliament more power in the decision making procedure. The Court, however, contrary to the view of the European Parliament, did not regard the Regulation as 'a harmonisation measure within the meaning of Article 100a of the EEC Treaty' (now art. 114 TFEU). It therefore concluded that the Regulation indeed was rightly based upon article 31 of the Euratom Treaty.[394]

Thus the European Parliament has so far, formally, not enjoyed great influence on nuclear legislation. Nevertheless it can be said that is has used its consultative role to an extent that allowed a certain influence on matters decided under the Euratom Treaty. This has been done by political means such as the publishing of reports in which it expressed its view on the European Parliament's role under Euratom.[395] Nevertheless, the European Parliament does not enjoy the same standing under the Euratom Treaty as it does under

391 Cenevska 2010, p. 418.

392 Hancher 1989, p. 496 + 499.

393 Council Regulation (Euratom) No. 3954/87 laying down maximum permitted levels of radioactive contamination of foodstuffs and of feedingstuffs following a nuclear accident or any other case of radiological emergency.

394 Case C-70/88 *European Parliament* v. *Council of the European Communities*[1990], para. 17+18.

395 Cenevska 2010, p. 418.

the TFEU. Consequently it can be said that the European Union has evolved into a (more) democratic Union, whilst Euratom seems to remain willingly undemocratic.[396]

4.2. A legal basis for a European nuclear liability regime

Concerning legislative competences, there are certain overlaps between the TFEU and Euratom and it is not always obvious which community of the two is empowered to legislate.[397] A Legal basis determines the balance of powers of the institutions involved. There is a tendency to construe Euratom's legal bases very broadly and furthermore the Commission has furthered harmonisation also via the use of soft law. The Court of Justice of the European Union justifies the broad approach by the objective of Euratom. The goals of the TFEU however can potentially also reach into the nuclear domain. Different nuclear rules can impede competition and can have an influence on the internal market. The question, however, is whether legal bases from the TFEU can also apply in the nuclear sector. The Court did not lay down general rules on this issue, but looks at it on a case by case basis.[398] The following sections will discuss some principles which are relevant when deciding on a legal basis and will then analyse potential legal bases for a nuclear liability regime both in the Euratom Treaty and the TFEU.

4.2.1. Criteria for an appropriate legal basis

Every piece of legislation has to be based upon a legal basis. The role of a legal basis is twofold. On the one hand it allows the European Union to legislate in that area and on the other hand it determines the role and powers of the institutions involved.[399] The choice of a legal basis must correspond to the stated objective and the content of the measure at stake. This assessment has to be an objective one.[400] Subjective motivations will not be taken into account since allowing political considerations to play a role would increase legal uncertainty.[401]

When setting out the criteria for an appropriate legal basis, the Court of Justice of the European Union also clarified the status of a dual legal basis. In *Commission v. European Parliament and Council*[402] the following conditions for the choice of a legal basis were confirmed by the Court: the choice must be based on objective factors, amenable to judicial review,[403] in the case of a twofold purpose the act shall be based on the legal basis

396 *Ibid.*, p. 424.
397 True 2010, p. 2.
398 True 2010, p. 6.
399 Chalmers 2010, p. 140.
400 Case C-45/86 *Commission of the European Communities* v. *Council of the European Communities* [1987], para. 11.
401 Barents 1993, p. 92–93.
402 Case C-178/03 *Commission of the European Communities* v. *European Parliament and the Council of the European Union* [2006].
403 *Ibid.*, para. 41.

appropriate for the main purpose if this can be identified,[404] and only in exceptional circumstances can a dual legal basis be used.[405] This recourse to a dual legal basis however is not possible if the two bases are incompatible with each other or liable to undermine the rights of the Parliament.[406] With regard to this last criterion is has to be added that it is not a problem if the two legal bases foresee different forms of involvement of the European Parliament as long as they ensure that the procedure will adhere to the strongest involvement possible under the used legal bases.[407] By pointing out that a dual legal basis will only exceptionally be used, the Court limited to a certain extent the possibility of the use of dual legal basis. This is also supported by the reference to the 'predominant purpose' of the measure which will be identified.[408] This approach focussing on the predominant aim however is not as straightforward as it may seem at first sight, given the flexibility with which one can phrase the objectives of a certain measure.[409] This can let the choice of the predominant aim seem arbitrary sometimes. In academic literature it has also been pointed out, that in the last years the Court of Justice of the European Union may have relied too much on the preamble of a new measure to identify the predominant aim.[410] The discretion in determining the predominant aim of a measure which results from this approach raises problems with regard to legal uncertainty.[411] A possible solution to that might be to rethink the use of a dual legal basis and focus on the advantages of a dual legal basis instead of only pointing at resulting complications and its exceptional character. If a single legal basis can only be found by a flexible approach to the predominant aim theory it might very well be legitimate to use dual legal bases more frequently if it is needed to achieve the objective at stake. Basing a measure on two legal bases should be preferred over artificially drawing a preamble or the objective of a certain measure in such a way that it can be covered by the single legal basis chosen.

These observations show that although using a dual legal basis has been described by the Court as exceptional, it sometimes may simply be necessary and should not be condemned right from the start. When analysing the possible legal bases for a nuclear liability regime in the following sections this will be kept in mind. The issue of a legal basis is particularly interesting in the field of nuclear liability since there are two possible applicable Treaties, the Euratom Treaty and the TFEU. Another interesting feature of the latter is that it has recently introduced a separate article on energy. Having a special article dealing with this area can easily lead to a presumption that this will automatically be the most appropriate legal basis. Whether this is indeed the case will be analysed when assessing the most appropriate legal basis for a nuclear liability regime.

404 *Ibid.*, para. 42.
405 *Ibid.*, para. 43.
406 *Ibid.*, para. 57.
407 Klamert 2010, p. 507.
408 Case C-178/03 Commission of the European Communities v European Parliament and the Council of the European Union [2006] ECR I-107, para. 42.
409 Emiliou 1994, p. 499.
410 Klamert 2010, p. 499.
411 *Ibid.*, p. 505.

4.2.2. *The principles of conferral of competences and subsidiarity*

Before turning to the discussion of concrete possible legal bases, attention has to be paid to the principles of conferral of competences and subsidiarity. Every European legislation has to be rooted in a legal basis to be found in specific Treaty provisions because the European Union does not possess general law-making competences *per se*.[412] This principle is called the principle of conferral and means that 'the Union shall act only within the limits of the competences conferred upon it by the Member States in the Treaties to attain the objectives set out therein.'[413] The question consequently arises, whether the European Union has competences to regulate matters dealing with nuclear liability. As apparent from article 3 TFEU which lists the exclusive competences, legislative action in the area of liability for nuclear accidents does not fall under the Union's exclusive competences. The Euratom Treaty does not mention nuclear liability either. It might however, as will be analysed in more detail below, fall under its shared competences listed in article 4 TFEU. In the area of shared competences one important condition for action at the level of the European Union has to be raised namely that it 'shall act only if and in so far as the objectives of the proposed action cannot be sufficiently achieved by the Member States'.[414] This principle is the principle of subsidiarity and is further explained in Protocol no. 2 attached to the Treaty on European Union and the Treaty on the Functioning of the European Union. Article 5 of the Protocol stresses once more the importance that it is necessary that the objective at stake can be better achieved at Union level. Having in mind the trans-border damage which would result from a nuclear accident within the European Union it becomes apparent that this condition should not pose any bigger problems.[415] Consequently it can be said that the principle of subsidiarity would not pose a problem for action at the level of the European Union if a legal basis for such action can be found in one of the two treaties which would also satisfy the principle of conferral of competences.

Whilst it is beyond doubt that in the environmental field the subsidiarity principle is not really a hurdle for EU action to take place because transboundary issues are clearly apparent in this field, de Sadeleer nuances this aspect with some pitfalls of the subsidiarity principle. Even if the EU is entitled to exercise its shared competence in the field of environmental law, the potential difficulties lie then in the way the environmental policy is designed and implemented by the Member States. In the area of shared competences and when EU action only aims at partial harmonisation there is of course the risk that the different approaches of the Member States nullify or at least weaken the initiatives from the Commission who is then only left with a 'marginal control over the proper implementation.'[416] However, it does not have to be that marginal after all. If we recall the policy linking clauses in the Lisbon Treaty and that environmental aspects have to be

412 Article 5(1) TEU.
413 *Ibid.*, Article 5(2).
414 *Ibid.*, Article 5(3).
415 Vedder 2008.
416 De Sadeleer 2012, p. 67.

taken into account in all policies, this gives the Commission appropriate power to monitor and if needed act against Member States and mitigates some pitfalls of the subsidiarity principle as described above.

4.2.3. Euratom

4.2.3.1. Article 98 – A dormant source of legislative power?

Article 98 of the Euratom Treaty deals with the facilitation of the conclusion of insurance contracts covering nuclear risks. The question which arises is whether this article is indeed only limited to this matter which would be a restrictive interpretation of it, or whether it might also serve as a legal basis for broader action. Another sub-question to be answered is whether the article imposes a duty on the European Union to act or the mere possibility.

With regard to the scope of the Article Handrlica points out that at the time of the Treaty's conclusion contemporary interpreters were proponents of a restrictive interpretation that 'Article 98 EuratomT aims exclusively towards eliminating any barriers the legal framework provides for concluding insurance contracts and setting the framework for these insurance contracts.'[417] He explains this by the legislative efforts in the field of nuclear liability going on during that time which let the drafters intentionally not include competences dealing with nuclear liability.[418]

Two recommendations however put article 98 Euratom Treaty in a different light. Commission Recommendation 65/42/Euratom and Commission Recommendation 66/22/Euratom both dealt generally speaking with the question of a harmonised nuclear liability regime.[419] These two recommendations clearly show a tendency of the Commission to use article 98 not only for insurance matters, but also in a more extensive manner.[420] This leads to a broader interpretation which has also been embraced by some scholars. At a workshop on nuclear liability Prof. Wathelet for example presented his opinion that article 98 can not only serve as a legal basis for matters dealing with insurance contracts but also for the harmonisation of a nuclear liability regime.[421]

With regard to the question of whether the article imposes a duty to act upon the Commission, the latter is of the opinion that it represent a mere right and no duty. In a reply to a question from a deputy of the European Parliament the Commission stated

417 Handrlica 2010, p. 5.

418 *Ibid.*

419 See *Ibid.*, p. 6f.

420 Legal Study for the Accession of Euratom to the Paris Convention on Third Party Liability in the Field of Nuclear Energy, TREN/CC/01-2005, p. 51–60.

421 See *Prospects of a Nuclear Liability Regime in the Framework of the European Union*, Bericht ueber einen Workshop der Europaeischen Kommission und der Brussels Nuclear Law Association, June 2010, Brussels in: EurUP,2010 p. 190.

that 'the Euratom Treaty, and in particular Article 98, does not impose any obligation to legislate in this field.'[422] Consequently Handrlica stresses that the Commission regards article 98 Euratom Treaty as a 'dormant source of legislative power' which does not have to be used, but if used it might well include issues to reconcile nuclear liability standards within the European Union.[423]

In contrast to the view of the Commission, the Gomez Acebo study interpreted article 98 differently and points out that it 'manifestly contains an obligation to act upon the Community.'[424] This shows that the issue seems not to be settled and diverging opinions on the issue can be found.

Considering all these observations together however, the conclusion that the Commission indeed is under a duty to act under article 98 Euratom seems reasonable. It is however not easy to agree with the proponents of the view that its scope would not only be limited to insurance contracts but could also cover a harmonised nuclear liability regime. With regard to the Euratom Treaty there is a tendency to construe its legal bases very broadly, and by way of extensive interpretation fit more subjects under certain legal bases as it might have been originally planned. It is preferable to resist such an extensive interpretation and rather look for alternatives which might be a more appropriate legal basis in line with core principles on the choice of such a legal basis.

4.2.3.2. Article 203

For the sake of completeness article 203 Euratom Treaty should be mentioned at this point as well. This article is the equivalent to article 352 TFEU which can be seen as a fall-back article for cases in which another legal basis cannot be found and yet action at Union level is necessary.[425] In the Gomez Acebo study Article 203 Euratom Treaty nevertheless has been seen as an appropriate legal basis when read in conjunction with article 2(g) Euratom Treaty.[426] This article however has the inherent flaw of needing unanimity which makes it not very attractive as a possible legal basis from the angle of political viability, a problem which has also been identified by the above mentioned study.[427] The author is of the opinion that unanimity is indeed unfeasible and therefore article 203 Euratom Treaty will not be further considered.

422 See Official Journal OJ C 158 1998, p. 191.
423 Handrlica 2010, p. 8.
424 Legal Study for the Accession of Euratom to the Paris Convention on Third Party Liability in the Field of Nuclear Energy, TREN/CC/01–2005, p. 37.
425 See Craig and de Burca 2008, p. 93.
426 Legal Study for the Accession of Euratom to the Paris Convention on Third Party Liability in the Field of Nuclear Energy, TREN/CC/01–2005, p. 49.
427 *Ibid.*, p. 69.

4.2.4. TFEU

4.2.4.1. Article 194 on Energy

In 1986 there was a Council Resolution laying down some objectives in the energy sector. It can be regarded as a market approach to energy. This market approach bears potential conflicts with issues of environmental protection which makes it all the more complex. The challenge within the Union has always been to strike an appropriate balance between environmental protection on the one hand, and energy supply on the other.[428]

In 1996 the Commission eventually suggested the introduction of a new chapter on Energy into the EC Treaty to have more coherent legal bases in the field of energy.[429] The introduction of a special legal basis for energy was also motivated by the desire not to use article 308 EC (now article 352 TFEU) any more in this field. Constant reliance on this fall-back article called for a separate article in the field of energy.[430] Through the Lisbon Treaty a specific chapter was eventually introduced and article 194 TFEU now deals specifically with energy matters. The introduction of a separate chapter on energy resulted partially in criticism from scholars who were of the opinion that it was doubtful whether there was really a need for a specific article on energy.[431] Questions were also raised whether the new article can indeed simplify matters or will only make things worse and complicate the matter even more.[432] However, the fact is that the article is now part of the primary law of the European Union and it has to be made sure that it will be applied correctly.

Article 194 TFEU states:

1. *In the context of the establishment and functioning of the internal market and with regard for the need to preserve and improve the environment, Union policy on energy shall aim, in a spirit of solidarity between Member States, to:*
   (a) ensure the functioning of the energy market;
   (b) ensure security of energy supply in the Union;
   (c) promote energy efficiency and energy saving and the development of new and renewable forms of energy; and
   (d) promote the interconnection of energy networks.

2. *Without prejudice to the application of other provisions of the Treaties, the European Parliament and the Council, acting in accordance with the ordinary legislative procedure, shall establish the measures necessary to achieve the objectives in paragraph 1. Such*

428 Hancher 1989, p. 476.
429 Rashbrooke 2004, p. 377.
430 *Ibid.*, p. 380.
431 Cameron 2007, p. 58.
432 Rashbrooke 2004, p. 377.

measures shall be adopted after consultation of the Economic and Social Committee and the Committee of the Regions.
Such measures shall not affect a Member State's right to determine the conditions for exploiting its energy resources, its choice between different energy sources and the general structure of its energy supply, without prejudice to Article 192(2)(c).
3. *By way of derogation from paragraph 2, the Council, acting in accordance with a special legislative procedure, shall unanimously and after consulting the European Parliament, establish the measures referred to therein when they are primarily of a fiscal nature.*

Paragraph 1 of this article lays down the general scope and objectives that it covers. Paragraph 2 deals with the legislative procedure and restricts the scope of the article to a certain extent. Paragraph 3 deals with measures which are of a fiscal nature and will be disregarded in the following analysis because a liability regime would not touch upon fiscal measures.

Concerning the scope one can say that paragraph 1 clearly mirrors the history of how the Union legislated in the area of energy before the Lisbon Treaty. The link to environmental policy and the internal market are indeed striking.[433] Unfortunately the article does not clarify the relation of this special article to the other articles which have previously been used in the area of energy which leads to the *prima facie* conclusion that according to the principle of *lex specialis* the energy title should prevail.[434] With regard to its suitability to serve as a legal basis for a harmonised liability regime for nuclear accidents it has to be pointed out that such a regime could fall under paragraph 1(a). The article does not define the term energy which means that nuclear energy can also fall under the scope of this article.[435] Given the preventive effect of a liability regime at European level, it could serve to preserve the environment and from an economic point of view the regime. If structured in a way to improve cost internalisation, it could also improve the functioning of the energy market since it would end the situation in which nuclear energy amounts to a subsidised industry. That the scope of this article might also cover a liability regime for nuclear accidents is also supported by the legislative history of the article which reveals that it was not intended to limit article 194 TFEU solely to measures aiming at the integration of the energy market within the European Union.[436]

The real obstacle one would be faced with when using article 194 as a legal basis however is to be found in article 194(2) TFEU. This section raises the caveat that measures taken under this article 'shall not affect a Member State's right to determine the conditions for exploiting its energy resources, its choice between different energy sources and the general structure of its energy supply'. If a liability regime led for example to higher prices for nuclear energy, which might indeed be the case depending on which principles the regime

433 Vedder 2008.
434 Rashbrooke 2004, p. 382.
435 Haghighi 2008, p. 472.
436 Rashbrooke 2004, p. 382.

would be built upon,[437] opponents of a harmonised liability regime at European level might argue that this would be contrary to article 194 (2) TFEU. Should such a system lead to higher prices this might indeed pose a problem with regard to the possibility of using article 194 TFEU as a legal basis, given that the wording of paragraph 2 simply states that the measures 'shall not affect a Member State's right'. A significant effect is not required and the threshold of simply affecting the Member State's choice will quickly be reached.

4.2.4.2. Article 192 on the Environment

Article 191 TFEU lays down some objectives in the field of environmental protection which include *inter alia* the objective of 'preserving, protecting and improving the quality of the environment' and 'protecting human health'. Article 192 then provides a legal basis for environmental measures taken to achieve these objectives:

1. *The European Parliament and the Council, acting in accordance with the ordinary legislative procedure and after consulting the Economic and Social Committee and the Committee of the Regions, shall decide what action is to be taken by the Union in order to achieve the objectives referred to in Article 191.*
2. *By way of derogation from the decision-making procedure provided for in paragraph 1 and without prejudice to Article 114, the Council acting unanimously in accordance with a special legislative procedure and after consulting the European Parliament, the Economic and Social Committee and the Committee of the Regions, shall adopt:*
   (a) provisions primarily of a fiscal nature;
   (b) measures affecting:
   - *town and country planning,*
   - *quantitative management of water resources or affecting, directly or indirectly, the availability of those resources,*
   - *land use, with the exception of waste management;*

   (c) measures significantly affecting a Member State's choice between different energy sources and the general structure of its energy supply.

   The Council, acting unanimously on a proposal from the Commission and after consulting the European Parliament, the Economic and Social Committee and the Committee of the Regions, may make the ordinary legislative procedure applicable to the matters referred to in the first subparagraph.
3. *General action programmes setting out priority objectives to be attained shall be adopted by the European Parliament and the Council, acting in accordance with the ordinary legislative procedure and after consulting the Economic and Social Committee and the Committee of the Regions.*
   The measures necessary for the implementation of these programmes shall be adopted under the terms of paragraph 1 or 2, as the case may be.

[437] In the case of more private money for accidents, this could lead to an increase in electricity prices.

4. *Without prejudice to certain measures adopted by the Union, the Member States shall finance and implement the environment policy.*
5. *Without prejudice to the principle that the polluter should pay, if a measure based on the provisions of paragraph 1 involves costs deemed disproportionate for the public authorities of a Member State, such measure shall lay down appropriate provisions in the form of:*
   - *temporary derogations, and/or*
   - *financial support from the Cohesion Fund set up pursuant to Article 177.*

The objectives mentioned in article 191 could be achieved by a strong nuclear liability regime given its preventive function. Picking up the constraint which the last section ended with, it is noteworthy that a similar formulation can be found in article 192 (2)(c). This paragraph of the legal basis for environmental measures makes the special legislative procedure applicable in case of 'measures significantly affecting a Member State's choice between different energy sources and the general structure of its energy supply'. The difference towards article 194(2) is that on the one hand, even if this criterion is fulfilled, the measures could still be adopted under the special legislative procedure, and on the other hand that measures must 'significantly' affect the Member State's choice which clearly sets a higher threshold.

Finally, another caveat with regard to the use of article 192 TFEU has to be raised. According to article 192(4) 'the Member States shall finance and implement the environment policy.' De Sadeleer points out that this referral to national competences can lead to a nationalisation of environmental policy, disempowering the Commission to a certain extent.[438] Such decentralisation could endanger a European wide approach to environmental protection and it has to be seen how in the area of nuclear law such danger can be prevented if article 192 TFEU were to be used as a legal basis.[439]

4.2.4.3. Article 114 on the Internal Market

Article 114(1) states:

> *'Save where otherwise provided in the Treaties, the following provisions shall apply for the achievement of the objectives set out in Article 26. The European Parliament and the Council shall, acting in accordance with the ordinary legislative procedure and after consulting the Economic and Social Committee, adopt the measures for the approximation of the provisions laid down by law, regulation or administrative action in Member States which have as their object the establishment and functioning of the internal market.'*

438 De Sadeleer 2012, p. 66.

439 One approach for example would be to issue more guidance. This would enable a common approach whilst enforcement would still be left with the Member States in accordance with article 192(4). More guidance could at least increase legal certainty and serve as a clearer benchmark to monitor performance and potentially open infringement proceedings.

The scope of this article is very broad, and the current situation of different national regulation of the issue of nuclear liability can indeed have an effect on the functioning of the internal market. Nuclear liability is currently regulated very differently in the Member States and liability limits of the operators and obligations to take out insurance differ quite tremendously.[440] If one regards the energy market as a European market, these different financial obligations have the potential to distort the functioning of the Internal Market and intervention under article 114 TFEU could be justified.

4.2.4.4. The *Titanium Dioxide* case law

Having introduced in the last two sections article 114 TFEU and article 192 TFEU as potential legal bases for a European nuclear liability system, it is necessary at this point to discuss the relationship of these two articles and their respective scope of application. This issue was raised in the Titanium Dioxide case which dealt with 'the borderline between the scope of article 100a [now Article 114 TFEU] and that of Article 130s [now article 192 TFEU] of the Treaty.'[441] In a very short judgment the Court followed the AG's opinion and ruled in favour of article 114 TFEU since 'the objectives of environmental protection referred to in Article 130r [now article 191 TFEU] may be effectively pursued by means of harmonising measures adopted on the basis of Article 100a [now Article 114 TFEU]'.[442]

Commenting on this judgment, Robinson describes the Titanium Dioxide Principle as follows: The first question that one needs to pose is whether the measure at stake is a harmonising measure in the sense of article 114 TFEU. If this is the case, it is capable of falling under the Internal Market Legal basis. If then one of its effects or purposes is to promote the internal market, the measure has to be adopted under article 114 TFEU even if the internal market component is only ancillary. Only if the second question can be completely denied could article 192 TFEU serve as a legal basis.[443]

Barnard points out that *Titanium Dioxide*[444] takes away the importance of what was at that time a newly introduced Environmental law title, and raises the question of why the Court was willing to take this route.[445] A strict application of this principle would indeed decrease the added value of article 192 TFEU. Robinson further points out that other judgments are hardly reconcilable with this principle.[446] It seems that an underlying reason for the Court's interpretation in *Titanium Dioxide* was its intent to give more

440 See section 3.3.5.2.
441 Advocate General Opinion Case C-300/89 *Commission of the European Communities* v. *Council of the European Communities*[1991], para. 1.
442 Case C-300/89, para. 24.
443 Robinson 1992, p. 115.
444 Case C-300/89.
445 Barnard 1992, p. 131+132.
446 Robinson 1992, p. 117.

power to the European Parliament.[447] It has to be recalled at this point, however, that since the time of this judgment the Treaties have been revised several times, leading also to crucial changes in the balance of powers between the institutions. Article 192 TFEU as it currently stands does not anymore merely foresee a consultative role for the Parliament but established it as a co-legislator. It can therefore be argued that nowadays the reasoning of the Court could have looked different, maybe even supporting a dual legal basis, an approach that seemed to have been supported by both the Court and the Advocate General already in Titanium Dioxide, but which was impossible at that time due to their incompatibility.[448]

4.2.5. *A dual legal basis*

Summing up it can be said that with regard to its material scope article 194 TFEU would also cover a liability regime for nuclear accidents. The restriction contained in paragraph 2 of this article however entails some problems, and the suitability of article 194 TFEU to serve as a legal basis for a harmonised regime of nuclear liability seems at the current moment at least questionable. More information on the influence of private funding on the prices of nuclear energy would be needed to give a conclusive answer to this.

With regard to article 114 TFEU and 192 TFEU it was shown that they could both serve as a possible legal basis. There is, however, no clear line of demarcation between these two legal bases when a measure touches upon on the internal market as well as on environmental protection and the question can be asked whether a dual legal basis would not be the most appropriate solution to this. Although the use of a dual legal basis is rather an exception than the rule, in certain cases it is simply necessary and a dual legal basis should be preferred over the use of one legal basis if this required an extensive interpretation of this legal basis. Also in the literature authors have pointed out that even the Court seems to have become less resistant towards the use of a dual legal basis, contrary to its approach in the past.[449]

4.3. A European nuclear liability regime – Aligning nuclear energy and environmental protection

As already discussed in section 4.1.2, environmental protection has a difficult and sometimes not entirely clear status in the nuclear sector. The unclear separation of competences between the Euratom Treaty and the TFEU arguably weakens environmental protection in this area. Furthermore, it is not entirely clear to what extent environmental protection can and should indeed be regarded as an inherent part of the nuclear sector and an objective of the regulation thereof. The following sections aim at shedding some

447 Barnard 1992, p. 131; see also AG Opinion Case C-300/89 para. 2+13 and the Court's reasoning at C-300/89 para. 18+19.

448 See AG Opinion Case C-300/89, para.11 and the Court's judgment C-300/89, para. 13+21.

449 De Sadeleer 2012a, p. 397.

additional light on the underlying complications and will also discuss how a nuclear liability regime based on the TFEU has the potential to solve these problems.

4.3.1. *Personal injury versus environmental damage*

Originally environmental law focussed on personal injury and the protection of private property. This definition of damage is also mirrored in the older nuclear liability conventions, focussing on

> '*i. damage to or loss of life of any person; and*
> *ii. damage to or loss of any property other than*
> *1. the nuclear installation itself and any other nuclear installation, including a nuclear installation under construction, on the site where that installation is located; and*
> *2. any property on that same site which is used or to be used in connection with any such installation'.*[450]

Over the last decades, however, one can witness a gradual shift towards the protection of the environment *per se*.[451] Whilst the main focus when dealing with more traditional heads of damages such as personal injury is on monetary compensation, environmental damage requires a different approach, putting more emphasis on restoration.[452] The development towards granting more protection to the environment as such, can also be seen to some extent in the nuclear sector. Whilst the exclusion of the nuclear sector from the Environmental Liability Directive[453] must still be regarded as a missed chance to achieve a more comprehensive system because under that directive the environment is offered protection *per se*,[454] the increased importance of environmental protection and the establishment of different international conventions and other liability regimes including environmental damage made it clear that also a modernisation of the definition of nuclear damage is necessary.[455] A broader definition of nuclear damage also needs to be seen in the light of a more developed nuclear sector and public expectations in such a mature sector.[456]

Consequently in the revised conventions the concept of nuclear damage was given a definition that does not exclusively focus on personal injury. The Paris Protocol from 2004 defines nuclear damage as

> '*1. loss of life or personal injury;*
> *2. loss of or damage to property;*

450 See Article 2a Paris Convention on Third Party Liability in the Field of Nuclear Energy.
451 Larsson 1999, p. 155.
452 Faure and Liu 2014, p. 230.
453 Directive 2004/35/EC of the European Parliament and of the Council of 21 April 2004 on environmental liability with regard to the prevention and remedying of environmental damage.
454 Danzi 2009, p. 22.
455 Soljan 2000, p. 63.
456 *Ibid.*, p. 64.

and each of the following to the extent determined by the law of the competent court,

3. *economic loss arising from loss or damage referred to in sub-paragraph 1 or 2 above insofar as not included in those sub-paragraphs, if incurred by a person entitled to claim in respect of such loss or damage;*
4. *the costs of measures of reinstatement of impaired environment, unless such impairment is insignificant, if such measures are actually taken or to be taken, and insofar as not included in sub-paragraph 2 above;*
5. *loss of income deriving from a direct economic interest in any use or enjoyment of the environment, incurred as a result of a significant impairment of that environment, and insofar as not included in sub-paragraph 2 above; 6. the costs of preventive measures, and further loss or damage caused by such measures'.*

Danzi points out that under the revised nuclear liability conventions the approach is to stipulate consequences of damage to the environment in economic terms. These economic impacts are then covered under the convention.[457] Thus the environment and damage to it is not covered *per se* as a part of nuclear damage.

Pelzer recalls that the nuclear liability conventions are part of the law of non-contractual obligations. A qualifying aspect of this area of law is a relationship between two actors, the tortfeasor and the victim, whilst the general public and its interests are normally not included.[458] He contrasts this with the Environmental Liability Directive which aims at the remediation and prevention of damage to the environment *per se*. The main relationship that the Directive deals with is not one between a victim and a tortfeasor but between an operator and a public authority, the latter being empowered to require certain actions as stipulated in the directive. This makes the Directive a public law instrument according to Pelzer because such a principle of subordination does not exist in private law.[459] Contrary to what the title of the Environmental Liability suggests, other authors also point at its rather hybrid nature with public law aspects playing arguably the more important role. De Smedt describes it as 'a mainly public law regime to be enforced by competent authorities, combined with private law aspects as strict liability and fault-based liability.'[460] Winter *et al.* point out that the more administrative approach of the Directive as it finally was adopted is in contrast to what originally had been planned when discussing and preparing the Directive.[461] Hence the absence of a protection of the environment as such under the liability conventions can also be explained by the private law nature of these conventions. Also according to Danzi it can be questioned whether environmental protection is something that can be the objective of a civil liability regime given the "public good" character of the environment.[462]

457 Danzi 2009, p. 8.
458 Pelzer 2010, p. 52.
459 *Ibid.*, p. 53.
460 De Smedt 2009, p. 2.
461 Winter *et al.* 2008, p. 164.
462 Danzi 2009, p. 10.

Regardless of the question of whether a private law instrument or a public law instrument is better equipped to deal with environmental damage or personal injury respectively, it is clear that in the case of a nuclear accident one would be faced with both of these two heads of damages. This also has to be taken into account when discussing a European regime for the regulation of nuclear accidents and appropriate tools that such a regime would need to make use of. Damage under such a regime would need to be defined appropriately and also the objectives of such a regime would be more varied, including not only compensation but also issues of restoration and prevention of damage.

4.3.2. Advantages of a more comprehensive regime

The Commission has always been very aware of the trans boundary problems coming along with the generation of nuclear energy, but has failed to introduce measures on nuclear power to remedy this problem. Recalling once more the promotional character of the Euratom Treaty this is not too surprising and it was even argued that this attitude enabled the support of nuclear energy to the detriment of renewable energy sources or other alternatives.[463] Although Chernobyl has led to a general reappraisal of nuclear energy within the European Union, far reaching changes or strict controls have not been introduced. This can also partially be explained by the complexity of the issue at stake, resulting from the unclear delineation of powers between Euratom on the one hand, and the European Union on the other hand. For certain issues it is not exactly clear to what extent each Treaty is applicable, whilst other areas such as radiation protection and nuclear safety clearly fall under the category of exclusive competences of Euratom and can apparently not be regulated under the TFEU. Nuclear liability, however, has not been regulated so far under the Euratom Treaty and would therewith not fall under this category. Arguably the regulation of nuclear liability therefore poses a chance to remedy the current shortcomings in the nuclear sector. Given the comprehensive and broad approach that is advocated throughout this thesis, finding an appropriate legal basis is a crucial aspect. Admittedly, the focus of a European regime would not exclusively be on liability but would also involve issues of regulation and more general concerns such as the inclusiveness of regulatory regimes concerning ultra-hazardous activities. The challenge in terms of a legal basis is not only to find a legal basis under which one can incorporate such a broad regime but also to avoid the problem that it might be claimed that certain aspects have already been regulated and might belong to the exclusive competences of Euratom. Relying primarily on nuclear liability, whilst at the same time accommodating broader aspects in a European initiative in that area increases the chances of avoiding a conflict between Euratom and the TFEU because liability issues have so far not been regulated under either of the two Treaties.

The dual legal basis relying both on Environmental Protection and on the Internal Market would on the one hand allow a broader scope of a liability regime, taking into account also the more recent paradigms and principles favouring environmental

[463] Hancher 1989, p. 487.

protection. This could reduce existing gaps in environmental protection that result from an unclear delineation of competences between the Euratom Treaty and the TFEU. It could also accommodate the discussion between personal injury on the one hand versus environmental damage, on the other hand, keeping in mind that in the case of a nuclear accident both of these kinds of damages will of course be at stake. On the other hand it could also remedy risks of a malfunctioning of the internal market which could be a result of the currently very different liability limits in the Member States. Facing different insurance obligations can have an influence on energy prices and if the energy sector is seen as a European sector such concerns need to be taken seriously, also from an Internal Market perspective.

The proposed dual legal basis would thus enable a stricter regulation of the nuclear sector, enabling the transition from an industry that is regulated according to a nuclear favourable treaty towards a regulation based upon a more restrictive and controlling treaty. This would be more in line with current realities and could close the gap between nuclear energy and environmental protection.

Chapter 5

HARMONISATION AT THE EUROPEAN LEVEL – A DESIRABLE OPTION?

5.1. The economics of Federalism

Following an economic approach, a discussion about the harmonisation of the nuclear sector in the European Union, has to start with an economic analysis of federalism. The main question that one is asking when engaging in such an analysis, is basically at what level regulation should take place so that this intervention can be regarded as optimal.[464] Translating this to the issue at stake this would mean it has to be checked whether powers should indeed be moved away from the Member States, giving the Commission or other European, centralised institutions more influence, or whether a decentralised solution should be preferred, with more reliance on Member States and national solutions.

When discussing the delineation of powers between central and decentralised levels, Tiebout's seminal article on the provision of public goods[465] is often mentioned in the literature as the starting point. According to Tiebout, citizens will under certain conditions move to the region which satisfies their preference the best.[466] Two assumptions made in Tiebout's analysis are of particular relevance, namely the one of full mobility of the citizens and complete knowledge of the options and different characteristics of the different regions.[467] If the assumptions made by Tiebout are given, citizens will be accumulated in different cities, depending on their preferences.[468]

A competition between different levels of expenditure on public goods in different regions as describes above, can also be transposed to the sphere of legal rules. The essence of regulatory competition is that the existence of different rules will lead to a competition between these rules which in the end will lead to an optimal rule.[469] Consequently the preferred choice from an economic standpoint would be decentralisation, because such a bottom up approach favours allocative efficiency, contrary to a top-down approach

464 Faure 2003, p. 34.
465 Tiebout 1956.
466 *Ibid.*, p. 418.
467 These two conditions will be picked up again below in 5.4.
468 Faure 2003, p. 34.
469 Bhagwati and Hudec 1997, p. 89.

which would be following if the European Commission engaged in harmonisation.[470] Van den Bergh argues that regulatory competition can also clarify the subsidiarity principle, which if taken seriously would always lead to a presumption that would support decentralised solutions.[471] He also points out that the call for regulatory competition is less supported if homogenous preferences are given. This is an especially interesting point in the area of environmental protection and more particularly nuclear liability because it can be argued that at least for the potential victims of a nuclear accident the interests and preferences will be relatively similar.[472]

5.2. The call for harmonisation

Following Tiebout's model, the starting point for the regulation of the nuclear sector in the European Union should be a decentralised approach. Esty and Geradin, however, maintain that contrary to what is often claimed in theory, experiences would have shown that decentralisation cannot be regarded *per se* as welfare enhancing.[473] The extreme alternative to decentralisation would be harmonisation of nuclear safety and nuclear liability in the European Union. When faced with the question whether a certain area should be harmonised it is not enough to show a sufficient legal basis to engage in harmonisation, but a substantial justification for it will be needed too.[474] Another important aspect which has to be kept in mind is that harmonisation might not always be needed because alternatives might achieve the same goals, such as for example the extra-territorial application of national law or more co-operation between different Member States and mutual recognition.[475] It has also been argued that harmonisation is a problem because it would favour those countries that already have stricter standards because they will face lower compliance costs to adapt to the stricter harmonised standard.[476]

Furthermore, a claim for harmonisation presupposes that different rules exist in a certain area of law. The logical starting question is thus why these differences exist in the first place. Differences in national laws always have to be seen in the context of the different cultures in which they came into existence.[477] The existing differences with regard to legal rules are the result of differing domestic preferences.[478] Such differences might consequently indeed be justified. This argumentation can of course also be applied to environmental regulation. Specific conditions of certain regions might justify less

470 Faure 2003, p. 38.
471 Van den Bergh 2000, p. 435.
472 For a classification of this statement see 5.4.
473 Esty and Geradin 2001, p. 31.
474 Van Dam 2006, p. 133.
475 See section 5.3.
476 Revesz 2001, p. 28.
477 Van Dam 2006, p. 125.
478 Van Boom 2009, p. 436.

stringent environmental standards than would be required in other regions.[479] However, with regard to the nuclear sector, an assumption can be made that throughout the European Union it is desirable to have at least a certain level of nuclear safety to minimise the risks of being exposed to radioactive releases and nuclear accidents.[480] Consequently the following sections will analyse whether arguments can be identified that would indeed justify a more centralised solution to the problems that the nuclear sector is facing. First the theoretical arguments will be presented. In section 5.4 these arguments will be applied to the issues of nuclear safety regulation and nuclear liability.

5.2.1. *Race to the bottom*

The first economic argument that will be discussed is the danger of a so-called race to the bottom. It has been pointed out in academic literature that regulatory competition which results from a decentralised approach, might bear this danger.[481] Revesz points out that the argument that there is a risk of a race to the bottom is a very common argument that is brought forward to justify environmental regulation being moved to a central level. This phenomenon describes a competition between different states to encourage companies to locate within their area. This competition would take place by continuously introducing laxer environmental regulations compared to the level of regulation introduced by other competing states.[482] The relaxation of standards would then induce companies to locate within the jurisdiction that follows such low standards which can lead to positive effects for that state in terms of for example tax revenue. As a response to this another state might lower its environmental standards even further to attract companies that are looking for an appropriate location to locate within their jurisdiction or even incite companies to relocate. This constant lowering of standards leads, however, in the end to welfare losses because the competing states would end up with environmental standards which would be too lax.[483] That is why another term for this type of competition for lower standards is destructive competition.[484] Given the welfare losses coming along with such a form of competition, believers of the race to the bottom do not regard regulation from a more central level as a problem or a restriction of the autonomy of decision makers at the decentralised level, but rather as a necessity to prevent welfare losses because by introducing a more stringent standard that also has to be complied with at the decentralised level, competition in the form of a race to the bottom is excluded.[485] As List and Gerking point out, however, decentralised regulation does not necessarily have to go along with a lowering of standards.[486]

479 See Esty and Geradin 1998, p. 11.
480 For a classification of this statement see section 5.4.
481 Faure 2009, p. 270.
482 Revesz 1992, p. 1210.
483 *Ibid.*, p. 1216.
484 See Oates and Schwab 1988.
485 Revesz 1992, p. 1217+1218.
486 List and Gerking 2000.

Revesz argues that often race to the bottom claims are used excessively and also in situations in which they are not appropriate. He calls for more careful analysis because different environmental standards could also simply be the result of an undervaluation of environmental quality by some states, it need not necessarily be the result of a race to the bottom.[487] Another criticism raised by Revesz is that even if one assumed that there was a possibility for a race to the bottom with regard to environmental regulation, the appropriate response would not be to transfer regulation to a central level. This would only lead to situations in which states would compete for industries by relaxing standards in other areas. Centralised environmental regulation would according to Revesz not solve the prisoner's dilemma that is at the heart of the race to the bottom claims.[488]

The argument that harmonisation at a central level is needed due to the risk of a race to the bottom, can only be successfully used if it can indeed be shown that there is a real possibility for states to attract industry by laxer regulation or legal rules.[489] Industries will migrate to countries with lower standards only when the reduced costs that result from the compliance with lesser standards will outweigh the costs that will need to be incurred to locate in another state than the home state of the respective company.[490] Obviously these costs will be higher for already established industries that are considering relocation than for new industries or companies that want to enter a certain market or are considering the construction of new plants.[491]

As apparent from these considerations, the crucial question is whether the race to the bottom is a real danger, or whether in practice it does not really take place. Esty and Geradin point out that there is little empirical evidence that would support a claim that industries would indeed relocate depending on the strictness of the respective environmental standards. As factors that can explain this they mention the high costs that a firm has to face when relocating.[492] Denying that the race to the bottom has any theoretical foundations, Revesz also states that the empirical evidence which would be needed to support such race to the bottom claims nonetheless is not really convincing[493] However, contrary to their findings in an older article, Esty and Geradin point in a more recent article to some authors that indeed provide empirical support for the hypothesis that lenient regulation will affect industry (re)location.[494] List and Co also demonstrate that environmental regulation and the stringency thereof has an influence on the location decisions of plants.[495] They explicitly make the point that globalisation and a continuous integration of markets fosters a potential competition between states to attract big

487 Revesz 1992, p. 1233–1235.
488 Revesz 1997, p. 540; Revesz 1992, p. 1245.
489 Faure 2003, p. 47.
490 Revesz 1992, p. 1215.
491 *Ibid.*, p. 1221.
492 Esty and Geradin 1998, p. 13; see also Faure 2001, p. 272.
493 Revesz 2001, p. 4.
494 Esty and Geradin 2001, p. 38.
495 List and Co 2000.

corporations.[496] Within the European Union there is a high level of market integration which further attaches relevance to this observation. With regard to the question of whether stringency of environmental regulation is related to the location decisions of enterprises, Xing and Kolstadt also provide some evidence that lenient environmental standards do attract investment.[497] They equally admit, however, that discourse on this is divided. This is also emphasised by Leiter *et al.* in a recent article, concluding that 'there is no consensus among environmental economists whether environmental regulation causes a positive or a negative impact on firm behaviour.'[498]

An argument for the absence of a real race to the bottom is that in some cases it might simply be the preference of a state to set a good example and protect certain values. This is certainly true in the field of environmental law where decision makers would have difficulties explaining why they support rules and regulations which endanger the well-being of the citizens.[499]

Vogel also argues that instead of a race to the bottom, regulatory competition can even lead to a race to the top. Enacting stricter regulatory standards would for example have the advantage that it can lead to new opportunities on the market for pollution control technologies.[500] Braithwaite and Drahos differentiate between different sectors. In some they observe that globalisation has led to a tightening of regulatory standards, whilst in other sectors the contrary is true. It is noteworthy that they classify the nuclear sector as one in which standards have become stricter. In their analysis they describe different factors that can contribute to the 'ratcheting up' of standards. Amongst these factors one is of particular interest namely the potential of the management philosophy of continuous improvement.[501] The relevance of this aspect will be picked up again below.[502]

In the discussion of the alleged advantages of regulatory competition on the one hand and risks for a race to the bottom on the other hand, Esty and Geradin reject both sides of the extreme. They argue that the race to the bottom line of argumentation has been overused but also the proponents of regulatory competition would not have provided much added value to the debate on centralisation and decentralisation. They suggest a more nuanced approach, focussing on 'a flexible mix of competition and co-operation between governmental actors, as well as between governmental and non-governmental actors.'[503]

496 *Ibid.*, p. 15.
497 Xing and Kolstadt 2002.
498 Leiter *et al.* 2011.
499 Faure 2003, p. 49.
500 Vogel 2001a, p. 334+335.
501 Braithwaite and Drahos 1999, p. 110.
502 See 5.4.
503 Esty and Geradin 2001, p. 31.

Another nuanced aspect which is brought forward by Esty and Geradin is that whilst they admit that cases in which one could speak of a real race to the bottom are not very frequent, another potentially welfare reducing phenomenon can result from regulatory competition. Regardless of a race to the bottom, states might nevertheless be inclined not to enact strict environmental standards because they are afraid that this could be harmful for their competitiveness. This political drag or regulatory chill makes it more difficult for governments to tighten regulatory standards.[504] Such hesitations can also materialise in a sub-optimal level of enforcement. Environmental rules that are in place and possibly even set at a strict level might simply not be properly enforced. Environmental offences which are not sanctioned are then the result of such an indirect lowering of standards.

5.2.2. Economies of scale

The call for regulatory competition according to the basic model of Tiebout has of course the inherent limit that it is only applicable if the issue at stake is a local one and has no influence on other communities. If one can identify a transboundary aspect in the problem to be regulated and thereby the issue goes beyond the competences of a local or national authority, a need to switch to a more centralised solution occurs to establish economies of scale better suited to deal with the problem. The central authority should be as high as to have sufficient authority to tackle the issue adequately in the entire territory concerned.[505]

Also with regard to environmental regulation an economies of scale argument can be made. One large well equipped institution can do research more efficiently than a multitude of different smaller institutions.[506] Revesz argues that the economies of scale rationale is particularly strong for regulatory processes that are still at an early stage, for example in the phase of information gathering and risk assessment, while later on in the process the economies of scale effect might not be as big anymore. When it comes to standard setting for example he argues that there is a lesser risk of a duplication of efforts and rather the regionally different preferences and conditions would need to be taken into account at the decentralised level.[507]

However, economies of scale advantages can also occur at later stages of the regulatory process. If, for example, similar environmental management systems can be developed and staff of power plants could be trained with the same seminars, and compliance programs would also be established across boundaries, significant economies of scale could be established.[508] For this to be possible however, a certain level of centralised

[504] Esty and Geradin 1998, p. 7.
[505] Faure 2003, p. 38.
[506] Kimber 1995, p. 1660.
[507] Revesz 1997, p. 543+544.
[508] Esty and Geradin 1998, p. 13.

regulation will be necessary. Furthermore, the argument that regulation at a later stage has to account for different preferences and conditions is also of lesser weight in some areas of environmental regulation, for example when it is clear that the exposure to a certain substance is a risk for human health.[509]

5.2.3. *Transboundary externalities*

Another argument that can be brought forward against the regulation at a decentralised level is the risk or existence of transboundary externalities. Even if prohibitive relocation costs might lead to a situation in which relocation is no option and therefore the risk of a race to the bottom is mitigated, states can have an incentive to introduce regulation that is not strict enough if certain harm can be externalised on other states.[510] Revesz provides a good definition of transboundary externalities stating that they 'arise because a state that sends pollution to another state obtains the labour and fiscal benefits of the economic activity that generates the pollution but does not suffer the full costs of the activity.'[511] If Coasian Bargaining between states is not possible to remedy such externalisation of harm, transboundary externalities are a strong argument for centralised environmental regulation according to Revesz. However, he also raises the caveat that this argument cannot be used for all forms of centralised environmental regulation.[512]

Faure also states that the transboundary nature of pollution is one of the strongest arguments for more harmonisation.[513] Inefficiencies will result from decentralised regulation of something with a transboundary character because if one state, or an entity within that state, has the possibility of externalising harm, there would be no incentive for stricter regulation within that state.[514] Consequently if there is a real danger of an externalisation of harm, there is an economic argument for centralisation to prevent this.

The argument of transboundary externalities as a justification for more centralised regulation can have a very broad scope if one takes into account the extension of this concept made by Esty and Geradin. They stress that externalities can also be of a psychological nature, stating that 'people in other countries may be greatly distressed by the disappearance of rare species or the loss of ecosystems that support biodiversity.'[515]

509 Esty and Geradin 2001, p. 36.
510 Revesz 1992, p. 1222.
511 Revesz 2001, p. 3.
512 Revesz 1997, p. 540.
513 Faure 2001, p. 269.
514 Faure 2003, p. 39.
515 Esty and Geradin 2001, p. 34.

5.2.4. *Public choice considerations*

When discussing reasons and arguments for harmonisation at the European level, one should also pay some attention to considerations of public choice, dealing with the influence of interest groups on decision making. If the European Commission itself is regarded as such an interest group, it could of course be argued that harmonisation sometimes also might take place to further the interest of the bureaucrats in Brussels. If regulation is centralised this means more power and influence for the actors at Brussels. Such an argument has for example been brought forward by Faure in his discussion of the Product Liability Directive.[516] Other considerations along the lines of public choice theory are at what level the influence of interest groups is bigger or at what level regulatory processes can be more transparent. If environmental protection can be strengthened, a relevant question would be at what level environmental considerations could be taken more effectively into consideration. If this was the case at a decentralised level an argument could be made against harmonisation, whilst the contrary is true if at EU level the influence of environmental interest groups could be greater than at national level.[517]

5.3. Alternatives to harmonisation

A claim for harmonisation will always imply a normative element because the underlying hypothesis is that one law is better than another.[518] Such a claim can be problematic because it is questionable whether one rule can simply be regarded as better. This is especially true if we recall that legal rules always have to be seen in the context of the culture and the system they operate in. These observations lead to the question whether harmonisation sometimes might indeed be an inadequate tool. The following sections will discuss some alternatives to harmonisation.

5.3.1. *Extra-territorial application of national law*

Harmonisation of environmental law was discussed above as a response to the risk of a race to the bottom and the inefficient lowering of environmental standards. As another response to a potential race to the bottom, and the fear that companies leave their home jurisdiction to operate in jurisdictions with laxer regulation, states could try to enforce their laws extra-territorially. This could for example include the application of domestic standards to national companies operating abroad. If indeed companies had to comply with the strict regulation of their home jurisdictions regardless of where they operate, the incentive to relocate to areas in which environmental standards are lower is lost.[519] Whether such an approach would indeed be effective is still questionable because

516 Faure 2000a, p. 495.
517 Revesz 2001, p. 10; Faure 2001, p. 282.
518 Bhagwati and Hudec 1997, p. 50.
519 Esty and Geradin 1998, p. 33.

corporate law offers enough tools to restructure corporate entities in a way to escape the application of strict standards from one's home jurisdiction.[520]

A more far-reaching option would be the application of domestic standards to foreign companies situated abroad.[521] Such considerations of extra-territoriality have a long tradition as an attempt to correct externalities that can arise from flawed foreign legal systems. This option, however, is quite controversial, because it displays a certain style of legal imperialism, trying to impose one's national rules on foreign states or companies.

The discussion of the extraterritorial application of national law in the environmental area requires some further attention to be paid to more general issues of private international law and also public international law, given that some issues of environmental protection are also regulated under international treaties.[522] One German example for the latter scenario is the *Chernobyl-case.*[523] After the Chernobyl accident, a farmer that lived in Bonn filed a claim at the Civil Court of First Instance to receive compensation due to a lack of an early warning about the accident at Chernobyl. Whilst an obligation to provide early warnings does exist under public international law, it was held that such an obligation only exists between states as the subject of public international law. An interesting aspect of this case is, that the court would have accepted jurisdiction if the farmer's land had been located in Bonn, which was, however, not the case. In that case, it would have provided a forum for a German applicant asking for compensation for an accident that happened in the Soviet Union.

Another example where an attempt was made by private individuals for a rule of international law to be tried in national courts is the case of the *Mines de Potasse d'Alsace.*[524] In this case the District Court of Rotterdam held that the international law principle of *sic utere tuo* could also apply between private parties. Whilst this judgment was overturned on appeal[525], Nollkaemper points out that the original reasoning of the District Court of Rotterdam was a sensible one, given that general principles of law, such as *sic utere tuo,* in many case originate from national law with individuals as their subject.[526]

520 *Ibid.*, p. 34.

521 *Ibid.*, p. 32.

522 The following discussion will focus on the possibility to invoke international laws and principles as an individual in national courts. Broader issues of private international law such as rules on jurisdiction and applicable law in general will be discussed below in section 5.4.2.

523 Discussion of this case will build on Rest 1997 and Nollkaemper 1998.

524 Handelskwekerij G.J. Bier B.V. and Stichting Reinwater v. Mines de Potasse d'Alsace S.A. (MDPA), District Court of Rotterdam, NJ 1979, 113.

525 Mines de Potasse d'Alsace S.A. (MDPA) v. Onroerend Goed Maatschappij Bier BV et al., Court of Appeal The Hague, 1986.

526 Nollkaemper 1998, p. 7.

A less intrusive way than the extra-territorial application of national law would be to focus on the enforcement of existing rules and regulations in other states.[527] This alternative as presented by Esty and Geradin shows that the transboundary character of a problem does necessitate more extensive co-operation, but not necessarily a full harmonisation of rules because other legal tools are available.[528] This approach, however, has the inherent weakness of depending on the existence of appropriately strict environmental regulations in other countries. If the main focus will be on proper enforcement, and non-enforcement could even lead to penalties, such a system could incentivise the adoption of low standards that are easy to comply with.[529] Nevertheless can closer collaboration between national authorities, including more intense exchange of information to increase mutual trust building, potentially be an alternative to harmonisation?[530]

5.3.2. The role of mutual recognition

Another alternative to harmonisation is mutual recognition. Originating from the case law of the CJEU on the internal market,[531] this principle is being regarded as the most prominent alternative to harmonisation. Proponents of this principle argue that it allows an increase in mobility and barriers to trade without requiring harmonisation or regulation at a more central level.[532] This sounds like the perfect solution in the debate between decentralised regulatory competition on the one hand and centralised harmonisation on the other hand. The exact relationship between harmonisation and mutual recognition and the consequences thereof, however, require a more sophisticated and nuanced approach. Armstrong for example indicates that mutual recognition always needs to be supplemented with on-going harmonisation.[533] He thereby does not regard mutual recognition and harmonisation as mutually exclusive alternatives. This is in line with the argumentation presented by Kerber and van den Bergh. They claim that contrary to what can mostly be found in literature, mutual recognition is not an alternative to harmonisation but rather leads to more harmonisation and fewer regulatory powers at de-centralised levels.[534] Referring to the experience made in the EU they show that mutual recognition which is conditioned on the equivalence of objectives or effects of different national measures will ultimately lead to more co-operation, less regulatory autonomy and eventually more harmonisation.[535] The condition of equivalent objectives of effects points also to another aspect of mutual recognition, namely that if we are indeed faced with rules that are fundamentally different and harmonisation is envisaged

527 Esty and Geradin 1998, p. 34.
528 Faure 2001; p. 268.
529 Esty and Geradin 1998, p. 35.
530 Armstrong 2002, p. 244.
531 Case 120/78 *Rewe-Zentral AG v Bundesmonopolverwaltung für Branntwein* [1979].
532 Kerber and van den Bergh 2008, p. 451.
533 Armstrong 2002, p. 242.
534 Kerber and van den Bergh 2008, p. 462.
535 *Ibid.*, p. 454.

to mitigate the shortcomings of some national rules, mutual recognition will not be a viable alternative because of the normative element involved. This can be nicely illustrated by the case of nuclear liability within the European Union. The majority of the liability regimes currently in force in Member States of the European Union rely on the principles of the international conventions. Some principles of these conventions, such as for example the limitation of liability, the reliance on public funds and the principle of legal channelling, are heavily criticised in economic literature because they raise concerns of insufficient cost internalisation, subsidies and lacking incentives for safety. It would therefore be desirable that a European regime would depart from these principles to come up with better rules and regulations. Such a normative element precludes the application of mutual recognition as a tool to uphold regulatory competition.[536] A re-conceptualisation of mutual recognition as suggested by Kerber and van den Bergh, however, could very well be relevant in that discussion. They suggest that mutual recognition should be understood as initiating a rethinking process of whether regulatory powers have been allocated correctly.[537] In the nuclear sector, for example, the difficulties of relying on mutual recognition due to very different national rules that also illustrate the inadequacy of some of these rules, could initiate a transfer of regulatory powers to a more central level, giving more powers to the European Commission.

5.4. Analysis

Having laid down the theoretical framework of harmonisation and different economic arguments that would justify harmonisation, this part will now apply the criteria to specific issue at stake. In previous sections it was stated that certain prohibitions or regulation stemming from a centralised level can be justified by reference to homogeneous preferences. The European Union for example can be classified as a region with a high level of homogeneity concerning releases that would have a significantly bad effect on the environment and health.[538] At first sight the main inclination is to assume that within the European Union preferences with regard to nuclear safety and a robust liability regime are certainly not as different between citizens would justify fundamental differences. However, these claims have to be nuanced to some extent, taking into account that differences in rules can also be the result of different preferences and cultures that can have an influence on the development of legal rules. Building upon the work of Hofstede,[539] van Dam discusses exactly this relationship.[540] In his article he links different cultures with the content of legal rules, stating that especially in the area of tort law 'national rules [...] are to a great extent the outward manifestation, the body, of the national culture, its soul.'[541] Relying on the 5 dimensions as discussed by Hofstede, namely individualism versus collectivism, masculinity versus femininity, uncertainty

536 Bhagwati and Hudec 1997, p. 91.
537 Kerber and van den Bergh 2008, p. 460.
538 Faure 2001, p. 281.
539 Hofstede 2001.
540 Van Dam 2009.
541 *Ibid.*, p. 281.

avoidance, power distance and long-term versus short-term orientation, van Dam sketches how different cultures can explain different developments in legal rules and different preferences in legal system as a whole.[542] Taking these considerations into account, it can be said that there indeed might not be a uniform desire for the same level of nuclear safety and victim protection throughout the European Union. However, taking into account the flaws of the current regime as outlined in previous chapters, a higher level of protection than the current one, and regulation that would minimise the results of nuclear accidents as much as possible, can be regarded as a goal that would be shared amongst potential victims of a nuclear accident within the European Union. Differences in cultures arguably have a lesser influence on minimum levels of protection, especially in the area of ultra-hazardous activities. That can also be seen in the universal choice of strict liability for nuclear accidents, despite the fact that in some jurisdictions a rule of strict liability is less common than in others.[543]

Another point that deserves some preliminary remarks refers to two assumptions of Tiebout's model that perfect mobility and full knowledge are taken as granted.[544] In the nuclear sector these two assumptions require some further qualification. With regard to mobility it can be said that European citizens can move relatively freely within the European Union. The free movement of persons is one of the fundamental freedoms of the European Union and administrative hurdles for European citizens to make use of these rights are continually lowered. Whether citizens indeed will make use of this right is of course another question. Even if other Member States offer better services or a higher level of environmental protection citizens might still not leave their home Member States due to a number of ties that could hold them back, such as for example friends or families. Also differences in culture or language barriers could constrain the mobility of citizens. Nevertheless, the mobility of citizens can be regarded as essentially given, certainly from a legal perspective, and citizens will also face fewer practical constraints in exercising this mobility than companies.

If we then look at companies that might want to choose the best location taking into account the different regulatory regimes applicable, from a strictly legal perspective it can also be said that mobility of companies in the European Union is possible, keeping in mind the relevant case law in this area.[545] However, some differentiations have to be made. Firstly a separation needs to be made between first location and relocation. For the latter category mobility is restricted by the quite substantive costs that companies would face in the case of relocation. Secondly, mobility can be impeded by the fact that many nuclear power plants are operated by state-owned enterprises. In these cases relocation will play a lesser role than if a power plant is run by private parties.

542 *Ibid.*, p. 291–299.

543 See in that regard also van Dam 2009, p. 288.

544 Section 5.1.

545 Case C-212/97 *Centros Ltd* v. *Erhvervs- og Selskabsstyrelsen* [1999]; Case C-208/00 *Überseering BV* v. *Nordic Construction Company Baumanagement GmbH* [2002]; Case C-167/01 *Kamer van Koophandel en Fabrieken voor Amsterdam* v. *Inspire Art Ltd* [2003].

The distinction between private parties on the one hand and state-owned enterprises on the other also has a more general relevance to the discussion at stake if the model of regulatory competition of Tiebout[546] is analysed together with Hirschmann's framework on exit, voice and loyalty as possible responses to changing circumstances.[547] As its title suggests, Hirschmann's theory discusses three different options to react to a decline in quality or changes in a regulatory environment. Actors could leave, they could express their dissatisfaction or they could stay. For the discussion at stake here, the most interesting aspect of this theory is the role that loyalty plays with regard to the two options of exit and voice. On the one hand it has been argued that the possibility of exit can decrease the frequency with which the opportunity to voice dissatisfaction is used effectively. Loyalty on the other hand can decrease the likelihood that actors do indeed vote with their feet and leave, thus activating the option to voice their concerns.[548] To increase the likelihood that voicing one's concern will be effective, however, an existing threat to exit can be regarded as a tool to increase one's bargaining power.[549] This power, however, is lost, if loyalty is so strong that exit actually becomes unlikely. Thus loyalty could repress both voice and exit at the same time.[550] If we draw now an analogy with the issue of state owned enterprises in the nuclear sector, state-ownership could be regarded as a form of dictated loyalty. As apparent from the discussion above, such loyalty can render the system of regulatory competition less effective. Exit is virtually impossible whilst voice might not always be an effective option either.[551]

Concerning the second assumption mentioned, namely the one of full knowledge, some clarification is needed to assess whether the actors involved can indeed 'vote with their feet' by moving to areas that fulfil their preferences as suggested by the model of Tiebout. Companies are in that regard in a better position than citizens. On the one hand companies are equipped with research departments and can invest resources in the accumulation of information about different regulatory regimes and their respective advantages and disadvantages. Also experts can be hired to take care of this. Whilst theoretically a private person could of course also do this, companies will have much more resources to engage in such activities. Another aspect with regard to the knowledge of companies is that they can also benefit from exchanges between different companies. In the nuclear sector for example, certain associations only meet with the exclusion of

546 Tiebout 1956.

547 Hirschmann 1970.

548 *Ibid.*, p. 76–78.

549 *Ibid.*, p. 82.

550 *Ibid.*, p. 92.

551 A nice example for this can be seen in the litigation in Germany that occurred as the result of the decision to phase out nuclear energy earlier than originally planned in the light of the accident at the Fukushima Daiichi nuclear power plant. Originally, EnBW, one of the four nuclear operators in Germany, did not want to legally question the legality of the phase-out decision, whilst the other operators were more eager to do so. Several sources saw the partial public ownership of EnBW as one of the main reasons for this, see for example www.sueddeutsche.de/wirtschaft/klage-gegen-atomausstieg-abgesagt-enbw-kneift-1.1426679 (last accessed on 21 August 2015); www.tagesspiegel.de/wirtschaft/atomausstieg-energiekonzerne-drohen-mit-klagen/10700058.html (last accessed on 21 August 2015).

the public, allowing companies to gather more information than it would be possible for an individual interested in the matters. In the case of nuclear safety and nuclear liability full knowledge of citizens is therefore arguably not given. There is a high likelihood that citizens will not be aware of the respective regulatory regimes and requirements for nuclear operators in their jurisdiction. This weakens the case for decentralisation, because at least one underlying assumption of the Tiebout model can be questioned for one of the actors involved.

Nevertheless a more detailed analysis in how far the economic arguments can be applicable to the discussion at stake is necessary. Therefore the following sections will first analyse whether there is indeed a need from an economic point of view to harmonise nuclear safety, before turning to the issue of nuclear liability. In a concluding session the findings will be summarised and also some attention will be paid to non-economic arguments for harmonisation in the nuclear sector.

5.4.1. Nuclear Safety Regulation

With regard to nuclear safety regulation the first argument that will be discussed is whether harmonisation in that area is justified due to the risk of a race to the bottom. Recalling the discussion above, such a risk would exist if there is a danger that different Member States within the European Union engage in destructive competition concerning their nuclear safety standards in order to attract nuclear power plants from other countries. It was pointed out that high relocation costs are a real obstacle for firms to relocate, which mitigates the danger of a destructive competition. With regard to relocation costs, the nuclear industry is a prime example for costs that would be too high for relocation to be efficient. It is inconceivable to find a jurisdiction in which the regulation of nuclear safety is so lenient that it would outweigh the immense costs an operator would incur in the case of relocation. This has to be seen together with the self-interest of an operator in preventing accidents. A certain amount of safety will always be in the interest of an operator so as not to risk losing their source of income. These observations weaken the race to the bottom argument in the area of nuclear safety. Another factor that needs to be taken into account is the general climate within the European Union with regard to nuclear power generation. Many Member States do not engage in nuclear power production and therefore will also not have an interest in attracting power plants to locate within their jurisdiction. Also with regard to Member States that are relying on nuclear power it has to be recalled that some of them already decided to phase it out or power plants are coming to the end of their life span. And even if it is decided to keep plants in operation longer, the more reasonable strategy is to go for a life time extension and not a relocation of the power plant to escape the strict regulatory regime of the home jurisdiction.

Another important issue is that some steps towards harmonisation of nuclear safety regulation have already been made within the European Union by the Nuclear Safety

Directives.[552] One principle installed in this Directive is of particular relevance for the race to the bottom claims. Article 1 of Directive 2009/71 states that one of the objectives of that Directive is 'to establish a Community framework in order to maintain and promote the continuous improvement of nuclear safety and its regulation'. As mentioned already above, Braithwaite and Drahos mention exactly this kind of a principle as a potential tool to not only work against a race to the bottom, but even initiate a race to the top.[553] For this to happen, there will still be the need to implement this principle. Mere incorporation of such a principle into the law will of course not suffice.

The discussion has so far mainly focussed on already existing power plants and whether a race to the bottom could attract relocation of existing plants. Given that within the European Union, however, there are also still plans to invest in new nuclear power plants, one has to analyse whether the risk of a race to the bottom might be bigger concerning new build. In such a case the relocation arguments of course lose weight because a company could decide right from the beginning to make use of its free movement rights within the European Union and set up a nuclear power plant in a Member State with a more lenient regulatory regime.[554] Whether this is indeed a serious risk, however, seems questionable. A competition between Member States in lax safety regulation to attract nuclear new builds is difficult to accommodate with public opinion on nuclear power generation. Given the strengthened role that the public can play by now in licensing processes, a policy that relies on the attraction of capital on the costs of nuclear safety will most likely be met with a lot of opposition by the citizens already living in that Member States. Furthermore, recent cases concerning new build have shown that it is not lax safety standards, but rather financial advantages guaranteeing security of investment that can play a crucial role in location decisions.[555]

An argument that could support harmonisation of nuclear safety at the European level, however, becomes apparent if we look at issues such as political drag and regulatory chill as discussed by Esty and Geradin.[556] This phenomenon, pointing to the unwillingness of governments to strengthen regulatory standards due to fears of losing competitiveness can be of particular relevance for the Eastern Member States in which nuclear safety is arguably not as high as in the old Member States. These Member States face more difficulties in enforcing the higher safety standards which are available in the old Member States, and therefore a tendency might be apparent to prefer less strict standards.[557] This

552 Council Directive 2009/71/EURATOM to be amended by Council Directive 2014/87/EURATOM.

553 Braithwaite and Drahos 1999, p. 110.

554 For state-owned enterprises this would again arguably play a lesser role. See section 5.4.

555 Http://blogs.ft.com/nick-butler/2014/10/08/hinkley-point-the-nuclear-winners-and-losers/ (last accessed on 21 August 2015), see also Press release IP/14/, State aid: Commission concludes modified UK measures for Hinkley Point nuclear power plant are compatible with EU rules.

556 Esty and Geradin 1998, p. 7.

557 See in that regard the Question for written answer E-002860/13 by MEP Dimitar Stoyanov, asking for a re-examination of the decision to close two older power plants in Bulgaria.

also explains that with regard to nuclear safety already some form of harmonisation has taken place in the European Union with the Nuclear Safety Directive.

Turning to the argument that economies of scale might justify harmonisation of nuclear safety within the European Union it has to be stated that indeed this could be a valid argument. If safety regulation is harmonised and also monitored and co-ordinated from a centralised level, this can create synergies and learning effects. If incidents happening in one power plant were registered in one European database and all reactors would have to be checked to see whether their safety standards would prevent a similar accident, this would enhance the status of nuclear safety. Efforts to that extent have for example been made in the chemical sector where the Seveso II Directive installed the Major Accident Reporting System and the Community Documentation Centre on Industrial Risks.[558] Further, the training of nuclear safety officers is facilitated if regulatory standards are harmonised in the European Union. Similar seminars and compliance programs could be developed which can lead to significant economies of scale.[559]

5.4.2. Nuclear liability

National boundaries are not respected by nature.[560] This is equally true for accidents in high risk sectors, given the likelihood of the transboundary character of the harm. This is further supported if we take into consideration that many power plants are located close to border regions, aggravating the issue of transboundary harm even further.[561] Also the experiences from past nuclear accidents have shown that nuclear pollution does not acknowledge or respect state borders. Harm resulting from a nuclear accident is of a transboundary nature. Therefore one local authority will not be sufficient to adequately deal with the problem. An argument therefore can be made that nuclear liability needs to be regulated by a more central authority with sufficient competences to approach the problem in the entire area that can be affected.[562] Such an argument for economies of scale could consequently justify harmonisation of nuclear liability in the European Union.

Faure, however, points out that even in the case of typically transboundary harm such as environmental liability, one should not be too quick with a call for centralisation because other appropriate tools may exist within national law to remedy the problem.[563] One possibility for example would be the extra-territorial application of national law if the national law follows higher standards than neighbouring countries which are potentially

558 See Chapter 2, section 2.2.1.3.
559 Esty and Geradin 1998, p. 13.
560 Preston and Hanson 2013, p. 1.
561 For an overview of the location of NPPs in Europe see http://news.bbc.co.uk/2/hi/europe/4713398.stm (last accessed on 21 August 2015).
562 Faure 2003, p. 38.
563 Faure 2003, p. 39.

externalising harm.[564] More monitoring between neighbouring countries has also been suggested in the literature, but the effectiveness of such proposals has also been questioned at the same time.[565]

The first option, an extraterritorial application of national law, plays an especially important role in the discussion of externalisation of harm as a potential economic justification for harmonisation. An externalisation of harm takes place if 'a state that emits pollution to another state obtains the labour and fiscal benefits of the economic activity that generates the pollution but does not suffer the full costs of the activity.'[566] This can equally be applied to companies in the nuclear sector. If an operator of a nuclear power plant can enjoy the profits from their activity whilst not having to face the full costs of damages that they might create, we can speak of an externalisation of harm. If a conflict of law rule enables a victim in a country with stricter liability rules or higher compensation amounts to impose this standard on actors from countries with softer rules, the argument of externalisation of harm does not hold.[567] This discussion leads to the question of how far the rules of private international law in the European Union enable such a process. Determining the applicable law and the competent courts to hear a case is of course of crucial importance in attempts of extra-territorial application of national law. With regard to jurisdiction it can be said on a general note that one would expect national courts in the state where the pollution created damage to be more favourable towards the claims of victims in that state.[568] Therefore victims might have an inclination to have their case heard in their national jurisdiction. In the European Union, jurisdiction in civil and commercial matters is dealt with under the so-called Brussels I regulation.[569] Article 5(3) of that regulation states that

> *'A person domiciled in a Member State may, in another Member State, be sued in matters relating to tort, delict or quasi-delict, in the courts for the place where the harmful event occurred or may occur'.*

This article created some ambiguity with regard to the question of whether 'the place where the harm occurred' refers to the place where the activity takes place (*Handlungsort*) or the place where the consequences of the activity materialise (*Erfolgsort*). This ambiguity was solved by the CJEU in the *Bier-case*.[570] In response to a reference for a preliminary ruling, the Court held that 'the expression "place where the harmful event occurred", in article 5(3) of the Convention, must be understood as being intended to cover both the place where the damage occurred and the place of the event giving rise to

564 See section 5.3.1.
565 See Esty and Geradin 1998.
566 Revesz 2001, p. 3.
567 Faure 2000a, p. 477.
568 Faure and Betlem 2008, p. 139.
569 Council Regulation 44/2001 on jurisdiction and the recognition and enforcement of judgments in civil and commercial matters.
570 Case 21/76 *Handelskwekerij G.J. Bier BV* v. *Mines de potasse d'Alsace SA* [1976].

it.'[571] With regard to the applicable law in a transboundary scenario, the Rome II regulation[572] codified a similar approach. Article 7 of this regulation states

> *'The law applicable to a non-contractual obligation arising out of environmental damage or damage sustained by persons or property as a result of such damage shall be the law determined pursuant to Article 4(1), unless the person seeking compensation for damage chooses to base his or her claim on the law of the country in which the event giving rise to the damage occurred'*

Since article 4(1) of the regulation refers to the *Erfolgsort*, together with article 7 again a choice is possible between the *Erfolgs-* or the *Handlungsort.*

In the nuclear sector, however, this discussion as presented above is of less relevance, because the international conventions on civil liability exclude the European rules on private international law. Victims of a nuclear accident can only sue the operator in the jurisdiction where the power plant is located according to the applicable rules of that jurisdiction. If a nuclear power plant is operated in a country with low liability limits for example, whilst the damage occurs in a country with higher liability limits, it can happen that victims in the second country are worse off than in a situation in which the accident would have happened in their jurisdiction, because the operator from the jurisdiction with less strict rules was able to externalise some harm on the victims in the neighbouring state. This is at odds with experiences in other areas as for example illustrated by the *Cockerill-case* as discussed by Faure and Betlem.[573] In that case emissions by a foreign polluter were judged according to the standard that would have been applicable for a polluter within the country of the court's jurisdiction. This would not be possible under the currently applicable civil liability regimes for nuclear accidents.[574] This is also contrary to the views of the Commission that explicitly stated in its proposal for the Rome II regulation that a high level of environmental protection and the wish to prevent the externalisation of harm was the reason for allowing a choice between the *Erfolgs-* and *Handlungsort as connecting factor for the applicable law.* Thus, a harmonisation of liability rules for nuclear accidents would not only be justified to fight against the externalisation of harm in the nuclear sector, but would also be more in accordance with the *acquis communautaire.*

The risk for a race to the bottom would be a less convincing argument for harmonisation of nuclear liability in the European Union. Already the existing regimes rely heavily on state funds. Lowering the limits that industry would have to pay for even further would lead to a situation in which the proportion of state funds would be increased. Making taxpayers pay for nuclear accidents would become even more difficult to defend against one's citizens if this is the result of a conscious decision to lower liability amounts to

571 *Ibid.*, para. 24.
572 Council Regulation (EC) 864/2007 on the law applicable to non-contractual obligations.
573 Faure and Betlem 2008, p. 162+163.
574 There are exceptions to this, as for example Austria, see above 3.3. Whether a judgment in Austria, applying its law on nuclear liability extraterritorially would be enforceable is, however, doubtful.

attract foreign industry. Lenient liability rules would further decrease the possibilities of appropriate compensation which can also not be in the interest of the Member States because it would limit possibilities of recourse in the case where an accident occurs.[575] A race to the bottom rationale therefore does not seem to provide a strong argument in favour of harmonisation of liability rules within the European Union.

5.4.3. Conclusion

As it was shown in the previous sections, whilst a call for harmonisation within the nuclear sector is easily made, finding an economic justification for such claims is not that straightforward. With regard to nuclear safety it was shown that especially considerations of political drag and regulatory chill can serve as a justification for harmonisation. The need for economies of scale provides an even stronger argument for harmonisation in that area. Economies of scale, which would enable a more efficient risk management of transboundary nuclear damage, can also be an argument to harmonise nuclear liability, but the strongest argument for harmonisation of nuclear liability can be found in the danger of an externalisation of harm.

As discussed in section 5.3, some alternatives to harmonisation are presented in the literature. At this point it will be useful to consider one aspect of this, namely the extra-territorial application of national law or alternatively the focus on the enforcement of existing, and also foreign, rules. Whilst there are also certain flaws with these alternatives it must nevertheless be recalled that they could serve as a compromise solution if combined with some form of minimum harmonisation. Centralised intervention at the European level could guarantee a certain harmonised level of environmental protection. Whilst states would still be able to go further, the joint supervision of enforcement of the existing rules would make sure that at least minimum standards are complied with.

Another point that has to be mentioned at this stage is that next to the economic arguments discussed in the previous sections, there also non-economic aspects that should be kept in mind when discussing the issue of more harmonisation of the nuclear sector at the European level. A very common argument that is often brought forward is the relatively loose term of levelling the playing field. In the academic literature, the current legislative landscape concerning nuclear liability has been described as a regime that is extremely patchy and complex.[576] This is a real problem, having in mind the uncertainties which come along with such a regime. Former Commissioner Piebalgs strengthens this point further by pointing out the special importance of legal certainty particularly in the field of nuclear energy.[577] Whilst it might be going too far to speak of

575 Faure 2003, p. 49.

576 Currie 2008, p. 85.

577 Europa Rapid Press Release, *Andris Piebalgs Energy Commissioner: The Euratom Treaty and development of the Nuclear Industry Keynote Speech at the 'International Nuclear Law Association'*, 3rd of October 2007, SPEECH/07/599.

legal uncertainty in the area of nuclear liability as it is currently regulated in the European Union, the multitude of liability regimes that are in existence certainly contribute to a high degree of legal complexity. A harmonised liability regime could solve this problem at the European level and end the co-existence of several different liability regimes.

Another justification for regulation to take place at the European level would be the wish to protect certain values that are deemed so fundamental that throughout the European Union a certain level of protection of these values needs to be guaranteed.[578] This argument is also supported by constitutional considerations, keeping in mind that environmental protection has constitutional status in some Member states and certainly also has a prominent role in the European Treaties.

5.4.4. Path dependence

Throughout this chapter the economics of federalism and potential harmonisation have been discussed. Different arguments, for and against the harmonisation of nuclear liability and nuclear safety regulation respectively, have been brought forward and it was shown that both economic and non-economic arguments for such harmonisation can be found. Another crucial point that still has to be added, however, concerns the question of how far the existing liability regimes will still have an effect on a new European system, given that the existing liability regimes that built on the international conventions have been in force for quite some time, and that the international conventions will also not simply disappear. Thus, a further problem that a call for harmonisation could face in this regard is a certain degree of path dependence.[579]

Starting with a non-legal example, Heine and Kerber discuss path dependence and the effects it has on the development of new technology. They show how temporal factors, such as for example that one certain technology was used first can have such strong 'lock-in' effects that it is possible that this technology even continues to prevail when already more efficient technology would be available.[580] A number of factors can impede the switch to a new standard, arguably a more efficient one, such as for example dynamic economies of scale or complementarities to other technologies. The latter means that a switch in technology would also necessitate a switch in other fields which are complementary to the first one. This can have a stabilising effect on existing technologies, making it difficult to substitute these with newer, more efficient ones.[581] Drawing an analogy to the legal sphere, Heine and Kerber also identify certain legal paradigms that once they are set will determine legal development and steer the approach to how certain problems are tackled.[582]

578 Faure 2001, p. 276.
579 For a legal analysis of how to integrate a European system into the international ones see section 7.2.
580 Heine and Kerber 2002, p. 53.
581 *Ibid.*, p. 54.
582 *Ibid.*, p. 57.

Path dependence can on the one hand be regarded as an obstacle to harmonisation if the aim of the harmonisation is to come up with new paradigms to replace the old existing ones. However, recognising path dependence can also be a chance to come up with new rules to replace inefficient existing ones which are only still in place due to the previously discussed stabilising factors. Applying this argumentation to the regulation of the nuclear sector one can argue that asking for a European initiative that would rethink the existing principles could be regarded as a way to break with path dependence. The following chapter will therefore analyse why a new, European system might indeed be needed and will discuss the core aspects that a European regime for nuclear liability should be built upon.

Part III

The Way Forward

Part II described the current status quo of the regulation of nuclear accidents within the European Union and provided an outlook that more competences than currently are being made use of, do exist also under the TFEU for a stricter and more comprehensive regulation of the nuclear sector. Further, economic justification for more harmonisation in the nuclear sector was identified.

Chapter 6 of this thesis will develop this thought further by assessing how a proposal for a different European regime for nuclear accidents should appear. It will reconsider the currently applicable core principles to identify which principles a European regime should adhere to. The European Union is homogeneous enough to establish its own liability regime and the extent to which this provides a unique chance to become the forerunner in nuclear liability and the safe regulation of the nuclear sector, will be assessed. This chapter will end with a proposal for what a European liability regime for nuclear accidents should look like.

Chapter 7 will deal with the question of the compatibility of a European system with the international conventions on nuclear liability and how a European liability system could be integrated into the existing ones. Further analysis will show how to increase the chances that the suggested proposal would indeed become part of the legislative agenda and how the relevant stakeholders could be convinced of its advantages to enhance the chances of its implementation.

Chapter 6

NUCLEAR LIABILITY IN THE EUROPEAN UNION – RETHINKING CURRENT PRINCIPLES

6.1. The need for a European system

As already discussed in previous chapters of this thesis, nuclear liability within the European Union is regulated mainly by reliance on different international conventions, leading to a multitude of liability regimes co-existing within the European Union. The result of this is a very complex and scattered picture. In his description of the international regimes, Currie draws an analogy with the labyrinth which was created to hold the Minotaur and rightly points out that in the nuclear sector one can speak of a situation in which 'the Minotaur largely constructed the labyrinth.'[583] This comparison illustrates nicely on the one hand the complexities of the currently liability regimes and on the other hand the role that the nuclear industry played in shaping them.

Given the current importance of international conventions in the area of nuclear liability, some general principles of international law should be used to set the scene for the analysis that will follow in this chapter. Principle 13 of the Rio Declaration from 1992 for example states that

> *'States shall develop national law regarding liability and compensation for the victims of pollution and other environmental damage. States shall also cooperate in an expeditious and more determined manner to develop further international law regarding liability and compensation for adverse effects of environmental damage caused by activities within their jurisdiction or control to areas beyond their jurisdiction.'*[584]

Further, it is well established international law that states must respect the integrity of the environment of neighbouring states and that a certain level of due diligence requires them to keep a regulatory system that enables sufficient control of potentially hazardous activities.[585] In the words of Birnie and Boyle there is a need for 'the introduction of

583 Currie 2006, p. 85.
584 Rio Declaration on Environment and Development.
585 Van Dyke 2006, p. 15.

legislation and administrative controls applicable to public and private conduct which are capable of effectively protecting other states and the global environment'.[586] It is doubtful whether we can speak of the existence of such a regime in the nuclear sector, and also Principle 13 of the Rio Declaration from 1992 does not really seem to be complied with in the nuclear sector. It needs to be noted that Principle 13 of the Rio Declaration deals with environmental damage. Whilst traditionally personal injury was the main concern of environmental law and certainly of the international nuclear liability conventions, in the last decades a development has been taking place that shifted the attention more towards environmental damage. In the area of liability for nuclear accidents of course both, personal injury as well as environmental damage would be at stake.[587]

The currently applicable liability regimes that originated from the international conventions on nuclear liability cannot be regarded as offering effective protection for the environment or potential victims of nuclear accident. This is because core features of environmental regulation and victim protection are not incorporated into the international regimes. Liability is often limited and the limits are not set at appropriate levels. Furthermore, focussing on the aspect of Principle 13 of the Rio Declaration that requires more co-operation between states to develop international law further, it can be said that in the nuclear area progress is very slow. Negotiations take a long time and even when a Convention is drafted often decades pass until the entry into force of such conventions. As an example for this, reference can be made to the Convention on Supplementary Compensation which was drafted in 1997 but almost needed 20 years to finally enter into force in April 2015.[588] This necessitates a call for a new impetus within the European Union to strengthen the rules on liability and compensation for nuclear accidents, also taking concerns of environmental protection more seriously than is currently done.

The past decades have shown that the creation and fostering of the nuclear industry happened at remarkable speed and with serious efforts. The real challenge, however, lies not in the promotion, but the control of nuclear energy.[589] Developments in the area of nuclear liability do not really present a promising picture. Some authors have pointed out that the lack of control of nuclear activities can be explained in part by the fact that the IAEA was created to support and promote the use of nuclear energy.[590] Whilst one cannot speak from a real lack of control on the European level, the initial focus on the promotion of nuclear energy can certainly explain the difficulties that we are currently facing with regard to a pro-active liability regime that truly fulfils the objectives of deterrence and victim protection. It has to be recalled at this time that the first conventions

586 Birnie and Boyle 2002, p. 112.
587 See section 4.3.1.
588 Https://www.iaea.org/sites/default/files/supcomp_status_15012015.pdf (last accessed on 21 August 2015).
589 Kiss 2006, p. 82.
590 Nanda and van Dyke 2006, p. 1.

in the area of nuclear liability stem from the 1960's. In the last decades many things have changed, given that the nuclear sector has matured. Looking at the European energy mix it is also apparent that nuclear is only one of many energy options. In 2007, nuclear energy made up only 13.4% of the energy mix. It was only the fourth most used energy, after oil (36.4%), gas (23.9%) and solid fuels (18.3%).[591] Nuclear is but one of many options in the European Union yet still remains regulated in isolation from the more dynamic field of general environmental law.

The Environmental Liability Directive (ELD)[592] arguably presents an approach that mirrors the increased importance of protecting environmental values as collective goods. The nuclear sector however, stayed outside of the scope of this Directive. Article 1 of the Euratom Treaty states

> *'It shall be the task of the Community to contribute to the raising of the standard of living in the Member States and to the development of relations with the other countries by creating the conditions necessary for the speedy establishment and growth of nuclear industries.'*

This commitment to nuclear energy as a pre-requisite for a flourishing and successful European Union cannot be upheld anymore. All these observations show that the nuclear sector is in need of reform and it is up to the European Union to live up to this challenge by providing a coherent and effective regulation of the nuclear sector along the lines of the same principles as other environmental sectors are regulated.

Whilst the major reigning principles of the international conventions dealing with nuclear liability have already been briefly introduced in section 3.2, the following parts will analyse them in more detail and assess their acceptability in a mature nuclear sector. This will be done in the context of a call for a new, European liability and compensation system for nuclear accidents. Before concluding this chapter with a summarised proposal how a European regime might look in section 6.7, the following parts will analyse some core features of nuclear liability and how they should be approached in the European Union. The examination will focus on the questions of which liability rule a European system should follow (6.2), what role the principle of legal channelling should play in a European system and whether viable alternatives could be thought of (6.3). Further the currently available liability and compensation limits will be scrutinised and problems experienced with the current limitations will be highlighted (6.4). Section 6.5 discusses how potentially higher amounts than the current ones could be financed before also some competition law considerations will be addressed (6.6).

591 Europe's energy position – markets and supply, European Union 2010, p. 8.

592 Directive 2004/35/EC of the European Parliament and of the Council of 21 April 2004 on environmental liability with regard to the prevention and remedying of environmental damage.

6.2. Strict liability and beyond – Ensuring deterrence

6.2.1. *Strict liability versus negligence*

The two main liability rules that will be discussed at this point are a rule of strict liability and a negligence rule. In a system that follows the latter, the decisive factor will be a behavioural standard which will be assessed by a judge. If a certain level of care was not taken, the injurer will be held liable.[593] Thus, if due care is exercised by the injurer, a victim will not be compensated for the suffered damages.[594] This points at a weakness of such a rule because it does not fulfil a compensatory role in such situations. Being based on a behavioural standard, a negligence rule can further lead to the problem that an inappropriate level of care will be set by a judge.[595] Cognitive illusions such as hindsight bias have the potential to aggravate such concerns further.[596]

From the point of view of administrative costs, it has to be mentioned that a negligence rule can be more burdensome and involve more costs than a rule of strict liability, because negligence needs to be proven.[597] This argument does arguably carry less weight, however, in the nuclear sector. Given that nuclear safety also relies very much on safety regulation, proving negligence can be facilitated if an operator is in clear breach of a well-defined obligation.[598] However, nuclear safety regulation within the European Union has the tendency to rely on principles which are too broad,[599] thus problems of proving negligence and proving whether indeed an operator had not been in compliance with a certain principle might still pose difficulties.

A strong point in favour of a liability rule based on negligence is its superiority over strict liability in the case of incomplete cost internalisation of the activity generating the accident risk.[600] This is of particular importance in the area of liability for nuclear accidents because the current regimes do not achieve a full cost internalisation.[601]

Another interesting point which was raised in academic literature is the potential of a negligence rule to distribute information on safety technology. If a negligence rule is followed the Court will assess different kinds of information to be brought forward by the accused operator. This exchange of information would not take place in a case where that liability would be strict.[602]

593 Shavell 2004, p. 180.
594 Schaefer and Mueller-Langer 2009, p. 10.
595 Faure 2008, p. 88; Schaefer and Mueller-Langer 2009, p. 7.
596 Guthrie *et al.* 2001, p. 799–805.
597 Schaefer and Mueller-Langer 2009, p. 10.
598 Faure 1995, p. 27.
599 See above chapter 2.
600 Schaefer and Mueller-Langer 2009, p. 35.
601 See Chapter 3 and also discussion below in 6.4.2.
602 Feess and Wohlschlegel 2006, p. 63–67.

Turning to a strict liability rule, the most striking aspect of such a rule is that an injurer will have to pay for the damages caused regardless of the care taken.[603] Complications as discussed above that could come along with phenomena such as hindsight bias will not carry any weight under a strict liability rule because it dictates the behaviour of a potential injurer *ex ante*.[604] Strict liability has been termed superior compared to a negligence rule when dealing with unilateral accidents.[605] An explanation for this is that contrary to the negligence rule where an injurer will never be held liable as long as due care is exercised,[606] a strict liability rule incorporates the activity level of the injurer as well. This can be explained by the risks that the injurer faces to be always held liable if an accident occurs under a rule of strict liability which will give incentives for the adoption of an efficient activity level.[607]

Fiore introduced an interesting nuance to the comparison between negligence and strict liability by the discussion of no-fault compensation systems.[608] She points out that tort law has its flaws with regard to victim protection, but it is a strong tool to ensure deterrence, whilst no-fault systems give priority to the compensation of victims.[609] Delimiting no-fault systems from strict liability, Fiore comes to the conclusion that strict liability combines the best aspects of tort law on the one hand and no-fault compensation systems on the other hand.[610] This can be seen as a further advantage of a strict liability system over a rule of negligence.

Next to these considerations, one also has to look at some very practical aspects. Generally it can be said that strict liability is easier to apply than a rule based on a behavioural standard.[611] This can also be of importance for possible victims in the case of a nuclear accident which would also speak for a system of strict liability if the angle of fairness and victim protection were taken. Furthermore, litigation costs will be lower if a rule of strict liability is used.[612]

Having these considerations in mind it becomes apparent why the current international regimes for nuclear liability do rely on a rule of strict liability. A European regime should also not depart from this path. Nevertheless, some qualifications and additions to a rule of strict liability for nuclear accidents should be made, as will be discussed in the following section.

603 Shavell 2004, p. 179.
604 Stavang 2010, p. 199; Korobkin and Ulen 2000, p. 1099.
605 Korobkin and Ulen 2000, p. 1098.
606 Schaefer and Mueller-Langer 2009, p. 9.
607 *Ibid.*, p. 12+13.
608 Fiore 2009, p. 406–427.
609 Fiore 2009, p. 407.
610 Fiore 2009, p. 416+417.
611 Shavell 1980, p. 25.
612 Schaefer and Mueller-Langer 2009, p. 10+11.

6.2.2. *Criminal law*

In the previous section the focus was on rules of tort law and their effect on incentivising the safe behaviour of nuclear operators. Liability rules can have an effect on internalising externalities and thereby have a preventive effect. However, the use of tort law has certain limits and, in literature, arguments can be found to supplement the use of tort law by the use of criminal law to increase the deterrent effect. Increasing deterrence, not only focussing on the compensatory aspect of liability rules, is of crucial importance especially in the area of nuclear liability, given that reliance on compensation ignores that the main problem is that pollution should be prevented in the first place.[613] Therefore this section will pay some attention to the question of whether the use of criminal law could supplement a civil liability regime for nuclear accidents within the European Union.

A preliminary remark that has to be made, however, is whether indeed the use of criminal law is needed, or whether in fact a call for public enforcement is what is being advocated, something which can also be achieved by other means and without resorting to criminal law.[614] When arguing for public enforcement, one argument that can be identified in literature is that victims might not always have the right incentives to bring a claim which leads to an imperfect detection by victims. This can for example be the result of widely dispersed harm which is especially the case in environmental pollution. In such a situation there might not be one individual victim who would have sufficient cause to indeed bring a claim which would necessitate public enforcement so that negative externalities can still be controlled.[615]

Next to the flaws of civil liability that could be remedied by the introduction of public enforcement, there are, however, also shortcomings of tort liability rules which can indeed only be mitigated by the introduction of criminal law. This becomes apparent if one looks at the sanctions that are available under a civil liability regime, being mainly of a monetary nature. Limited financial resources, however, do limit the scope of monetary sanctions. If there exists a risk of insolvency, the introduction of non-monetary sanctions is warranted to increase or achieve sufficient deterrence.[616] Faure also points to this problem when discussing the use of criminal law in the maritime sector to prevent oil pollution.[617] Potentially the insufficient wealth of an injurer is obviously as much a problem in the case of nuclear accidents as in the field of oil pollution, as recently demonstrated by the Fukushima accident and the magnitude of the resulting damages. In May 2015, more than € 35 billion had been paid out in compensation.[618] A study from

613 Spier 2013, p. 234.
614 Bowles *et al.* 2008, p. 390.
615 *Ibid.*, p. 400+401.
616 *Ibid.*, p. 405.
617 Faure 2010, p. 164.
618 For the most recent status of paid copmpensation see http://translate.googleusercontent.com/translate_c?anno=2&depth=1&hl=nl&rurl=translate.google.com&sl=en&tl=nl&u=www.tepco.co.jp/en/comp/index-e.html&usg=ALkJrhgo2XS-xKB_SBLLOCA73c4MMOpNJQ.

the end of 2014 estimated the entire cost related to the Fukushima accident at almost € 100 billion.[619] The risk of insolvency and problems coming along with this can be mitigated by insurance solutions,[620] but insufficient capacity on the insurance market or an inefficient liability limit can weaken the incentive effects of civil liability rules in this regard. Next to these issues that have an influence on the choice of monetary versus non-monetary sanctions such as imprisonment, it also has to be stressed that there are certain crimes which simply cannot be compensated for due to their horrific nature.[621] In times where environmental protection is high on the agenda of an increasing number of governments, this moral implications of criminal law could also be of relevance in the nuclear sector.

Coming back to the argument that the use of criminal law can increase the deterrent effect of a liability system, it has to be mentioned that this argument relies on the assumption that potential injurers are rational utility maximisers and would weigh the costs and benefits of their actions against each other. If it is possible to resort to non-monetary sanctions such as imprisonment this can increase the deterrent effect because this represents significant opportunity costs for the potential injurer which could outweigh the benefits.[622] According to Becker's deterrence hypothesis both the probability of detection (p) and the severity of punishment (S) will influence the decision of a potential injurer, because the higher the costs of committing a crime (C), which consist of the product of p and S, the more unlikely it will be that these costs are outweighed by the benefits. Applying this deterrence hypothesis to maritime pollution, Faure points out that the probability of detection in that area can often be lower than 100% which then necessitates higher sanctions, following the model of Becker. This, however, is not possible under tort law because the sanction can only be as high as the damage that was caused.[623] Making the link to the area of nuclear liability, however, the picture is rather different. The probability of detecting a nuclear accident leading to off-site damages is arguably 1 because it is hardly imaginable that such an accident could not be detected.[624] Following this reasoning, one could reason that criminal law is maybe not necessarily needed, because the limited potential of S can be remedied by a very high, actually constant, p which would be equal to 1. These considerations lead to an argument that could be made against the use of criminal law, namely that it can lead to over-deterrence, meaning that, in the context of running a business, decision takers might act too carefully, thereby also not taking acceptable risks anymore.[625] This has to be seen together with the fact that industrial activities will of course always have certain negative

619 Http://rt.com/news/183052-japan-fukushima-costs-study/ (last accessed on 21 August 2015).

620 Faure 2010, p. 168.

621 Becker 1968, p. 196.

622 Becker 1968.

623 Faure 2010, p. 165.

624 This will change, however, if criminal liability is not used as the primary liability but only as an additional aspect as the result of a violation of a safety regulation. In that case probability of detection can be lower.

625 Bowles *et al.* 2008, p. 412.

effects on the environment and this also seems to be accepted. The principle of *Restrisiko*[626] in Germany for example is an embodiment of this perception. Criminal law will therefore only play a role in situations where harm has occurred as the result of behaviour which is not deemed acceptable by society. Therefore criminal law should only be used in instances of very serious violations which threaten values that are deemed worthy of protection by society. This also explains that it should only be used as an *ultimum remedium* when other mechanisms have failed. Nevertheless, sometimes it can also be used to make a point and to send a message that certain behaviour will not be tolerated.[627] With regard to the question of when and under what circumstances criminal law could, or should, be used to supplement tort law, one can link the discussion to the issue of an arguably high detection rate in the area of nuclear liability which, as mentioned above, could question the need for criminal liability. If, however, criminal liability is indeed seen as an additional layer and could also be used for situations in which individual persons within a nuclear power plant, due to their behaviour, contributed significantly to an accident, criminal liability for these actions could work as a meaningful supplement focussing on behaviour and incidents that might not be as easily detected as the resulting nuclear accident and thereby also work as an additional incentive for safety amongst people in charge of the operation of a nuclear power plant. Also in case of breach of safety regulations criminal law could be an adequate supplement, because the probability of detecting such breaches is certainly less than 1, contrary to the observations made above with regard to nuclear accidents as such.

Making the link to a different high-risk sector, it is interesting to see that the Commission is well aware of the additional role that criminal law can play in supporting and if necessary increasing the deterrent effect of a civil liability regime. In the field of marine pollution it argued strongly for an additional layer of criminal law to mitigate the shortcomings of the international regime.[628] In the nuclear sector the attitude is still more conservative. An illustrative example for this the introduction of an article on sanctions in the draft for a new Safety Directive[629], which later again was removed after claims that the Commission lacked the competences to regulate such issues. With regard to this question of competences, not only on laying down sanctions but also on requiring the use of criminal law, reference has to be made to some case law of the Court of Justice of the European Union. In Case 176/03[630] the Court stated that 'as a general rule, neither

626 See Kalkar decision 1978: 'Vom Gesetzgeber im Hinblick auf seine Schutzpflicht eine Regelung zu fordern, die mit absoluter Sicherheit Grundrechtsgefährdungen ausschließt, die aus der Zulassung technischer Anlagen und ihrem Betrieb möglicherweise entstehen können, hieße die Grenzen menschlichen Erkenntnisvermögens verkennen und würde weithin jede staatliche Zulassung der Nutzung von Technik verbannen. Für die Gestaltung der Sozialordnung muß es insoweit bei Abschätzungen anhand praktischer Vernunft bewenden. Ungewißheiten jenseits dieser Schwelle praktischer Vernunft sind unentrinnbar und insofern als sozialadäquate Lasten von allen Bürgern zu tragen.'

627 Bowles *et al.* 2008, p. 393+394.

628 COM (2003)92 final, p. 6.

629 COM(2013) 343 final.

630 Case 176/03 *Commission of the European Communities* v. *Council of the European Union* [2005].

criminal law nor the rules of criminal procedure fall within the Community competence'.[631] It continued, however, by stating that

> *'the last mentioned finding does not prevent the Community legislature, when the application of effective, proportionate and dissuasive criminal penalties by the competent national authorities is an essential measure for combating serious environmental offences, from taking measures that relate to the criminal law of the Member States that it considers necessary to ensure that the rules it lays down on environmental protection are fully effective'.*[632]

This judgment has to be seen together with a later decision by the Court, however, in which it stated that 'the determination of the type and level of the criminal penalties to be applied does not fall within the Community's sphere of competence.'[633] Today this case law needs to be seen together with the legislative changes that resulted from the Lisbon Treaty. Article 83(2) TFEU states that

> *'If the approximation of criminal laws and regulations of the Member States proves essential to ensure the effective implementation of a Union policy in an area which has been subject to harmonisation measures, directives may establish minimum rules with regard to the definition of criminal offences and sanctions in the area concerned.'*

Consequently with regard to the use of criminal law in the nuclear sector and how far this could be prescribed by the EU, it can be concluded that whilst the issue of criminal sanctions could not be dealt with exhaustively by the Community legislature, it can certainly require the use of criminal law to achieve a more robust legal framework for nuclear activities.[634]

6.3. Legal channelling – Necessity or obstruction?

The international conventions dealing with nuclear liability have not been amended very often and basic principles have remained the same since the start of the nuclear industry. On some instances, reforms were initiated leading sometimes even to relatively big changes, such as for example the reforms under the Paris Protocol which broaden the scope of damage and increase both the financial and the temporal limits to quite a significant extent. However, such occasions were never used to really question the principle of legal channelling as one of the cornerstones of the international nuclear liability conventions.[635] The following sections will briefly discuss the origins of this

631 *Ibid.*, para. 47.
632 *Ibid.*, para. 48.
633 Case C-440/05 *Commission of the European Communities* v. *Council of the European Union* [2007], para. 70.
634 For a succinct and very comprehensible summary of the case law pre-dating the Lisbon Treaty see also Faure 2010, p. 181+182; see also Herlin-Karnell 2008 and Peers 2008 for the scope and limits of article 82 and 83 Lisbon Treaty.
635 Ameye 2010, p. 34.

principle before turning to a critical analysis thereof and whether it could be changed or even replaced by alternatives.

6.3.1. *Reasons and justifications for legal channelling*

Starting from an historical perspective, Ameye points out how the principle of legal channelling was introduced to the European market by US suppliers.[636] When in the late 1950's nuclear material was also about to be exported to countries outside the US, suppliers were concerned that they could potentially face liability for the use of the exported products. In their eyes this could be unfair because well-designed material could still result in accidents if it was used in an improper way. They therefore felt the need to protect themselves and 'managed to impose legal channelling upon Europe's nuclear industry and to secure their business without taking any risks on the liability front.'[637] Against this background it can consequently be said that historically the principle of legal channelling was introduced to protect the industry of nuclear suppliers.

With regard to the international conventions Vanden Borre points at the two main justifications for legal channelling that can be found in the Exposé des Motifs of the Paris Convention. On the one hand, one wanted to avoid complications coming along with complex determinations of who exactly is liable, and on the other hand it would enable them to focus only on one party with regard to insurance obligations.[638] With regard to the latter argument that channelling would facilitate the taking out of insurance because the operator would be in the best position to do so, Liu *et al.*, however, argue in an analysis of another high risk sector, namely oil pollution, that this argument does not hold and that actually all parties that are influencing the risk for an incident would be in a position to take out insurance.[639] The first argument is also phrased along the lines of alleged victim protection, because it would be easier for victims to claim damages if they could always go to one party and would not have to identify the exact party that they can hold liable. Contrary to these claims it has also been argued in the literature that legal channelling weakens the positions of victims. This can be explained by the reduced number of people that victims can go after in case they have a claim for compensation. Victims will prefer to have as many pockets as possible from which they could get compensation. The argument that legal channelling will facilitate the procedure for victims because they do not have to identify against whom a claim has to be directed is also not convincing given assistance that victims can receive from lawyers specialised in this.[640] The argument of facilitating claims for potential victims does further also only provide an explanation for the fact that a victim can only sue one party, and it fails to explain why this party should then not have a right of recourse against other parties.[641]

636 *Ibid.*, p. 35.
637 *Ibid.*
638 Vanden Borre 2007, p. 273+274; Exposé des Motifs, para. 15–18.
639 Liu *et al.* 2014, p. 176.
640 Currie 2006, p. 9; Ameye 2010, p. 37.
641 Ameye 2010, p. 38.

As other arguments in favour of this principle, Kohlemainen mentions that channelling leads to a situation in which the person who is liable is also in the best position to control the nuclear risk. It further created incentives for the operator to monitor the entire supply chain to prevent possible harm from occurring.[642] These arguments cannot however be simply accepted like that. It may be true that the operator is in a superior position to control nuclear risks because it is him after all that engages in that activity. Nevertheless, this does not exclude the possibility that nuclear accidents can be the result of design flaws and in a globalised and interdependent industry it remains questionable if suppliers should be shielded from possible claims upfront and in its entirety. Picking up the argumentation that the one who is in the best position to control the risk should also bear the risk of liability does only lead to the same conclusion.

As apparent from these observations, even the basic arguments that were brought forward as a justification for legal channelling are highly questionable. The following sections will therefore shed some more light on the disadvantages of this principle and discuss alternatives.

6.3.2. *Disadvantages of legal channelling and alternatives*

Whilst the previous section mainly focused on the most commonly heard justifications for legal channelling, this section will look at some wider effects that legal channelling can have and ask the question whether in a mature nuclear industry this principle should indeed still be applicable.[643] In current debates about the core principles of nuclear liability there is also at least some first sign of concerns whether legal channelling in its most absolute and purest form can still be upheld or might need some adjustments to alleviate its consequences.[644]

As a first point of concern one has to turn to the question of what incentives a rule of legal channelling gives. This also needs to be seen together with other principles that currently are present on the nuclear liability landscape, such as for example the limitation of liability.[645] If liability is legally channelled, this further aggravates the negative effects of limitations in liability because the limits thereby apply to all actors which can transfer their liability to the one actor, in our scenario the nuclear operator, to whom liability is channelled. This further increases the inefficiencies and Winter and Trebilcock therefore plead for a system in which suppliers also could be held liable under a negligence standard. The negligence standard would mean that in a case where accepted production processes were complied with, a supplier would still have the possibility of escaping liability.[646]

642 Kohlemainen 1999, p. 457–458.
643 Ameye 2010, p. 40.
644 Pelzer 1999, 428–429.
645 See section 6.4.2.
646 Trebilcock and Winter 1997, p. 233–235.

With regard to setting the right incentives for safe operation and to prevent accidents from happening, it can be said that legal channelling weakens the potential of a civil liability regime to set the right incentives. This is also pointed out by Faure referring to the maritime sector.[647] The same reasoning is also followed by the European Commission, acknowledging that the channelling as rooted in the International Convention on Civil Liability for Oil Pollution does not incentivise all main actors involved and was in need of reconsideration.[648]

The accident of Fukushima also revealed the flaws which are inherent to the currently applicable rule of legal channelling. As Ramseyer points out, the generators that should function as a back -up to cool the Fukushima power plant were placed in the basement which made them vulnerable to flooding in the case of a tsunami.[649] There are even voices that General Electric had been explicitly warned about its flawed design and the potentially devastating consequences.[650] Consequently Faure and Liu stress that if the inappropriate placement of the generators can be seen as a negligent act of the designer, the weaknesses and disadvantages of a rule of legal channelling have been illustrated in a dramatic way by the Fukushima accident.[651] Following this example, it could still be questioned whether in the end it was not still the operator who had taken the final decision and whether therefore that party would be the proper party to hold liable, as done under a regime of legal channelling. This line of argumentation focuses on the responsibility of an operator to monitor and choose the safest suppliers, who then again on their side would have an incentive for high safety levels because this would lead to reputational advantages.[652] However, it is highly questionable whether the nuclear operator would be in the best position to monitor the supply chain, because suppliers will have more information about their products and the respective risks they cause. Trebilcock and Winter also point out that indirect incentives for suppliers will not lead to an appropriate level of safety.[653] Therefore direct incentives should also be given to suppliers and designers.

One way of incentivising suppliers and designers would be to expose them also to the probability of a claim against them. In line with this argumentation the US Oil pollution Act is not following a rule of legal channelling, but rather established a system of joint and several liability of operator, demise charterer and ship owner.[654] With regard to the efficiency of joint and several liability, some qualifications have to be made. In such a system, the solvency of the respective parties is of crucial importance, because in the case

647 Faure 2010, p. 170.

648 COM (2003)92 final, p. 6.

649 Ramseyer 2012, p. 476.

650 Http://abcnews.go.com/Blotter/fukushima-mark-nuclear-reactor-design-caused-ge-scientist/story?id=13141287 (last accessed on 21 August 2015).

651 Faure and Liu 2012, p. 203.

652 Goedde 2003, p. 230.

653 Trebilcock and Winter 1997, p. 234.

654 Liu *et al.* 2014, p. 147.

of insolvency of one party, this party would have the possibility to externalise its risks on the other parties. If solvency is given, or insolvency is not very likely for all the parties, a rule of joint and several liability can lead to incentives for mutual monitoring, something which would also be very desirable in the nuclear sector and which is not being incentivised under a rule of legal channelling.

Another alternative to legal channelling would be economic channelling. A rule of economic channelling allows victims to sue any party involved in the nuclear accidents, including also parties such as suppliers and designers. The operator, however, remains under an obligation to indemnify these parties. The operator therefore has to cover not only his, but also the liabilities of the other parties under an 'omnibus coverage'.[655] A prominent example for economic channelling can be found within the Price-Anderson Act in the US. This Act was originally established in 1957 and has been amended several times since then. It does not legally channel the liability of a nuclear accident to the operator. Consequently, by also allowing suppliers or designers to be held liable, the Price-Anderson Act prevents the situation in which there is a lack of incentives for other parties that also could have contributed to the accident risk.[656] The omnibus coverage provided by the operator furthermore reduces administrative costs and mitigates problems of duplication of insurance because 'anyone who can be held liable for the damage of a nuclear accident, including, for example, the supplier, can benefit from the liability insurance coverage of the nuclear operator.'[657] Given that economic channelling under the Price-Anderson Act creates more safety incentives and also limits tertiary accident costs, Faure and vanden Borre conclude that this rule is more efficient than the rule of legal channelling as rooted in the international conventions on nuclear liability.[658]

Both the introduction of a rule of joint and several liability and the introduction of economic channelling would necessitate a complete departure from the principle of legal channelling. A less drastic approach would be to change the principle of legal channelling and adapt it to a mature nuclear industry and incorporate the lessons learned from accidents that have happened so far. One possibility would be to strengthen the right of recourse of an operator against suppliers. The international conventions currently in force only allow a right of recourse in case of an existing written agreement or if a nuclear accident was the result of an intentional act or omission to cause such an accident.[659] One option would be to change the default setting to one that legal channelling would only apply if contractually agreed upon.[660] Another possibility focussing more on the harsh standard to invoke a right of recourse based on the contribution of another party to the accident risk would be to introduce a standard of gross negligence or even negligence.

655 Ameye 2010, p. 34.
656 Faure and vanden Borre 2008, p. 264.
657 *Ibid.*, p. 242.
658 *Ibid.*, p. 265.
659 Article 6 Paris Convention; Article X Vienna Convention.
660 Ameye 2010, p. 56.

This would also set more incentives for suppliers to invest in safety and provide the safest equipment possible.

6.4. Liability amounts

At the beginning of the commercial exploitation of nuclear power for energy production, a major challenge that operators and governments were faced with was the need for sufficient amounts of compensation in case an accident occurred. This was a real challenge, given the potentially huge damages that can occur and the considerations of insurability coming along with these magnitudes of damages.[661]

In a Communication to the Council and the European Parliament in 2007, the Commission already pointed to the importance of the availability of sufficient funds to compensate for the damage in case of a nuclear accident.[662] Having in mind the dimension of a possible nuclear accident it becomes apparent that this might cause problems with regard to insuring such risks. This has been brought forward in literature as an explanation for the tendency to limit the liability of nuclear operators and to rely on public funds.[663] The following sections will focus on the currently available amounts under the international regimes and analyse the effects that a limitation of liability can have.

6.4.1. Current nuclear liability amounts

As already shown in chapter 3, international conventions in the area of nuclear liability are split up in one system that is administered by the OECD in Paris and one that is under the auspices of the IAEA in Vienna.

Within the OECD regime the most recent convention that is in force is the 1960 Paris Convention as supplemented by the 1963 Brussels Supplementary Convention. Under this regime, the amount available in case of a nuclear accident is 300 million SDR. This amount consists of three different layers. Under the first layer the operator faces a minimum liability of SDR 5 million for which insurance or another financial guarantee has to be taken out. A second tier which will amount to the difference between the amount for which the operator is liable and SDR 175 million has to be provided by public funds of the installation state. The remaining SDR 125 million has to be made available from joint contributions of signatory states to the Convention according to a predetermined formula.[664]

It should be recalled that there exists an amendment to the Brussels Supplementary Convention which increases liability amounts significantly, but this Protocol is not yet in

661 Carroll 2008, p. 76.
662 COM(2006) 844 final.
663 Carroll 2009, p. 18.
664 Article 3 Convention of 31st January 1963 Supplementary to the Paris Convention.

force. Under the 2004 Protocol the minimum liability of the operator would be increased to € 700 million, the public funds from the installation state would be increased in as much as needed to make up for the difference between the operator's liability and € 1.2 billion, and the collectively financed layer by all parties to the Convention would be an additional € 300 million. Thus the total amount available in case of a nuclear accident would increase to € 1.5 billion.[665]

The most recent development under the IAEA regime is the 1997 Protocol to amend the Vienna Conventions. Under this Protocol the liability of the operator will be not less than SDR 300 million. The Member States can decrease this amount if public funds are made available to make up for the difference.[666] This amended version of the Vienna Convention entered into force in 2003 but does not have many members.[667]

The Convention on Supplementary Compensation further established additional means to have more funds available in case of a nuclear accident. It obliges the installation state to provide SDR 300 million or a higher amount. Next to this it also introduces a collective fund from Contracting Parties. Almost 20 years after its adoption, the CSC recently entered into force on the 15th of April 2015.[668]

Table 3. Schematic overview of the different liability limits[669]

What Convention	Who pays?	First generation	Second generation
Paris Convention	Nuclear operator	5.9	700
Brussels Supplementary Convention	Installation State	202.13	500
	Collective State Fund	148.62	300
Total NEA regime		**356.7**	**1500**
Vienna Convention	Nuclear operator	4.2	189.04
	Collective State Fund	–	189.04
Total Vienna Convention		**4.2**	**378.08**
Convention of Supplementary Compensation	Operator/installation state		378.08
	Collective State Fund		378.08
Total CSC			**756.16**

665 Article 3 2004 Paris Protocol.
666 Article 7 Protocol to amend the Vienna Convention on civil liability for nuclear damage.
667 Www.world-nuclear.org/info/Safety-and-Security/Safety-of-Plants/Liability-for-Nuclear-Damage/ (last accessed on 21 August 2015).
668 Https://www.iaea.org/newscenter/news/convention-supplementary-compensation-nuclear-damage-enters-force (last accessed on 21 August 2015).
669 See also Vanden Borre 2007, p. 298. Amounts in € million and adapted in time.

Summing up it can be said that even the highest amounts currently foreseen, are the ones in the 2004 Paris Protocol which would increase available compensation to € 1.5 billion, € 700 million of which would be private money whilst the remaining € 800 million would come from public funds.

6.4.2. *Limitation of liability*

If one speaks about potential damage that could occur to people, states or the environment at large as a result of a nuclear accident, it is important to stress that there is no given limitation.[670] Such damages are potentially unlimited, and catastrophes that have already occurred in the nuclear sector have shown that they indeed lead to very high damages. Nevertheless, as already introduced in chapter 3, it is still common practice in the area of nuclear liability to set a limitation.

Linking available insurance with the amounts of liability under the nuclear liability conventions led to a limitation of liability both in time and amount because it was argued that the insurance market would face serious difficulties in providing coverage if these two limitations were not met. Another rationale of this limitation, however, was also to protect the nuclear industry.[671] Liability of course will always be limited by resources and admittedly this question cannot be regarded as entirely independent from the insurance capacity available on the market. The current limits as they exist in many national systems, however, do not reflect amounts that are close to what could be insured. Further, it is important to recall the possibility of decoupling the obligation to insure from the question of whether liability should be limited, holding an operator liable beyond limits available on the insurance market.[672]

From an economic point of view the limitation of liability is very problematic because it does not lead to full cost internalisation. It has already been discussed above that liability rules can also have an incentivising effect to internalise externalities. To achieve this, however, a potential injurer has to face the full costs of his actions. In the case of nuclear liability this would mean he needs to be liable for the damages caused without limitations.[673] Faure and Fiore discuss three consequences of a limitation of liability namely that it supports nuclear energy by hiding its real costs, it does not set efficient incentives for preventive measures and it also leads to insufficient amounts for the compensation of victims. Furthermore it is questionable whether limiting liability is in full compliance with the polluter pays principle.[674] Keeping in mind these considerations, the limits of the international conventions are in urgent need of a revision and should be abolished in a European system.

670 Currie 2006, p. 91.
671 Carroll 2008, p. 84.
672 Pelzer 2007, p. 47; See also section 3.2.4.
673 Faure and Fiore 2009, p. 425.
674 Van Dyke 2006, p. 36; vanden Borre 2007, p. 297.

An interesting approach towards the limitation of liability can be found in the Oil Pollution Act in the US. Under this legislative instrument liability is also capped. However, there exists the threat that a party responsible for damage which has occurred loses the right to rely on this limitation if they acted with gross negligence or their behaviour can be classified as wilful misconduct. The caps will further not apply if an applicable Federal safety, construction, or operating regulation was violated. Another important feature of the OPA in this regard is that it does not pre-empt state laws, which could still hold a party liable without limitation, although under federal law the liability limit would apply.[675] Further, costs that have to be incurred as removal costs do not fall within the financial cap.[676] Another aspect of OPA which is worth mentioning at this point, is that it links the liability limit to the type of ship that is used. Safer double-hull tankers benefit from a lower limit than one-hull tanker which are less safe. Such a rule gives incentives for increasing preventive measures such as using safer ships.[677] At the European level these experiences can stimulate further debate in the area of nuclear liability and the deterrent effect of liability rules which is based on rather remote consequences, namely potential liability in the future, could be supplemented by more immediate incentives. Coupling for example a limitation of liability to conditions on siting or specific designs to be used could set further incentives for prevention. Whilst from the perspective of cost-internalisation the use of a rule of unlimited liability still remains the preferred option, the approach of OPA shows at least some possibilities and alternatives how the negative effects of limited liability can be mitigated. Limitation of liability could also be coupled to the licensing process of nuclear power plants. The right of limitation for example could be lost if an accident could have been prevented or mitigated if concerns that were voiced during a consultation process were not taken into account. This would combine *ex ante* and *ex post* incentives and also increase the role and importance of public participation in the nuclear sector.[678]

Coming back to the international conventions it also has to be mentioned that the international Conventions as amended in the meanwhile do provide for the option of unlimited liability.[679] It thus also depends on the initiative of the national states that are members of the international conventions whether a true commitment in the form of unlimited liability is made. Once more it has to be kept in mind, however, that the mere introduction of unlimited liability will not entirely solve the problem. Corporate law principles such as limited liability will work as a shield against truly unlimited liability because liability will only be limited by the assets of the operator,[680] as also demonstrated by the Fukushima accident in Japan which already indeed follows a rule of unlimited liability.[681] Therefore the following section will discuss how far a rethinking of the

675 Liu *et al.* 2014, p. 148+149.
676 Faure *et al.* 2014, p. 13.
677 Liu *et al.* 2014, p. 181.
678 See section 1.3.2.4.
679 Carroll 2008, p. 93.
680 See on this also the discussion in 6.3.3.
681 Faure and Liu 2012, p. 202–205.

principle of limited liability could be an option worth considering in the area of liability for nuclear accidents.

6.4.3. Unlimited liability

Limited liability means that a corporation does not have to pay for the entire damage that its activities might have caused. Such a principle could encourage executives to take too many risks.[682] However, even in the case of a nuclear accident that did not result from excessive risk taking, the corporate law principle of limited liability can lead to situations in which the operator is shielded from the entire amount of damages. Especially in the area of nuclear liability the potential magnitude of damages and resulting need for financial compensation can be huge. Therefore it is possible that damages go beyond the assets of the firm and it has also been argued that nuclear liability also poses problems of insurability. Introducing a system of unlimited liability for such situations could mitigate these problems.[683]

In their proposal to introduce unlimited liability for corporate torts, Hansmann and Kraakman do not suggest a form of joint and several liability of shareholders, but rather a pro rata liability which could be triggered if a company is not able to cover the damages after an accident that it has caused.[684] Such a rule of unlimited liability could create incentives for an increased distribution of information. Given that shareholders are also facing a liability risk under such a rule, they will demand more insight into the risky activities of a corporation.[685] This could enhance the transparency in the nuclear sector. Whilst this would be a positive effect, Coffey argues that a pro rata rule would have a negative effect with regard to information sharing and monitoring. He argues that such a rule of unlimited liability would create incentives to keep the stock invested in a company low to not unnecessarily increase the pro rata share because this would also increase potential liability. Consequently monitoring by big institutional investors would decrease, simply because no big investors would exist anymore.[686]

Since the principle of limited liability is one of the most fundamental principles of corporate law, it is important to note that Hansmann and Kraakman make a distinction between contract creditors and tort creditors, not questioning the principle of limited liability for the former category of creditors.[687] Contract creditors can be regarded as voluntary creditors. There the limited liability does not pose a problem because voluntary creditors, for example a bank, have the opportunity to negotiate in advance and let for example interest rates mirror the risks at stake. Such Coasian bargaining, however, is not possible in the case of involuntary creditors. According to Hansmann and Kraakman for

682 Hansmann and Kraakman 1991, p. 1894.
683 *Ibid.*
684 *Ibid.*, p. 1896.
685 *Ibid.*, p. 1907.
686 Coffey 1994, p. 80.
687 Hansmann and Kraakman 1991, p. 1921.

this group a rule of unlimited liability should apply to protect victims of an accident who did not have the chance to make a reasoned and conscious decision whether they agreed to accept the risks resulting from some form of interaction with the company that created certain damage.[688] This distinction has been criticised by Coffey, pointing at difficulties in distinguishing between these two classes of victims and arguing that relying on the courts to make this distinction as suggested by Hansmann and Kraakman would lead to undesirable vagueness and unpredictability.[689] Taking the perspective of victim protection, however, one can argue that it is exactly this differentiation which makes the proposal from Hansmann and Kraakman attractive because victims of a nuclear accident can indeed be seen as such involuntary creditors which in case of insufficient capital to compensate for damages caused could benefit from an unlimited liability. An argument against this has been made by Coffey. Referring explicitly to the nuclear sector, he raises the point that certain industries might simply not exist if liability would always be unlimited. According to his argument, society is willing to accept that certain externalities will have to be borne by it, if society can thereby profit from the positive aspects of the industrial activity.[690] Whilst there is some truth in this statement, it also has to be recalled that attitudes towards the generation of nuclear powers have changed in the last years and that within the European Union there also exists the risk that even people that would not be willing to tolerate this risk might ultimately have to bear the risks due to the transboundary nature of the problem.

Another argument of Coffey against the abolition of unlimited liability is that the principle of limited liability is not without exceptions. Tools such as for example veil piercing are always at the disposal of a judge and using them when needed would create a situation that would on the one hand allow corporations to benefit from limited liability, whilst on the other hand it would still be possible to disregard limited liability in certain situations, thereby also having the potential to mitigate abuses.[691] This is of course true and from a practical point of view this objection is an important one. Instead of substituting a fundamental principle by a new one, it might be worthwhile to look for strategies to mitigate the flaws of this principle. This is a tendency that to some extent has also already been happening in the past. There is for example Irish case-law which shows how principles such as the polluter pays principle have been indeed used to pierce the corporate veil.[692]

Discussions about veil piercing and unlimited liability have often taken place in the framework of corporate abuses. It is not in this area for which the above discussions are relevant. Rather, the observations in this section can serve as an inspiration for a European liability regime for nuclear accidents. There is a need for tools to mitigate the undesirable consequences of the corporate law principle of limited liability which can also serve as an additional tool to tackle the flaws of the currently existing regimes.

688 *Ibid.*
689 Coffey 1994, p. 61+62.
690 *Ibid.*, p. 69+70.
691 Coffey 1994, p. 71–73.
692 Wicklow County Council v. Fenton [2002] IEHC 102.

6.5. Different ways of financing

As pointed out in section 6.4, the currently available liability amounts are clearly insufficient and a European liability system for nuclear accidents should strive for higher amounts. The following sections will discuss different means of financing to cover the liability of nuclear operators. As a preliminary remark it is worth pointing out that compared to insurance coverage that currently is offered for ultra-hazardous activities, the financial resources of the corporations active in this area often surpass this coverage. In other words, companies are apparently in a better position to self-insure themselves than asking for available insurance on the market.[693] Self-insurance therefore would also provide a means of financing, which at least would be able to cover current amounts.

6.5.1. Insurance and re-insurance markets

Reliance on the traditional insurance and re-insurance market is one option to cover a certain amount of liability. However, concerns of insurability have been raised with regard to nuclear liability. This was especially the case with the Paris Protocol from 2004 which extended the definition of damage.[694] Limited possibility to provide insurance was also seen as a reason for the relatively low liability limits that are rooted in the Conventions. It has to be emphasised, however, that recent developments on the insurance and re-insurance market question this argumentation. One of the most prominent examples which points out that much higher amounts could be made available is a recent proposal from re-insurance company Munich Re. In the area of oil pollution it announced that it could develop a mechanism with which it would be able to cover $10–20 billion for Sudden Oil Spills (SOS). It would not provide this coverage alone, but foresees three different scenarios in which this amount could be guaranteed. One option would be to rely on a consortium of parties from the insurance and re-insurance. Every party would have uniform prices and conditions and a fixed capacity. Relying on traditional insurance and re-insurance on a subscription basis would be another option and the SOS-Proposal also introduces the option of a pool for companies engaged in oil drilling who would contribute to this pool according to their market share.[695] These high amounts, however, can only be guaranteed under a set of conditions that come along with the SOS proposal which can be summarised as follows:[696]

- there is a high retention rate of $1–1.5 billion. This would be more than the total amounts available under the conventions currently in force and as much as the highest amounts that are currently foreseen in the amended conventions and protocols;

693 Abraham 2011, p. 1778.
694 See for example Tetley 2006.
695 Www.businessinsurance.com/article/20100912/NEWS/100919977 (last accessed on 21 August 2015).
696 See Metro Report 2014, p. 267+268.

- the coverage provided would be triggered by a certain event with a certain magnitude that has to be determined beforehand;
- Coverage would not be a general liability cover for companies but for specific scenarios which increases predictability;
- long tail liability risks are excluded to guarantee certainty.

The condition specified in the second bullet point is the so called parametric trigger. It also shows that the coverage offered is constructed as a cover for natural catastrophes. As in the case of natcat cover, particular events will trigger the coverage.[697] With regard to the third bullet point it can be added that such a coverage that focuses on specific scenarios and not one particular party has some resemblance with the concept of economic channelling under the Price Anderson-Act and its omnibus coverage.

Looking at the special conditions and disclaimers of the proposal, one can understand that it was also received with mixed feelings by stakeholders, pointing to some of its flaws, such as for example the exclusion of long tail risks. Another point raised was that such a system might come along with very high prices, which industry might not be willing to pay. This is of special importance in the context of potential self-insurance. In the area of oil spills the Deepwater Horizon accident had shown that BP would actually have been in a better situation to self-insure itself compared to the amounts that would have been available under the SOS proposals. This of course leads to the question of why there should be an interest in this model which would be available only subject to high premiums when self-insurance could lead to bigger amounts. These considerations are equally applicable to the nuclear sector. Nevertheless the Munich Re proposal shows that there is still more potential on the insurance market and higher amounts could be insured than are currently done.

6.5.2. *Public funding*

As already apparent in section 6.4.1, the current international conventions rely heavily on public funds. From the € 1.5 billion under the Paris Protocol, for example, € 800 million would come from public funds. Governments are also being lobbied by operators not to ratify Conventions with higher liability amounts unless warranties are given that government will support the operators in the form of public funds.[698] The problem with public funding however is that it amounts to a subsidy; costs are not internalised and are borne ultimately by the general public.[699]

Whilst it should be avoided that governments simply take over big parts of the financial risks, there is nevertheless a role for governments to play if their interventions take place

697 Metro Report p. 267.
698 Carroll 2008, p. 85.
699 Carroll 2009, p. 21–22.

in a way to facilitate insurability. Governments could stimulate insurability as a reaction to failing insurance markets due to too little supply.[700]

Concerning a more facilitative role that could be played by the government to increase available funds, the British Government states in a consultation paper from 2007 that 'Government will explore the alternative options available – including providing cover from public funds in return for a charge.'[701] Carroll is critical with regard to such mechanisms, arguing that they would go against the polluter pays principle and that guarantees by the state would likely not be entirely market-based, thereby not properly internalising the real liabilities.[702]

Another example for such a more facilitative intervention can be taken from Japan. In Japan, the operator has to provide a financial guarantee up to 120 billion Yen which is approximately € 0.81 billion. The operator also has the option to ask for an indemnity agreement for this amount. The government can provide the operator with such an agreement to cover its liabilities. The operator, however, has to pay a fee for this.[703] That is in clear contrast to the international regime in which state intervention so far only takes place in the form of an outright subsidy to the nuclear industry. Nevertheless there remain some doubts with regard to the extent to which the Japanese type of intervention is indeed desirable because it is not clear whether the fee charged by the government is indeed market based.[704]

Given the subsidising character of state funds, a shift is needed away from public funding towards more private funding. It is interesting to see that the currently existing regimes also do not entirely exclude this possibility.[705] Under the existing Conventions it would be possible that states that do take over certain amounts of liability recoup this money from other market participants. This could either be again the nuclear operator or also other players such as for example designers or suppliers. The latter is an option that was chosen by the US who will recover the money that they have to contribute under the Convention for Supplementary Compensation from nuclear suppliers.[706]

It also has to be stressed that avoiding the use of public funds could furthermore also have a positive impact on public acceptability of nuclear energy.[707] In academic literature

700 Faure 2007a, p. 356+357.

701 UK Consultation Paper 2007, p. 61+62; see also Bruggemann *et al.* 2012 on the role and conditions of facilitative government intervention.

702 Carroll 2008, p. 87.

703 Liu and Faure 2014, p. 17.

704 *Ibid.*, p. 20.

705 Vanden Borre 2007, p. 306+307.

706 Vanden Borre 2007, p. 296+304.

707 COM(2006) 844 final.

several alternatives to public funds have been discussed.[708] A pooling scheme between nuclear operators is one option of those alternatives and the following section will analyse the core features of such a scheme and what its advantages could be.

6.5.3. *Operator pooling*

Reducing the importance of public funds to ensure sufficient coverage for the compensation of victims is an important factor of an efficient liability regime at the European level. Having in mind considerations of cost internalisation, intervention by the State should be avoided.[709] One of the main advantages of a pooling scheme is that large amounts of private money can be made available in such a system which can be used for the compensation of victims.[710] It consequently does not only get rid of the subsidies of public funds, but also increases coverage. An interesting example for a national pooling system can be found in the United States. Under the Price-Anderson Act of 1957 the US system initially also allowed for public funds to compensate victims in the case of an accident.[711] This however was gradually changed, leading to the situation that in 1982 public funds were completely replaced by private funds but the same amount as in 1957 was available.[712] The pooling scheme is based on a collective tier which is financed by all American nuclear operators. Another special feature of the *Price-Anderson Act* is that nuclear operators do not finance the collective tier *ex ante*, but via retrospective premiums. In case of an accident, the Nuclear Regulatory Commission will compensate the victims and claim back the money retrospectively.[713] The *Price-Anderson Act* is a good example of how a pooling scheme can ensure higher amounts of compensation and at the same time reduce the use of public funds.[714]

Recalling that a pooling scheme will be financed by private money, the question arises how this would correlate with the prices for nuclear energy. Taking the US example, one cannot come to a clear conclusion. It is not clear whether the retrospective premiums are already taken into account in the calculation of energy prices. If this has not been done yet this poses indeed a problem because future generations would have to pay higher prices to compensate for this.[715] These considerations will also have to be taken into account when designing a European regime because an increase in prices for nuclear energy might also have an influence on the choice of a legal basis.[716]

708 Faure and Skogh 1992, p. 499–513; Tyran and Zweifel 1993, p. 431–444; Faure 1995, p. 21–43; Pelzer 2007, p. 48ff.
709 Faure and Fiore 2008, p. 297.
710 Carroll 2009, p. 22.
711 *Ibid.*, p. 23.
712 *Ibid.*, p. 24.
713 Faure and Fiore 2008, p. 307.
714 Faure and vanden Borre 2008, p. 286.
715 Faure and Fiore 2008, p. 308.
716 See chapter 4.

6.5.3.1. European wide pooling – Preliminary observations

A pooling system can create win-win situations for the different stakeholders involved in the nuclear sector.[717] It can generate higher amounts, thereby strengthening the position of victims of a potential accident, it can also be beneficial for operators and the energy industry in general and also for government, removing some of the funding obligations from them.

A pooling system between all nuclear operators within the European Union would also have the added value that it provides a cross border solution for a cross border risk.[718] Such a mechanism can further tackle some of the challenges posed by ultra-hazardous activities. As already discussed in this chapter, when it comes to the insurability of nuclear damages, the potentially high amounts on the one hand, but also the uncertainty and difficulty with regard to calculating actuarially fair premiums, are posing difficulties. With regard to the latter, a pooling between operators would circumvent this problem because it can be structured in a way not relying on actuarial premiums that have to be calculated *ex ante* but could work with contributions from the operators.[719] This also means that no premiums are lost if no accident happens as it would be the case in a traditional insurance solution. Thus, such a mechanism reduces administrative costs and further has the advantage that it is rather flexible, because if an accident happens and agreed contributions turn out not to be enough one could still negotiate additional contributions *ex post*.[720]

6.5.3.2. Coverage and available amounts

Given the multitude of operators within the European Union, one can very well imagine how an EU pooling mechanism could significantly increase the available amounts to compensate for a nuclear accident. To increase this amount of money even further, one could argue for pooling on an international scale because this would also increase the contributors to such a pool. Nevertheless, the starting point should be a more geographically limited approach, focussing on an area that is relatively homogeneous and that could be classified as a 'natural transboundary risk community'.[721] Pooling on a European level is also more feasible because it might be difficult to explain the solidarity of European operators with operators overseas due to the distance between them.[722] Also a pooling mechanism between operators from the European Union, however, would only be possible if the participating operators face comparable risks.[723] In the absence of

717 Carroll 2008, p. 76.
718 Faure and Fiore 2008, p. 303.
719 See Skogh 1998.
720 Faure *et al.*2014, p. 16.
721 Carroll 2008, p. 94.
722 Pelzer 2008, p. 279.
723 Skogh 1998, p. 254.

common, or at least comparable safety levels, such a pooling mechanism will not be feasible.

With regard to the amounts resulting from a pooling scheme, Carroll rightly points out that also in the case of pooling between operators and higher amounts resulting from that, the insufficiency of these amounts to fully cover the damages of a large scale nuclear accident cannot be excluded. Therefore he argues for the need for a system of unlimited liability of the operator beyond the amounts that could be generated via an operator pooling.[724] The mechanism of retrospective premiums as mentioned above as one of the key features of the *Price-Anderson Act* could also serve as a means to increase liability amounts and even live up to unlimited liability because premiums could be levied retrospectively as long as it is needed to cover the amount that was paid to compensate for a nuclear accident.

6.5.3.3. Mutual monitoring and risk diversification

Given that within such a pooling scheme nuclear operators might become liable for other operators, the system would have to be structured in a way to guarantee acceptance of all nuclear operators and solidarity towards each other. If a pooling mechanism is structured in a bad way and not taking into account these considerations, it could lead to a situation in which operators could spread their risks through the pool, thereby free-riding on the amounts provided by the other operators. Such a risk would of course also lead to incentives for increased monitoring of the operators by each other which could lead to better safety levels.[725] Arguably operators are also in a better position to engage in monitoring, given the information advantages they can have compared to an external party.

In the area of pooling for Offshore Oil and Gas Activities, however, the Metro Report[726] points out that such an increase in safety levels is only a realistic scenario if risk differentiation between the parties is indeed possible to such an extent that lower premiums would encourage more investment in safety, and if the risks that are posed by the different operators are of a similar nature. With regard to the first aspect it has to be stressed that especially risk sectors which represent low probability risks are facing difficulties to engage in a meaningful system of risk diversification.[727] With regard to the second aspect, it has to be recalled that different safety standards within the European Union could indeed be a hurdle to a European wide pooling scheme. Faure *et al.* for example argue that operator pooling is not a realistic option in the area of nuclear liability, because of the absence of European wide safety standards.[728]

724 Carroll 2008, p. 93.
725 Carroll 2008, p. 95.
726 Metro report 2014.
727 *Ibid.*, p. 281.
728 Faure *et al.* 2014, p. 19.

6.5.4. *Concluding remarks*

As apparent from the discussion above, different means of financing are available and also the currently applicable conventions allow the Member States to use different methods than reliance on public funds to cover certain amounts. It seems that one problem also lies in the fact that different options available are sometimes seen as mutually exclusive or in competition to each other. A European regime for nuclear liability should try to make use of different kinds of financing mechanisms that are available. Such a multi-layered approach would increase the available amounts as much as possible.

6.6. Competition law

The following sections will focus on possible competition law problems which result from the current liability regimes. On the one hand an assessment will be made of whether the reliance on public funds creates problems under the aspect of potential state aid. On the other hand the possible applicability of article 101 TFEU to the currently existing nuclear pools will be analysed. This will require a preliminary discussion on the applicability of European Competition rules to the nuclear sector.

6.6.1. *Applicability of European competition rules to the nuclear sector*

According to article 106a(3) of the Euratom Treaty, 'the provisions of the Treaty on the European Union and of the Treaty on the Functioning of the European Union shall not derogate from the provisions of this Treaty.' This implies that in case of a conflict between the Euratom Treaty and the TFEU or if an issue has exhaustively been dealt with by the Euratom treaty, it will prevail. With regard to state aid and competition law, however, the Euratom Treaty does not contain any specific provisions which would be applicable to a nuclear liability regime. This leads to the conclusion that the rules to be found in the TFEU on these matters will also be applied to the nuclear sector.[729] Goyder describes the application of these rules to matters covered by the Euratom Treaty as softer.[730] An explanation for this could be that in these cases the general objectives of the Euratom Treaty as set out in its articles 1 and 2 were taken into account as well.[731] This has also

[729] Ahner *et al.* 2012, p. 261+262.

[730] Goyder 1992, p. 78.

[731] Article 1 states: 'It shall be the task of the Community to contribute to the raising of the standard of living in the Member States and to the development of relations with the other countries by creating the conditions necessary for the speedy establishment and growth of nuclear industries.';
Article 2 states: 'In order to perform its task, the Community shall, as provided in this Treaty:
a) promote research and ensure the dissemination of technical information;
b) establish uniform safety standards to protect the health of workers and of the general public and ensure that they are applied;

been supported by Cusack, pointing to the intention of the founders of the Treaty which should be taken into account in the absence of rules on state aid and competition.[732]

Having in mind that the current regime is based upon international conventions, it is also necessary to consider the application of European competition rules to these international agreements. On the relation between international conventions and obligations stemming from European law, the *Mesquer*[733] case is of special importance. Interestingly the background of this case can be compared nicely to the situation with regard to nuclear liability. Dealing with compensation for an oil spill, the issue at stake was whether the provisions of the International Convention on Civil Liability for Oil Pollution Damage from 1969[734] and the International Convention on the Establishment of an International Fund for Compensation for Oil Pollution Damage[735] were applicable, or the conflicting provisions of the *Waste Directive*.[736] The CJEU pointed out that neither the EU nor all members of the EU acceded to the conventions at stake and was therefore not bound by them.[737] With regard to the applicable law the CJEU stressed that the Member State first has an obligation to interpret its national law in accordance with the Directive even if it derived from an international agreement.[738] It thereby established that international agreements indeed have to be interpreted in accordance with European law. Having in mind the similar legal situation in *Mesquer* and the current situation concerning nuclear liability one can conclude that the European rules on competition and state aid indeed do apply to international conventions on nuclear liability.

c) facilitate investment an ensure, particularly by encouraging ventures on the part of undertakings, the establishment of the basic installations necessary for the development of nuclear energy in the Community;
d) ensure that all users in the Community receive a regular and equitable supply of ores and nuclear fuels;
e) make certain, by appropriate supervision, that nuclear materials are not diverted to purposes other than those for which they are intended;
f) exercise the right of ownership conferred upon it with respect to special fissile materials;
g) ensure wide commercial outlets and access to the best technical facilities by the creation of a common market in specialised materials and equipment, by the free movement of capital for investment in the field of nuclear energy and by freedom of employment for specialists within the Community;
h) establish with other countries and international organizations such relations as will foster progress in the peaceful use of nuclear energy.'

732 Cusack 2003, p. 130.
733 Case C-188/07 *Commune de Mesquer* v. *Total France SA and Total International Ltd* [2008].
734 International Convention on Civil Liability for Oil Pollution Damage, 29th of November 1969, available at: http://sedac.ciesin.columbia.edu/entri/texts/civil.liability.oil.pollution.damage.1969.html (last accessed on 21 August 2015).
735 International Convention on the Establishment of an International Fund for Compensation for Oil Pollution Damage, 18th of December 1971, available at: www.admiraltylawguide.com/conven/oilpolfund1971.html (last accessed on 21 August 2015).
736 Directive 75/442/8EEC was as amended codified by Directive 2006/12/EC on waste which was repealed by Directive 2008/98/EC on waste and repealing certain Directives.
737 Case C-188/07 *Commune de Mesquer* v. *Total France SA and Total International Ltd* [2008], para. 85.
738 *Ibid.*, para. 84.

6.6.2. *State aid*

According to article 107 TFEU

> *'any aid granted by a Member State or through Member State resources in any form whatsoever which distorts or threatens to distort competition by favouring certain undertakings or the production of certain goods shall, in so far as it affects trade between Member States, be incompatible with the internal market.'*

This article contains several aspects. Firstly, the aid indeed has to be classified as aid, secondly it has to be financed by the Member State or through Member State resources, thirdly there must be an effect on competition and fourthly an element of selectivity is needed. If we look at the current nuclear liability regimes which heavily rely on public funds, three criteria seem obviously to be fulfilled. The funds are provided by the Member States, an effect on competition is also given and only the nuclear sector is subsidised. The question of whether the funds however can indeed be classified as aid deserves some further attention.

The wording 'any form whatsoever' in the article is very broad and Commission and CJEU indeed follow a broad interpretation of this article.[739] However, to be classified as aid the financial transfer has to grant the recipient an artificial advantage. This has been termed as the 'market investor criterion', meaning that if a private investor would have acted like the state that is accused of granting state aid, it will not be classified as such.[740] In the case of public funds to guarantee sufficient coverage to compensate victims of nuclear liability, this principle it rather difficult to apply. As was argued by some authors, increased limits of compensation can indeed be uninsurable.[741] One could argue that the market investor criterion cannot be applied to something for which there is no market, which would lead the state aid analysis into very vague, difficult and doctrinal unsound areas. The Commission has taken another approach. In a decision from September 2007[742] it stated that the fact that there is no market for the measure in question does not have an automatic influence on the assessment of an artificial advantage.[743] The measure at stake was a loan guarantee for which there was no market. By comparing the situation with public intervention to a similar situation how it would have looked like in the absence of public intervention, the Commission concluded that the guarantee did not amount to state aid.[744] In this case however the measure at stake was a loan guarantee and not public funds. It seems difficult to interpret the current public funds in a way that they would not amount to state aid since the Member States simply will compensate

739 Craig and de Burca 2008, p. 1087.

740 See Case C-308/88 *Italy* v. *Commission* [1991]; Case C-305/89 *Italy* v *Commission* [1991]; Case C-42/93 *Spain* v. *Commission* [1994].

741 Pelzer 2007, p. 39.

742 Commission decision 2008/281/EC, [2008].

743 *Ibid.*, para. 68.

744 Commission decision 2008/281/EC, para. 66–75.

victims in case of an accident if damages exceed a certain level without charging the nuclear operators for the costs. The existence of alternative means in the form of a pooling scheme further supports the conclusion that public funding creates an artificial advantage.

Having established that public funds indeed can be qualified as state aid, the next step would be to analyse whether this way of funding can be exempted under one of the exemptions to be found in article 107(2) TFEU[745] or article 107(3).[746] It is rather straightforward that the automatic exemptions of article 107(2) (a)+(c) will not apply. With regard to article 107(2)(b) the question could be raised whether a nuclear accident could be regarded as an exceptional occurrence. Under certain reservations the Commission has indicated a willingness to indeed qualify major nuclear accidents as exceptional occurrences. It made also clear, however, that nuclear accidents are not always covered by this exemption. This also has to be seen together with the fact that article 107(2) is an exemption to the general prohibition of state aid and therefore has to be interpreted restrictively.[747] The international conventions in the area of nuclear liability do not make public funding dependent on any specific nature or degree of severity of a nuclear accident. They therefore foresee public funding for all nuclear accidents in general. Whether such public funding can indeed be exempted by article 107(2)(b) is therefore doubtful.

Amongst the facultative exemptions, article 107(3)(c) might serve as a possible exemption. Furthermore it has to be kept in mind that, as was mentioned above, the provisions on state aid will only apply in its strict sense in the case of a liability regime based exclusively on the TFEU. Under the current regime, articles 1 and 2 of the Euratom Treaty would

745 Article 107(2) TFEU states: 'The following shall be compatible with the internal market:
a) aid having a social character, granted to individual consumers, provided that such aid is granted without discrimination related to the origin of the products concerned;
b) aid to make good the damage caused by natural disasters or exceptional occurrences;
c) aid granted to the economy of certain areas of the Federal Republic of Germany, in so far as such aid is required in order to compensate for the economic disadvantages caused by that division. Five years after the entry into force of the Treaty of Lisbon, the Council, acting on a proposal from the Commission, may adopt a decision repealing this point.

746 Article 107(3) TFEU states: 'The following may be considered to be compatible with the internal market:
a) aid to promote economic development of areas where the standard of living is abnormally low or where there is serious under-employment, and of the regions referred to in Article 349 TFEU, in view of their structural, economic and social situation;
b) aid to promote the execution of an important project of common European interest or to remedy serious disturbance in the economy of a Member State;
c) aid to facilitate the development of certain economic activities or of certain economic areas, where such aid does not adversely affect trading conditions to an extent contrary to the common interest;
d) aid to promote culture and heritage conservation where such aid does not affect trading conditions and competition in the Union to an extent that is contrary to the common interest;
e) such other categories of aid as may be specified by decision of the Council on a proposal from the Commission.'

747 Community guidelines for State Aid in the Agriculture and Forestry sector, p. 18.

also have to be taken into account which might expand the scope of article 107(3)(c) even further. Whether however such intensive funding, as it is at stake in the current regimes, could be exempted under these articles, remains questionable, having also in mind the alternatives that do exist to such a system.

The analysis above has shown that the question of state aid is a difficult topic to address in the field of nuclear liability. As a cautious conclusion it is at least fair to say that many current liability regimes, if relying on public funds, do indeed raise concerns with regard to state aid and it is questionable whether they could be exempted.

6.6.3. Nuclear pools and article 101 TFEU

Insuring nuclear risks is a difficult task. On the one hand the probability of an accident is very low whilst potential damages can be huge. On the other hand, a relatively small number of operators that would need insurance creates difficulties in creating coverage that is high enough, and also adequate risk spreading is complicated by this limited amount of potential policy holders.[748] Ameye and Arregui explain that this was the reason why 'pools of insurers and re-insurers were set up world-wide to provide the necessary coverage to the operators of nuclear power plants.'[749]

With regard to the question whether nuclear pools are in line with European Competition rules, Ameye and Arregui are of the opinion that they do not fall within the scope of article 101 TFEU. Their main line of argument is that, given the capacity problem that the private insurance market faces with regard to the insurability of nuclear risks, a pooling between insurers and re-insurers does not create an anti-trust problem because it answers to a failure of the market and provides a service which could not be provided without the nuclear pools. It thereby does not only have the advantage of providing coverage for nuclear risks but also enables capacity building and knowledge distribution to increase the insurability thereof.[750] In the maritime sector, another sector that has to deal with catastrophic and potentially huge damages, this reasoning is also apparent. With regard to maritime insurance pools the Commission held in the P&I Clubs case[751] that

> *'such an agreement cannot be considered anti-competitive, at least when the claim sharing is necessary to allow its members to provide a type of insurance that they could not provide alone. Indeed there cannot be a restriction of competition when the members of the pool are not actual or potential competitors, because they are unable to insure alone the risks covered by the pool'.*[752]

748 Ameye and Arregui 2012, p. 266.
749 *Ibid.*
750 Ameye and Arregui 2012, p. 276+277.
751 Commission Decision 1999/329/EC.
752 *Ibid.*, para. 66.

Also in decisions relating to nuclear insurance pools a similar reasoning is apparent. 'The Commission concluded that without the pooling arrangements there would be no supply of nuclear liability insurance with adequate coverage for the risks involved, and therefore the pooling agreements do not restrict competition in that respect.'[753] This conclusion is also once more confirmed in the report on the functioning of the old Block Exemption for the insurance sector.[754] This view however, could be questioned to some extent, keeping in mind recent developments in the oil sector and also in the nuclear sector. The SOS proposal from Munich Re for example does theoretically provide an alternative. It is therefore questionable whether one can indeed still speak of an absolute necessity and that the national pools are indeed needed to provide sufficient coverage for a nuclear accident.

If this was the case, the question would pose itself, whether nuclear insurance pool can benefit from the Block Exemption for the insurance sector (IBER).[755] It has to be noted at this point that the 2010 IBER is of a narrower scope than the 2003 IBER.[756] Whilst the old IBER still exempted 4 different categories namely Joint Calculations, Tables and Studies, Common Coverage of certain types of risks, Standard Policy Conditions, and Security devices, the 2010 IBER only renewed the exemption for the first two categories. In its report on the functioning of the IBER 2003, the Commission expressed an interest in increasing the scrutiny of the insurance sector. The reduced scope of the 2010 IBER is also a logical consequence to this.

As just stated, the category of common coverage of certain types of risks remained exempted in the 2010 IBER. Nuclear insurance pools could be covered under article 5 of the exemption:

> *'Pursuant to Article 101(3) of the Treaty and subject to the provisions of this Regulation, Article 101(1) of the Treaty shall not apply to agreements entered into between two or more undertakings in the insurance sector with respect to the setting-up and operation of pools of insurance undertakings or of insurance undertakings and reinsurance undertakings for the common coverage of a specific category of risks in the form of co-insurance or co-reinsurance.'*

This exemption is subject to fulfilling the conditions as stated in article 6 of the regulation. Pools to cover new risks are, pursuant to article 6(1), exempted for three years regardless of any market share considerations. Nuclear pools, however, would not fall under article 6(2) but would have to satisfy the market share conditions as laid down in the remainder of article 6. The threshold for co-insurance and co-reinsurance pools is basically 20% and 25% respectively. Any pools that would surpass these thresholds would not benefit from the block exemption.

753 XXXIst Report on Competition Policy 2001, p. 63.

754 COM(2009) 138 final.

755 Commission Regulation 267/2010 on the application of Article 101(3) of the Treaty on the Functioning of the European Union to certain categories of agreements, decisions and concerted practices in the insurance sector.

756 Commission Regulation 358/2003 on the application of Article 81(3) of the Treaty to certain categories of agreements, decisions and concerted practices in the insurance sector.

In summary, it can be said that doubts can be raised whether nuclear insurance and re-insurance pools still fall outside the scope of competition law. Next to this it can also be said that if this is the case they will only benefit from the block exemption if the threshold in market shares is not exceeded. Given the very high market share of currently existing pools this leads to the conclusion that if, due to existing alternatives, nuclear insurance pools do not fall any more outside the scope of competition law because they are not a pre-requisite any more to offer coverage for nuclear risks, such pools would have to be assessed according to the criteria of article 101(3) if they do not fulfil the conditions of the 2010 IBER.

6.7. Proposal for a European regime

Keeping in mind the observations made throughout this chapter, a European regime for nuclear liability should be built around the following core principles:

- Liability of the nuclear operator shall be strict. To further increase the deterrent effect of a liability regime there shall be the possibility of introducing criminal sanctions if it can be shown that safety regulations have been violated;
- If negligent acts or omissions have caused or contributed to a nuclear accident, operators shall have a right of recourse against the persons acting or omitting to act with such negligence;
- Liability shall be unlimited;
    - Alternatively if liability was to be limited, limits shall be made conditional:
        - To the use of specific design standards;
        - A breach of safety regulation will break the right to limitation of liability;
        - If concerns that were raised during the licensing procedure either by experts or by the public in the course of a consultation were not taken into account but could have prevented or mitigated an accident the right to limit liability shall also be lost.

- The highest amounts of available funds shall be guaranteed by using a multi-layered system;
    - The first layer shall consist of insurance taken out by the operator;
    - The second layer shall consist of a European pooling arrangement between nuclear operators, participation in which will be a pre-requisite to operate a nuclear power plant within the European Union. Contributions shall be made by retrospective premiums;
    - If the first two layers turn out to be insufficient the unlimited liability of the operator shall serve as a means to guarantee further funds. In that regard also mother companies of subsidiaries shall contribute to compensate the damage caused;
    - Government intervention shall only take place as a means of last resort and in a facilitative manner, subject to charging a price for its intervention.

If a European regime complied with these core principles, such a regime would have the potential to increase public acceptance of nuclear energy and accommodate the interests between nuclear and non-nuclear member States. It would further significantly increase the available amounts to compensate for a nuclear accident. It would also have a greater deterrent effect than the current international regimes with an increased level of cost internalisation and true commitments not only to victim protection but also environmental protection, thereby realising that nuclear accidents will lead to both personal injury and environmental damage. Further it would allow for a meaningful interplay of *ex ante* incentives and *ex post* liability rules.

Chapter 7

THE FUTURE OF THE NUCLEAR SECTOR IN THE EUROPEAN UNION

7.1. Challenges on the way towards a European liability system for nuclear accidents

The last chapter ended with a proposal of how nuclear liability should be regulated within the European Union (hereinafter: the proposal). It has to be admitted that the proposal departs from existing rules in the area of nuclear liability and suggests the introduction of new principles within the European Union. As a result of this, two challenges present themselves which will be the main focus of this chapter. On the one hand, there needs to be analysis of how far it is possible to reconsider and adapt some of the core principles of nuclear liability as currently regulated in the international conventions, and whether and to what extent the suggested regime would still be in compliance with international obligations, and to what extent the European Union is free to deviate from international principles. This analysis will be done in section 7.2. On the other hand, one has to be aware that the proposal is far from being accepted, let alone implemented throughout the European Union. Ways need to be found to introduce the proposal within the European Union to move towards a more uniform European approach to nuclear safety and liability. Section 7.3 will focus on this and will suggest some tools that could increase the chances that the proposal as presented in chapter 6 will also make the next step from a mere proposal to its actual acceptance and implementation within the European Union.

7.2. A European initiative in the area of nuclear liability – Chances and challenges in the light of existing international obligations

The following sections have a double focus. Firstly, they will highlight the degree of harmonisation in the area of nuclear liability at the international level to discuss the extent to which there is indeed a convergence with regard to the main principles in the international area. This has also to be seen against the background of pleas for a global regime and concerns that a European approach to nuclear liability would lead to further fragmentation. Such a claim loses its weight, however, if a global regime was maybe a goal too far and not a realistic one. Secondly, the relation between international and European law will be analysed to see to what extent the European Union still enjoys a certain margin of manoeuvre in designing a European liability regime for nuclear accidents. The compatibility of the proposal as suggested in chapter 6 with the international conventions will be checked and it will include discussion of how a European regime could be structured in such a way that it will not prejudice Member States' international commitments towards third countries which are not a part of the European regime.

7.2.1. Degree of harmonisation at the international level

As already discussed in section 3.2, there are a number of principles that are common to the international conventions that are in force in the area of nuclear liability. As common cores one can mention the strict liability of the nuclear operator, legal channelling and the possibility to limit liability. As apparent from this, nuclear liability has at least with regard to basic principles been harmonised on an international scale. As always, however, the devil lies in the detail.

With regard to the possibility to limit liability it has to be recalled that a multitude of different liability limits apply, depending on the convention of which a country is Member and also depending on the way the Member States have dealt with this issue under their national laws. So whilst an almost universal choice for a limitation of liability can be found, the amounts have not been harmonised at all. Also on a more regional scale differences persist as was shown by the comparative overview in section 3.3. In France and the UK for example liability remains limited whilst in Germany and Austria liability is in principle unlimited. Austria is of course a special case, because it is not party to any of the international conventions.

Also the principle of legal channelling is by no means universal in its application. The US is neither party to the Paris nor the Vienna Convention. In their national law, the Price Anderson Act follows a rule of economic channelling.[757] Also the recent legislation in India has introduced a recourse right for operators, thereby departing from legal channelling *stricto sensu*.[758] With the introduction of its Law on Civil liability for damages caused by radioactivity, Austria also moved away from the principle of legal channelling.[759]

The only issue that indeed has reached global consensus is that the liability of the nuclear operator should be strict. The remaining aspects of a liability regime have only been partially harmonised by the international regime, and a European regime could go further than this in terms of the harmonisation achieved. Such a European approach has been criticised due to alleged dangers of increasing fragmentation in the area of nuclear

[757] See Faure and vanden Borre 2008.
[758] See Ameye 2014.
[759] See section 3.3.

liability?[760] As shown in the previous paragraphs, however, on the international level the degree of harmonisation is not that advanced that one could speak of an existing global or nearly global liability regime. It has also been pointed out in literature that such a global regime might indeed not be feasible.[761] Thus, it could be argued that a harmonised regime at the European level does not make the situation worse, but would achieve the best solution possible at the moment by creating a strong regional liability regime for nuclear accidents, thereby at least ending the patchy situation as it exists at the moment within the European Union. This more modest goal of a second-best solution of a well-functioning regional regime seems to be more realistic than the first-best, solution of a global regime. A European regime could also have the potential to trigger improvements at the international level, as was for example the case in the oil sector with regard to the liability amounts for oil pollution.[762] The following sections will therefore deal with the relation of international law and European law and address the question of compatibility of the proposal for a European approach as it was suggested in chapter 6 with the international conventions.

7.2.2. The relation between international law and European law

When discussing the relationship between European law and international law, a first distinction that needs to be made is whether the European Union has acceded to an international agreement or whether only the Member States, or some of the Member States are parties to an international agreement. With regard to the first scenario, article 216(2) TFEU states that 'agreements concluded by the Union are binding upon the institutions of the Union and on its Member States.' In the area of nuclear liability, however, this article does not apply, because the European Union did not accede to any of the international conventions on nuclear liability.

Article 351 TFEU deals with the relation between EU law and international agreements concluded by the Member States prior to their accession to the European Union. It states that

> *'The rights and obligations arising from agreements concluded before 1 January 1958 or, for acceding States, before the date of their accession, between one or more Member States on the one hand, and one or more third countries on the other, shall not be affected by the provisions of the Treaties.*
>
> *To the extent that such agreements are not compatible with the Treaties, the Member State or States concerned shall take all appropriate steps to eliminate the incompatibilities established. Member States shall, where necessary, assist each other to this end and shall, where appropriate, adopt a common attitude.*

760 Nießen 2010, p. 188.
761 Pelzer 2008, p. 280.
762 See Chapter 2.

In applying the agreements referred to in the first paragraph, Member States shall take into account the fact that the advantages accorded under the Treaties by each Member State form an integral part of the establishment of the Union and are thereby inseparably linked with the creation of common institutions, the conferring of powers upon them and the granting of the same advantages by all the other Member States.'

This article covers the situation where international agreements were concluded before 1st of January 1958 for the founding Member States and before accession to the Union for the other Member States respectively. It does not, however, deal with the relation between a European measure which is adopted subsequent to the conclusion of international agreements by the Member States. Thus article 216(2) and 351 TFEU do not provide an answer to the question of how to define the relationship between existing international obligations and any planned action by the European Union in an area already covered by an international agreement. An analysis of some relevant case law of the CJEU, however, provides important guidance on this issue.

With regard to the general relation between European and international law, the CJEU ruled more than two decades ago in *Poulsen*[763] 'that the European Community must respect international law in the exercise of its powers'. It continued to point out that the provision at stake has to be interpreted and limited in the light of the relevant rules of international law.[764] However, the following paragraph seems to limit this restriction to rules of customary international law.[765] More recent case law does indeed support this limitation and even clarifies also that written agreements cannot bind the Union, unless they represent customary international law.[766] It also has to be stressed that in such a case the Union is still not bound by the agreement as such but by the rules of customary law that it represents.[767]

In *Intertanko*[768] the Court was asked to rule on the compatibility of Directive 2005/35/EC on ship-source pollution[769] and the Marpol Convention.[770] The Directive laid down in some regards a stricter legal framework than the Convention, and therefore the Court was asked whether the Directive is in violation of the international convention.[771] In its judgement, the Court stated that secondary legislation of the European Union can be reviewed in the light of international agreements provided that two conditions are fulfilled: The Union must be bound by the agreement and the agreement must not be too

763 Case C-286/90 *Anklagemyndigheden* v. *Peter Michael Poulsen and Diva Navigation Corp* [1992].
764 *Ibid.*, para. 9.
765 *Ibid.*, para. 10; see also Case C-162/96 *A. Racke GmbH & Co.* v. *Hauptzollamt Mainz* [1998].
766 Hachez 2007, p. 147.
767 Rosas 2011, p. 1325.
768 Case C-308/06 *The Queen ex parte Intertanko et al.* v. *Secretary of State for Transport* [2008].
769 Directive 2005/35/EC on ship-source pollution and on the introduction of penalties for infringements.
770 International Convention for the Prevention of Pollution from Ships, 1973.
771 For an in-depth analysis of this case see for example Hachez 2008 and Pereira 2008.

broad and thus sufficiently precise and unconditional.[772] Given that the Union was not party to Marpol, the first condition was not fulfilled and the Court refused to review the validity of Directive 2005/35/EC in light of the Marpol Convention.[773]

The relation between International and European law was also at stake in the *Mesquer*[774] decision. In this case the CJEU had to rule on the relation between international conventions in the field of oil pollution and the Waste Directive 75/442.[775] In its judgement the Court came to the conclusion that national law always has to be interpreted in the light of the directive even if it derives from an international agreement.[776] Further it opened the door for liability beyond the limitations laid down in international conventions.[777] Thus also the *Mesquer* case could be regarded as an example where deviation from international commitments was not seen as a sufficient reason to question the validity of European secondary legislation.

The case law of the Court that was briefly discussed in the previous paragraph showed that one cannot speak of a general primacy of international law over secondary legislation from the European Union. Legally, the review of Union measures in the light of international agreements to which the European Union has not acceded would not be in line with the case law of the CJEU. Van Rossem even describes the approach of the Court in its decisions over the last years as 'indicative of the subordinate place reserved for international law within the bounds of the Community in general.'[778] Whilst these observations can be regarded as providing the European Union with some leeway with regard to the content of a potential initiative in the area of nuclear liability, the European Union and its secondary legislation can obviously not be regarded in complete isolation from international law and obligations arising thereof. This is also apparent in the Court's judgement in *Intertanko* where the Court also ruled that secondary legislation that deals with a subject matter that is covered by an international Convention has to be interpreted by taking into account the international convention.[779] Whilst the issue that is at stake in this part of the thesis is not the interpretation of an existing Union measure, but the question of how far a European approach to nuclear liability has to respect existing international obligations, this re-iteration of the principle of good faith as also rooted in article 26 of the Vienna Convention on the Law of Treaties[780] can of course not be disregarded when speaking about the design of a liability regime for nuclear accidents in the European Union.

772 Case C-308/06, para. 43–45; see also Joined Cases 21–24/72 *International Fruit Company NV and others* v. *Produktschap voor Groenten en Fruit* [1972].

773 Case C-308/06, para. 47+66.

774 Case C-188/07 *Commune de Mesquer v Total France SA and Total International Ltd* [2008].

775 Directive 75/442/8EEC was as amended codified by Directive 2006/12/EC on waste which was repealed by Directive 2008/98/EC on waste and repealing certain Directives.

776 Case C-188/07, para. 84.

777 *Ibid.*, para. 82.

778 Van Rossem 2009, p. 191.

779 Case C-308/06, para. 52.

780 Vienna Convention on the Law of Treaties, 22nd of May 1969, available at http://legal.un.org/ilc/texts/instruments/english/conventions/1_1_1969.pdf (last accessed on 21 August 2015).

The principle of *pacta sunt servanda* therefore requires that a European regime on nuclear liability shall not prejudice the Member States' commitments resulting from international agreements towards other parties to these agreements. Therefore the following section will turn its attention to an analysis of how far a European regime as suggested in the proposal of chapter 6 deviates from existing principles of nuclear liability as laid down in international conventions, and whether as a result of such deviation a European regime would not be in compliance with international law and how potential conflicts could be accommodated from a legal point of view.

7.2.3. Compatibility of the proposal with the international nuclear liability conventions

At the outset of this section, reference has to be made to the Preambles of both the Paris and the Vienna Convention. The Paris Convention refers to 'the need for unifying the basic rules applying in the various countries to the liability incurred for such damage, whilst leaving these countries free to take, on a national basis, any additional measures which they deem appropriate'. The Vienna Convention refers in its preamble to 'the desirability of establishing some minimum standards to provide financial protection against damage resulting from certain peaceful uses of nuclear energy'. As apparent in both these preambles, the conventions do not aim at laying down maximum norms, but are tools of a form of minimum harmonisation, leaving the Member States still with some freedom to adopt additional measures in their national laws. An analysis of the compatibility of the proposal as suggested in chapter 6 with the international conventions has to be seen in that light.[781] The following analysis will take provisions from the liability conventions of the two main systems as a benchmark. This will be on the one hand the Paris Convention as amended by the Protocols of 1964 and 1982.[782] Reference will also be made to the 2004 Paris Protocol[783] which is not in force yet, but eventually could enter into force and can therefore not be ignored. On the other hand the analysis will also rely on provisions from the consolidated version of the Vienna Convention as amended by the Protocol of 1997.[784]

7.2.3.1. Strict liability of the operator

As also stated above in section 7.2.1, there is international consensus with regard to the liability rule for nuclear accidents. Article 3(a) Paris Convention establishes liability of the nuclear operator without the requirement of fault, and article IV(1) Vienna Convention also follows a rule of strict liability. This rule is the universally accepted standard and also

781 Allowing for a certain degree of differentiation could also be a feature of a European regime, thereby potentially increasing the feasibility of such a regime. See section 7.3.1.1.

782 Available at https://www.oecd-nea.org/law/nlparis_conv.html (last accessed on 21 August 2015).

783 Available at https://www.oecd-nea.org/law/paris_convention.pdf (last accessed on 21 August 2015).

784 Available at www-pub.iaea.org/MTCD/publications/PDF/Pub1279_web.pdf from p. 127 onwards (last accessed on 21 August 2015).

under the proposal this would not be any different. Thus, with regard to the main liability rule compatibility with the international liability regimes will not be an issue.

7.2.3.2. Liability limits

With regard to the possibility of limiting liability under the international conventions, a certain evolution has taken place over the last decades. Article 7 of the Paris Convention states that

> 'a) *The aggregate of compensation required to be paid in respect of damage caused by a nuclear incident shall not exceed the maximum liability established in accordance with this Article.*
> b) *The maximum liability of the operator in respect of damage caused by a nuclear incident shall be 15 000 000 Special Drawing Rights as defined by the International Monetary Fund.*'

Article 7 thus limits the liability of a nuclear operator. However, Article 15 Paris Convention states that 'any Contracting Party may take such measures as it deems necessary to provide for an increase in the amount of compensation specified in this Convention.' The liability limits are therefore not mandatory, which is also in line with the preamble of the Convention, granting Contracting Parties the right to go beyond the standards as laid down in the Convention. The 2004 Paris Protocol would increase the minimum liability of a nuclear operator, stating that 'each Contracting Party shall provide under its legislation that the liability of the operator in respect of nuclear damage caused by any one nuclear incident shall not be less than 700 million euro'.[785]

Whilst the Paris Convention does not explicitly foresee in its current form the introduction of unlimited liability, it could nevertheless accommodate this as shown by the example of Germany that introduced unlimited liability in its national laws already decades ago.[786] Rehbinder points out that the introduction of unlimited liability could be regarded as increasing the amount of liability in the most extensive way and an increase in liability limits is explicitly allowed.[787] Under the 2004 Paris Protocol the introduction of unlimited liability is clearly possible. The new article 10(b) of the Paris Convention as it would be introduced by the 2004 Paris Protocol states that 'where the liability of the operator is not limited in amount, the Contracting Party within whose territory the nuclear installation of the liable operator is situated shall establish a limit upon the financial security of the operator liable'. It thereby explicitly refers to the possibility of unlimited liability. A similar wording can also be found in article VII(1)a of the Vienna Convention which consequently also allows the introduction of unlimited liability. Higher liability amounts and also unlimited liability as called for in principle under the proposal as presented in chapter 6 would therefore also be compatible with the international conventions

785 Section I. H 2004 Paris Protocol, available at https://www.oecd-nea.org/law/paris_convention.pdf (last accessed on 21 August 2015).
786 See Schwartz 2006, p. 54.
787 Rehbinder 2010, p. 428.

It is also interesting to note that the 2004 Paris Protocol would introduce a slightly revised article 15(b). Concerning additional measures taken to increase liability beyond the limits laid down in the Convention it states that 'in so far as compensation for nuclear damage is in excess of the 700 million euro referred to in Article 7(*a*), any such measure in whatever form may be applied under conditions which may derogate from the provisions of this Convention.' This article can be regarded as giving substantial freedom to the Member States in coming up with solutions how to cover the increased amounts. Hence, the multi-layered approach to strive for the highest amounts of compensation possible as suggested under the proposal of chapter 6 does not seem to raise issues of incompatibility either.

7.2.3.3. The role of legal channelling

An important aspect of the proposal as presented in chapter 6 is that operators shall have a right of recourse, if the damage that resulted from a nuclear accident was caused negligently by an act or omission, against the person that was acting or omitting to act with such negligence. It would thereby not hold the nuclear operator exclusively liable, but would foresee a right of recourse also against for example suppliers and designers. Article 6(a) Paris Convention states that

> *'The right to compensation for damage caused by a nuclear incident may be exercised only against an operator liable for the damage in accordance with this Convention.'*

With regard to a possible right of recourse, Article 6(f) specifies that

> *'The operator shall have a right of recourse only:*
>
> 1. *if the damage caused by a nuclear incident results from an act or omission done with intent to cause damage, against the individual acting or omitting to act with such intent;*
> 2. *if and to the extent that it is so provided expressly by contract.'*

Article II(5) and article X of the Vienna Convention lay down the same rules concerning legal channelling and a right of recourse. Before assessing the compatibility of these provisions with the waiver of the principle of exclusive liability of the nuclear operator under the proposal of chapter 6, reference needs to be made to the fact that also under the Conventions one could argue that the principle of exclusive liability is not an absolute one. Germany for example made a reservation to the application of article 6(a) which allows it to introduce national laws that hold other persons than the nuclear operator liable.[788] Seeing the reservation in conjunction with article 19(c) of the Vienna Convention

[788] See Annex I Paris Convention, available at https://www.oecd-nea.org/law/nlparis_conv.html (last accessed on 21 August 2015).

on the Law of Treaties[789] which forbids reservations that are 'incompatible with the object and purpose of the Treaty' one could regard the fact that this reservation was accepted as an indication that the principle of legal channelling is not an absolute principle. In a way this is also supported by the fact that a right of recourse is foreseen under the Conventions, admittedly, however, in very limited instances. This makes the bridge with the discussion of the actual content of the proposal from chapter 6 concerning the issue of legal channelling. The proposal foresees a strengthened right of recourse for the nuclear operator because it would not any more depend on a written agreement, but such a right of recourse would be the default rule under the conditions of negligent acts or omissions causing or contributing to the nuclear accident. It would thereby also not require the intent to cause harm any more as required under the Conventions. Rather the threshold that needed to be passed would be establishing negligence. Since the preamble of the Paris Convention explicitly allows national states to introduce 'any additional measures which they deem appropriate', one could argue that changing the required intent into a standard of negligence could be regarded as such an additional measure. The measure being the lowering of the standard needed to invoke a right of recourse to a negligence standard. Thus, by means of an extensive interpretation of the articles of the Convention and especially in the light of the fact that the Conventions only lay down minimum rules, a strengthened right of recourse for the nuclear operator as foreseen under the proposal could be regarded as compatible with the international conventions.

7.2.3.4. Summary

In summary it can be said that strict liability would also under the European regime, as it was suggested in chapter 6, remain the main liability rule. There is no difference between this and the international conventions. Higher liability amounts and also unlimited liability would also be compatible with the international conventions, given that the conventions only provide minimum standards and states can go beyond these obligations. Furthermore, the more recent developments in the area of nuclear liability even foresee the introduction of unlimited liability in the international conventions. With regard to the introduction of a general right of recourse for nuclear operators against actors whose negligence has caused or contributed to a nuclear accident, it was argued that an extensive interpretation of the provisions of the international conventions could accommodate such a rule.

7.2.4. A European nuclear liability system and existing obligations towards non-Member States of the European Union

To conclude the discussion on how to integrate a European nuclear liability regime into the currently existing liability regimes, a differentiation needs to be made between accident scenarios involving only Member States of the European Union, and situations

789 Vienna Convention on the Law of Treaties, 22nd of May 1969, available at http://legal.un.org/ilc/texts/instruments/english/conventions/1_1_1969.pdf (last accessed on 21 August 2015).

in which non-Member States of the European Union are also involved. With regard to the former situation, the extent to which certain provisions of a European regime would be compatible with the international conventions, is an issue which would play a legally subordinate role. As it was shown in section 7.2.2, the validity of European measures cannot be reviewed in the light of international agreements. In internal situations there would also not be a need for this, given that all Member States would be covered by the European regime. With regard to situations in which also non-Member Sates are involved, these would be different because commitments made towards these States would still need to be honoured in accordance with more general principles of law such as *pacta sunt servanda* and the obligation to perform international agreements in good faith.

Whilst it was argued in the previous sections that the European regime as suggested in chapter 6 is compatible with the international conventions, States that are not Members of the European Union could nevertheless have a preference for the continuation of the legal regime as it is laid down in the international conventions also after a potential harmonisation of nuclear liability in the European Union. One option to achieve that would be the use of a disconnection clause. Such a clause allows the setting aside of the application of international Conventions because of the mutual relations between two or more Contracting Parties to the Convention that want to engage in further and more far reaching harmonisation. This covers for example the situations of Members of the European Union that want to engage in further harmonisation than foreseen in international conventions. As a logical consequence from this it also enables the international convention to remain applicable for situations that involve States which are not party to the European Union but to the international conventions.[790] Thus, also in the area of nuclear liability the introduction of a disconnection clause could enable a situation between the Member States of the European Union in which the European regime would be applicable, whilst the international conventions would remain applicable in the case where a state which is not a member to the European Union is involved.

7.3. From proposal to implementation

Having dealt with the issue of compatibility of a European regime with the international conventions and how to accommodate a European regime within the existing nuclear liability regimes in the previous sections, the following parts will pick up the issue that was already pointed out in the beginning of this chapter, namely the question of how to realise the proposal within the European Union and to provide an explanation why currently the nuclear sector is not regulated along the principles that were identified in chapter 6 as core principles of the proposal for a European nuclear liability regime.

As already discussed in section 2.5.3, public choice analysis can provide an answer to this. The nuclear sector currently is a sector in which industry is able to influence

[790] For a more detailed description and analysis of the use of disconnection clauses see for example Verdejo 2001, Smrkolj 2008, Dawar 2010.

regulation by rent seeking behaviour to such an extent that the outcome is very one-sided and in favour of industry interests whilst neglecting the concerns of victim protection, efficient accident prevention and protection of the environment. As Becker points out, interest groups and their influence on law making is particularly problematic when there is an imbalance between powerful and weak interest groups, with unequal possibilities to engage in the political process.[791] Means need to be identified to counterbalance this discrepancy. If the institutional set up allows for equal influence of different interest groups, and different interest groups are indeed present, the competition between these groups can lead to an equilibrium which would prevent single issue oriented regulation.[792] Given that the current regulation of the nuclear sector particularly favours business interests, the question can be asked why no stronger opposition to this has surfaced. According to Walker an interest group that furthers interests to the detriment of others will cause 'a social disturbance that affects the interests of other potential groups, and these groups may be stimulated, in turn, to form associations that will represent them.'[793] The formation of different interest groups can balance the situation to such an extent that if groups that favour not only industry interests but for example the interests of the environment or society as a whole were more active, a countervailing power would be given to ensure that law making in the nuclear sector does not only follow the interests of one or a few stakeholders whilst neglecting the others.[794] For the proposal from the previous chapter to succeed, this will also be of crucial importance. An alternative to the actual formation of interest groups can be found in the theory of shadow interest groups as described *inter alia* by Keenan and Rubin.[795] Even in the absence of an existing interest group, the potential that after a regulatory failure or after an accident the victims thereof would claim compensation and become more active in the political process can have an effect on the regulatory decisions taken and the outcome of the law-making process.

Without making a claim to provide an exhaustive list of possible solutions to the problems sketched above, there will be a focus on 4 approaches throughout the remainder of this chapter that could increase the chances of a successful change and the implementation of new regulation of the nuclear sector as suggested throughout the previous chapters of this thesis. Section 7.3.1 will assess the role of the different stakeholders within the European Union, and assess the balance of powers between them and how far their relationship has an influence on the implementation of the proposal suggested in the previous chapter. Section 7.3.2 will analyse the potential of CSR to impede single issue oriented policy making at the European level and to increase the costs of rent seeking behaviour of the nuclear industry. It will also pay attention to the question of how CSR can have a positive influence on corporate interests in the nuclear sector. Part 7.3.3 will focus particularly on one stakeholder, namely the nuclear industry. It will apply the

791 Becker 1989, p. 23.
792 Buchanan and Tullock 1965, p. 288.
793 Walker 1983, p. 391.
794 Becker 1989, p. 18.
795 Keenan and Rubin 1988.

findings of the Porter Hypothesis to the issues of nuclear liability and nuclear safety regulation to check whether an argument can be made that implementing the suggested changes would also advance business interests which would further enhance the chances of a successful implementation. Finally, section 7.3.4 will address an administrative tool, namely the creation of an independent agency in the nuclear sector to assess what role such an agency could have on the realisation of the proposal.

7.3.1. *Improving multi-level governance*

Intervention from the European Union in the nuclear sector is a sensitive issue because it triggers discussions of national sovereignty and governance of such a complex regional institution as the European Union with its Member States. This complexity is further highlighted when dealing with environmental concerns that transcend national borders.[796] Furthermore, the proposal as presented in chapter 6 would lead to quite significant changes with regard to the approach of the European Union towards nuclear liability and nuclear safety. It is therefore necessary to analyse what role the different actors within the European Union can play in the transition from the current system towards a new European system.

Any discussion on governance has to be done against the background that in times of globalisation the old perceptions are no longer workable. Static hierarchical structures with national constitutions at the top have to be reconsidered, taking sufficient account of the influence of different actors at different levels. All actors, be they public or private, individual or collective have to be involved in order to implement policies for environmental protection successfully.[797] Taking this broader view enables one to grasp the 'multi-layered dynamics of power exercise and policy making beyond a narrow, rigid and national structure.'[798] This is of course of special relevance in the nuclear sector, when one keeps in mind the transboundary effects that nuclear power generation can have within the European Union. As Ebbesson puts it, taking a purely national perspective will not enable decision makers to cope with 'human environmental interactions that in most cases fully disregard state borders.'[799]

One definition of governance, as provided by Treib, Bähr and Falkner, describes governance as 'a process of governing which departs from the traditional model where collectively binding decisions are taken by elected representatives within parliaments and implemented by bureaucrats within public administrations.'[800] When discussing the aspects and merits of governance, focus is often on the relationship between society and its government.[801] Thus, at the heart is the interplay between the different actors involved.

796 Ebbesson 2010, p. 420.
797 Salles 2011, p. 2.
798 Popelier and Vandenbruwaene 2014, p. 225.
799 Ebbesson 2010, p. 420.
800 Treib, Bähr and Falkner 2007, p. 3.
801 *Ibid.*, p. 5.

The following sections will focus on the three main actors within the European Union, namely the Member States (7.3.1.1), European institutions (7.3.1.2) and civil society (7.3.1.3) and their respective relevance for the acceptance of the proposal from chapter 6. Within the framework of the economics of federalism, section 7.3.1.1 will discuss how to convince the Member States to accept the proposal and the relinquishment of certain competences as a consequence thereof. When turning to the European institutions the main focus will be the question of how the powers of the European institutions and pressures to which they are exposed have an influence on the policy making of the European Union, and assess against this background how the chances of accepting the proposal can be increased. Lastly, section 7.3.1.3 will analyse what role civil society can play to enhance the acceptance of the proposal. Particular focus will be paid to issues of inclusiveness and transparency and to what extent these factors can work in favour of the proposal being adopted.

7.3.1.1. Member States

The decisive question that an economic analysis of federalism wants to solve is at what level legal intervention should take place in order to be regarded as optimal.[802] The different possibilities would be intervention at a centralised or decentralised level. For the sake of this section it is relevant to identify arguments for centralised intervention because such arguments can be used to convince Member States to agree to more European competences in the nuclear sector.[803]

The economic model of federalism as presented by Tiebout starts from the assumption that a decentralised approach should be favoured, allowing for regulatory competition, the result of which would be an efficient system.[804] Arguing for a centralised solution, some authors point out that such regulatory competition, however, does not always lead to welfare enhancing results.[805] Proponents of centralised intervention rely mainly on 3 factors that would justify centralisation: The risk of a race to the bottom and a regulatory chill, the need and advantages of economies of scale and transboundary externalities allowing harm to be externalised.[806] As apparent from section 5.4 above, some of these arguments can support European intervention in the area of nuclear liability and nuclear safety and thereby strengthen the proposal as presented in chapter 6. The risk of regulatory chill is an argument for moving competences about nuclear safety to a centralised level. Even more support for this is provided by the need for economies of scale. If the problem to be regulated entails a transboundary element and is not confined to the competences of a local or national authority, a need to switch to a more centralised

802 Faure 2003, p. 34.
803 See chapter 5 for an in-depth analysis of the economics of federalism.
804 See Tiebout 1956.
805 Esty and Geradin 2001, p. 31.
806 See e.g. Oates and Schwab 1988; Revesz 1992; Revesz 1997; Revesz 2001; Esty and Geradin 1998; Esty and Geradin 2001; Vogel 2001a; Faure 2003.

solution occurs[807] Also the advantages of a European system, with regard to knowledge pooling and joint research, support such a claim.[808] The need for economies of scale can also support centralised intervention in the area of nuclear liability, keeping in mind improved risk management of transboundary nuclear damage that would come along with a European approach. Also the risk of an externalisation of harm supports intervention at the European level in the area of nuclear liability.[809]

As apparent from the discussion above, the economic analysis of federalism does provide arguments that could be used to convince Member States to support more European intervention in the area of nuclear safety and nuclear liability. It is thus a factor that can enhance the chances of the proposal being accepted with regard to a shift of competences away from the Member States towards the European level.

Next to the issue of determining the best level at which legislative action should take place, a legal initiative to reform the nuclear sector and its regulation in the European Union faces another challenge. With regard to the enforcement of Union law Lee points out that the Commission's power under article 258 TFEU has its limits because it is a form of indirect enforcement. The Commission will address the Member States, but for European Union law to be complied with, the Commission then depends on the willingness and ability of the national governments to guarantee compliance.[810] This obstacle to implementation can be seen as a typical aspect of multi-level settings such as the EU. Jordan and Tosun observe that 'poor implementation in the EU remains very much a "safety valve"', meaning thereby that it is a tool to accommodate different interests whilst not disrupting the integration process as a whole.[811] They are further of the opinion that such '"post decisional" politics are an integral, and we suspect, never-ending part of the wider struggle between actors at different governance levels to shape the European integration process.'[812] This struggle also needs to be accommodated.

In the beginning of the creation of the European Community, the Member States might not have been aware of what kind of revolutionary changes this process would bring with it over the following decades. Notions of sovereignty, democracy and the rule of law have been under a constant process of revision since the founding treaties were signed.[813] The European Union consists of 28 Member States with different, independent legal systems. This constitutional plurality within the European Union can be approached in two ways. One way is to argue that the plurality is something that needs to be overcome, and will eventually be substituted by one European Constitution. The other approach is to take the plurality of constitutions as an inherent part of the European Union. Every

807 Faure 2003, p. 38.
808 Kimber 1995, p. 1660.
809 Faure 2001, p. 269; Faure 2003, p. 39.
810 Lee 2014, p. 127.
811 Jordan and Tosun 2013, p. 262.
812 *Ibid.*
813 Popelier 2014, p. 300.

initiative coming from the European Union would have to take this diversity into account when designing its policies and legislative instruments.[814] With regard to a reform of the regulation of the nuclear sector this could potentially also mean to allow for some degree of differentiation between the Member States. Differentiation can have the advantage of accommodating different interest and coping with diversity.[815] This is of special importance in the nuclear sector given the differing attitudes of Member States to the use of nuclear energy. A European system aiming at maximum harmonisation might have a smaller chance of success than an approach that guarantees a certain common denominator but at the same time allows some Member States to go even further than that. Also the exact content of a European regime will of course have an influence on the feasibility and success of a European intervention. A differentiated approach could accommodate these concerns. If this route were to be followed it has to be emphasised, however, that the common standard would still need to comply with the major principles as presented in chapter 6 to be able to remedy the flaws of the currently existing regimes.

More specifically this would entail the following conditions. Obviously a rule of strict liability would need to be followed. Also the right of recourse for nuclear operators against persons whose negligence has caused or contributed to a nuclear accident should be the default rule in a differentiated approach. One could, however, think of the possibility to allow operators to waive such a right. With regard to the liability amounts a general preference should be given to unlimited liability. In case a Member State would only join the European regime if it is allowed to limit liability, such a limitation should only be accepted if the right to such a limitation can easily be lost for example in case of a breach of safety regulations. The limited liability amount, however, will in any case be still a significantly increased amount compared to the liability limits as laid down in the international conventions.

Whilst a fully harmonised European system should be strived for as the first-best solution within the European Union, as a second best solution such a differentiated approach would still be preferable to approaches such as enhanced co-operation. Using this tool bears the risk of splitting up the European Union for example into an East-West divide on the issue of nuclear liability. Western states being willing to follow the stricter criteria whilst the Eastern Member States want to stick to the more lenient international conventions. Another possible divide would be between Member States making use of nuclear power generation and Member States opposing nuclear energy. Such situations would of course not be an enhancement of the current status quo with regard to the level of harmonisation of nuclear liability in the European Union.

814 Simoncini 2014, p. 244.
815 Martinico 2014, p. 295.

7.3.1.2. European institutions

On the one hand there are institutions on the European level that are clearly intergovernmental, such as the Council or directly elected such as the European parliament, and on the other hand there is the Commission with a more 'technocratic mission'.[816] There is disagreement whether these two components are always are well balanced or whether 'there is a constant risk that the technocratic and undemocratic dimension will trump the more democratic aspects of the institutional balancing act'.[817] With regard to the balance of powers between the institutions it can be said that both Council and Commission have significant powers. The European Parliament is still less influential than these two bodies, although its role has continuously been strengthened in the past. The weaker position of the Parliament is somewhat paradoxical because only the European Parliament is an elected body.[818]

The institutional set up within the European Union, with a relatively small Commission and a European Parliament not enjoying sufficient competences leads to a situation in which external expertise and influence can be very common.[819] This can lead to a situation in which private bodies have a very big influence on policy making at the European level. If standards are set by technical experts and in an opaque manner, there is a need to accommodate accountability issues. In a transnational setting this becomes even more problematic because whilst an ever continuing move towards globalisation has increased the inter-dependence between nation states and public and private actors, there is a lack of effective transnational mechanisms that can co-ordinate such regulatory developments, taking into account all interests involved, public and private.[820]

If all interests were indeed taken into account and had equal influence on the policy making process at the European level, the influence of interest groups would not necessarily need to be a bad thing. If different interest groups are competing for influence such competition can prevent legislation that furthers only one interest because the influence of the different interest groups can lead to equilibrium.[821] Becker also highlights that the influence of interest groups on the legislative process is particularly problematic if stronger interest groups can dominate weaker ones.[822]

According to Adelle and Anderson, half of the interest groups active in Brussels represent business interests, whilst only one third deals with the interests of citizens. Part of the latter group are also environmental interest groups.[823] In the past there have been instances

816 Scott 2009, p. 171.
817 *Ibid.*
818 Lee 2014, p. 184.
819 Lee 2014, p. 194.
820 Curtin and Senden 2011, p. 168.
821 Buchanan and Tullock 1965, p. 288.
822 Becker 1989, p. 23.
823 Adelle and Anderson 2013, p. 152.

where lobbying by environmental interests groups has been very successful. The process leading up to the REACH regulation, for example has been referred to as being very much influenced by environmental pressure groups which also led to some severe consequences for the industry that would not have been realised without the role of the environmental interest groups.[824] One can thus not generally say that environmental interests are overall sacrificed for business interests. However, an interesting point is that environmental interest groups mainly have good links with the environmental bodies of the Commission, whilst industry interests are well represented throughout the Commission and its different DGs.[825] This is an interesting aspect and can also be linked to the issue at stake of a possible imbalance of influence of interest groups in the nuclear sector. Currently initiatives in the nuclear sector originate from the DG Energy and Transport and not the DG Environment. Under the proposal this would change, given the increased emphasis on environmental protection, which is also mirrored in the legal basis.[826]

Whilst the preceding paragraph clarified that one cannot generally speak of an under-representation of environmental interests in the decision-making process at Brussels, the nuclear sector seems to present a different picture. According to a report by Corporate Europe Observatory, there are up to 200 lobbyists that try to enhance the interests of the nuclear industry in Brussels and they are very successful in doing so.[827] The most recent initiative in the nuclear sector, the revision of the Nuclear Safety Directive, supports this claim. The adopted version of the amending Directive is weaker and introduces fewer far-reaching changes than the original version.[828] According to MEP Rivasi 'the lack of any real substance in this directive shows just how much pressure lobbyists can exert on legislators.'[829]

As apparent from above, in the area of nuclear law there are legitimate concerns that industry views are better represented than other interest such as environmental ones. Giving more influence to environmental interest groups is crucial to achieve a more balanced law-making. This can also have positive effects on the legislation because more aspects and perspectives will be taken into account.[830] By the creation or empowerment of interest groups not pursuing industry interests, countervailing powers can be established to decrease the likelihood that only the interests of one group of stakeholders is taken into account whilst others are neglected.[831] Also after the legislative process,

824 *Ibid.*, p. 158.

825 *Ibid.*, p. 161.

826 As discussed in section 4.2 the proposal would be based on a dual legal basis of article 192 TFEU and 114 TFEU.

827 CEO report 2012, p. 1–3, Nuclear Contamination: A year after Fukushima, why does Brussels still back nuclear power?, Corporate Europe Observatory, 2012, http://corporateeurope.org/sites/default/files/publications/nuclear_contamination_march2012_0.pdf (last accessed on 21 August 2015).

828 See section 2.4.4.

829 Https://www.theparliamentmagazine.eu/articles/opinion/nuclear-safety-directive-accused-%E2%80%98lacking-substance%E2%80%99 (last accessed on 21 August 2015).

830 Lee 2014, p. 202.

831 Becker 1989, p. 18.

environmental groups and individuals can play an important role. If their rights were strengthened they could play an enhanced role in the implementation of environmental law because this allows them to work as watchdogs.[832] Such interventions could remedy situations where only industry interests had been taken into consideration during the decision making process. Following the theory of shadow interest groups, such empowerment could even prevent one-sided legislation, because it might not be passed in the first place due to a risk of later scrutiny and protest by other interest groups.[833]

7.3.1.3. Civil society

Given that the general public also plays an important role in the changes as proposed in chapter 6, this section will focus its attention on civil society. The effects of the proposals would be twofold. On the one hand the public would benefit from a stricter regulation of the nuclear sector if this leads to more nuclear safety, fewer environmental risks and more available compensation in the event of a nuclear accident. On the other hand civil society also plays a stronger role in the proposal because the suggested changes foresee a more inclusive regulatory style. Therefore the following sections will discuss two aspects. Justifications for stronger involvement of civil society will be discussed and also the effect that such an increased involvement would have on the legitimacy and acceptance of the proposal as a whole.

7.3.1.3.1. Legitimacy concerns

In times of increasing anti-EU attitudes amongst people, there is a need to increase the legitimacy of the European Union and to bring civil society closer to the decision making in Brussels.[834] Mere dialogue between societal actors and institutions at the EU level is of course not enough to increase the democratic legitimisation of the EU.[835] Civil society has to be given a more substantial role, allowing European citizens to have a meaningful involvement in the core issues on the European agenda. An inclusive approach and more public participation for example could play its role to achieve this. In the environmental field, however, Krämer regrets that this potential has not been realised so far, leading to a situation in which 'citizens and civil society as a whole are in desperate need to see the EU moving to more openness, transparency and democracy.'[836] The need for more democracy at the European level is also a result of the phenomenon that 'traditional democratic processes at national level [...] simply cannot keep up with the migration of power and authority to the transnational level.'[837] Transnational governance can thus be felt as illegitimate. There is therefore a need to democratise decision making at the

832 Lee 2014, p. 128.
833 See Keenan and Rubin 1988.
834 Kohler-Koch 2012, p. 811.
835 *Ibid.*, p. 814.
836 Krämer 2013, p. 473.
837 Curtin and Senden 2011, p. 186.

European level and an increased role of civil society can counter such negative perceptions of transnational governance.

Lee identifies three aspects of newer forms of governance within the EU: firstly, flexible approaches, with sometimes rather softer than hard rules, are to be preferred over top-down regulation in a command and control style, Secondly, governance is more inclusive and thirdly increased access to information and the dissemination of knowledge facilitates an adaptive and reflexive process.[838] The last two points support a further empowerment of the general public. If civil society has the possibility to control the decision making processes this can have a positive influence on the perceived legitimacy of decisions taken and the actors taking these decisions. More democratic and dialectic decision making process can also bridge the distance between decision takers on the one hand and people being affected by these decisions on the other hand.[839]

There is, however, still a lack of inclusiveness and a true participatory approach has not yet been realised within the European Union.[840] Kohler-Koch identifies the institutional conditions that civil society is facing in the European Union as one of the major reasons for that.[841]

At this point it is interesting to make a reference to the Citizens' initiative, which could arguably play a role in this. It was introduced by the Lisbon Treaty, more specifically by Article 11 TEU:

'1. *The institutions shall, by appropriate means, give citizens and representative associations the opportunity to make known and publicly exchange their views in all areas of Union action.*
2. *The institutions shall maintain an open, transparent and regular dialogue with representative associations and civil society.*
3. *The European Commission shall carry out broad consultations with parties concerned in order to ensure that the Union's actions are coherent and transparent.*
4. *Not less than one million citizens who are nationals of a significant number of Member States may take the initiative of inviting the European Commission, within the framework of its powers, to submit any appropriate proposal on matters where citizens consider that a legal act of the Union is required for the purpose of implementing the Treaties.*
The procedures and conditions required for such a citizens' initiative shall be determined in accordance with the first paragraph of Article 24 of the Treaty on the Functioning of the European Union.'

838 Lee 2014, p. 81.
839 Curtin and Meijer, p. 111–114.
840 Kohler-Koch 2012, p. 816.
841 *Ibid.*, p. 819.

This initiative has been described by Lee as 'not a true form of direct democracy'.[842] It is also amongst other authors not really regarded as a well-functioning mechanism that could allow a more meaningful involvement of civil society.[843] An advantage of the European Citizens' initiative is that it is structured in a relatively simple way which theoretically would also allow ordinary citizens to take action. It is in that regard different to more complicated participatory mechanisms that favour more professionally organised interest groups.[844]

In 2012 this initiative was tried in the nuclear sector. It did not get very far however, since the Commission rejected it.[845] The attempt to use the European Citizens' initiative, based on the TEU, to fundamentally change subject matter of the Euratom Treaty can indeed be regarded as going a bit too far. It nevertheless shows that civil society still has a difficult standing within the structure of the European Union and especially within the nuclear sector. This is a pity because involving society in a more meaningful way can reduce the democratic deficit of the European Union.[846] The enhanced role of civil society as foreseen under the proposal could remedy these flaws. From the perspective of increasing the legitimacy of the regulation of the nuclear sector, the arguments presented throughout this section thus support the adoption of the proposal.

7.3.1.3.2. Inclusiveness of regulation

As it was already apparent from the section above, the role of the general public in the decision making processes in the European Union is under-developed. This does not only lead to problems with regard to legitimacy, but can also have more substantive influence. Civil society is just as important as other stakeholders, and can also have an important role to play. This enables a dynamic interplay of different actors involved, leading to more dialectics.[847] As one of these actors, civil society can also play its role in enhancing the level of implementation and enforcement.[848]When administrative law is used to control and restrict certain behaviour, transparency, authorisation, representation and participation can be regarded as core principles of such procedural rules.[849] Therefore an increased role for civil society can also have positive effects on the effectiveness of the regulatory regime under the proposal.

In an attempt to democratise transnational regulation, de Burca also argues for more influence and participation of people who are affected by the regulation in question.[850]

842 Lee 2014, p. 187.
843 See De Witte *et al.* 2010.
844 Lee 2014, p. 192.
845 Www.citizens-initiative.eu/?p=1141 (last accessed on 21 August 2015).
846 Popelier 2014, p. 319.
847 Simoncini 2014, p. 247+248.
848 McBarnet 2007, p. 46.
849 Curtin and Senden 2011, p. 165.
850 De Burca 2008, p. 248–256.

Participation should be kept as open as possible, preventing a form of participation by specific groups that were defined beforehand. This would guarantee a higher level of inclusion because some interest groups would not arbitrarily be excluded.[851] If public participation is facilitated, this has furthermore the potential that regulatory processes can be enriched by the knowledge of other interested and affected parties, as for example environmental interest groups.[852] In democratic decision making processes one cannot solely rely on experts and ignore public opinion. Expert opinion is furthermore not always the absolute truth, just as public opinion does not always need to be a hindrance and obstacle in decision making processes.[853] Therefore a higher level of inclusiveness does not only increase the legitimacy of regulatory processes but also has the potential to increase the quality thereof.

7.3.2. The role of Corporate Social Responsibility (CSR)[854]

Whilst there might be a trend in environmental law towards more private standards and an increased reliance on private environmental governance[855], it has to be emphasised from the very start that the following sections are not intended to promote the regulation of the nuclear sector by soft law or voluntary approaches. The analysis will indeed rely on findings from areas that currently can be termed as softer forms of regulation given the voluntary nature of CSR, but these findings will be used to make some hard recommendations about how some features of CSR can be used to challenge the current status quo of the nuclear sector.

7.3.2.1. CSR and public choice

Taking Olson's criteria for successful rent-seeking behaviour as a starting point, it has to be recalled that interest groups will be most likely to successfully influence the policy making process if they are small, share similar interests, can easily coordinate their actions and possess superior or more information than the general public. Such rent-seeeking behaviour will particularly be successful if the public is furthermore faced with financial or other hurdles for obtaining information about the negative effects of the single issue oriented policies resulting from the influence of a respective pressure group.[856] As apparent from these conditions, one option to impede such rent seeking by industry groups would be to increase the costs that they have to incur during the process or to enable other affected groups to mitigate their information disadvantage compared to the groups trying to influence the policy-making process. Increasing the transparency

851 *Ibid.*, p. 248–252.
852 Lee 2014, p. 84.
853 *Ibid.*, p. 27+38/.
854 This section focuses on the potential of CSR to impede rent seeking by the nuclear industry and in how far CSR could motivate industry to make stronger environmental commitment in the nuclear sector. For a more general discussion of CSR and its relevance in the nuclear sector see Heldt 2014.
855 See e.g. Vandenbergh 2013.
856 Olson 1965.

of the sector, for example would be one tool. This option links the discussion to CSR initiatives, keeping in mind the focus on increased transparency as an important aspect of CSR.

It is indeed the aspect of transparency that seems to be the most valuable aspect of the discussion about CSR for the purposes of this section. Tietenberg has termed the reliance on more disclosure the third phase of regulation after more traditional command and control (first phase) and market based incentives (second phase) have not reached the desired regulatory goals.[857] Publishing for example more information about the environmental performance of firms can have an effect on consumers and society as a whole, eventually leading to pressure on firms to change their policy. This, however, presupposes a certain level of interest of the public. If the public is indifferent towards the behaviour of firms this will not be a strong tool.[858]

Lee points out, that increased transparency can also stimulate changes in legal rules: If more information is available this can show the need for improvement which can create pressure that rules be revised. An increased amount of information that is made available for affected parties can also enable these parties to enforce the 'social license' of companies.[859] This argument can also be found in more general literature on the role of CSR and its relation to the industry. Wesley *et al.*, for example, argue for a re-conceptualisation of CSR. They describe it as a political phenomenon and all actions are being influenced by different factors and CSR should be regarded as a 'governable space'.[860] Business is linked with state and civil society and this has an effect on how it operates.[861] Thus increased reliance on transparency provides the chance for the nuclear sector to become more inclusive and transparent. Such an increased transparency can then also lead to more information being available about the harm and damage caused by pollution to the public. This can also mitigate collective choice problems because the increase of information can create incentives for collective action.[862] Increased transparency can thus also increase the amount of shadow interest groups which can mitigate single issue oriented law making.[863]

7.3.2.2. CSR and corporate interests

Since the first initiatives focussing on CSR there has always been the question of why companies should engage in it and whether it would provide added value for them. Okpara and Idowu identify four main motivations from companies to engage themselves in CSR: company reputation and legitimacy, cost and risk reduction, competitive

857 Tietenberg 1998, p. 588.
858 Konar and Cohen 1997, p. 110.
859 Lee 2014, p. 92–105.
860 Wesley *et al.* 2013, p. 36.
861 Sitnikov 2013, p. 117.
862 Cohen and Santhakumar 2007, p. 615+616.
863 Keenan and Rubin 188, p. 32; See also section 7.3.

advantage, and value creation by establishing synergies with stakeholders.[864] These motivations can also be linked to some extent. Strengthening one's reputation and legitimacy can also help to create new business opportunities and winning more customers, thereby ultimately also increasing shareholder value. A possible tool to increase one's reputation is increased dissemination of information about a firm's environmental and social performance. Having a good record with regard to CSR can also facilitate the attraction of more capital. This can be one of the competitive advantages that a firm can motivate to engage in CSR in the first place. Part of such a competitive advantage can be for example the fact that stakeholders will be more inclined to support the interests of the company if it is acting in an acceptable, socially responsible way.[865] This is also in line with findings from Kitzmueller and Shimshack who confirm that CSR records have an influence on the assessment of firms and their products and consumption decisions.[866] Corporate social performance can thus be advantageous for a firm's financial performance. Another interesting aspect brought forward by Porter, is that a responsible company might also be seen as a better employer by offering better working conditions due to increased monitoring and maintenance. This would provide an advantage in recruiting and retaining skilled employees.[867] As another potential benefit, engagement in CSR and being committed to stricter regulatory requirements can lead to an improved relationship with the regulator. Innes and Sam for example show a relationship between less regulatory scrutiny as a result of earlier over-compliance.[868]

European institutions have always been a driving force with regard to an agenda for CSR within the European Union.[869] Three recent documents give a good overview of the European approach to CSR and main considerations at stake. These are the Commission Communication on CSR from 2011[870] and two reports from the European Parliament dating from 2013.[871] These documents present CSR and its potential along similar lines to the academic literature. In its communication the European Commission also recognises the importance of incentivising corporations by market rewards to commit to good business conduct.[872] CSR can only play a meaningful role if it is translated into tangible advantages for businesses. To enable such rewards, however, better information for consumers will be necessary to allow them to make informed choices.[873] Also the Commission recognises the potential of CSR to provide reputational benefits for companies engaging in it.[874] In its opinion to the Parliament's report, the Committee of Legal Affairs further pointed at the need for more dialectics. More exchange and dialogue

864 Okpara and Idowu 2013, p. 13; Schmidpeter 2013, p. 176.
865 *Ibid.*, p. 8 ff.
866 Kitzmueller and Shimshack 2012, p. 74.
867 Porter 1995, p. 101.
868 Innes and Sam 2008.
869 Rahim and Nasrullah 2013, p. 184.
870 COM(2011) 681 final.
871 A7–0017/2013; A7–0023/2013.
872 COM(2011) 681 final, p. 5.
873 *Ibid.*, p. 10.
874 A7–0017/2013, p. 12.

between civil society and industry can increase the common knowledge base and come up with common strategies.[875]

There are studies that indeed provide some evidence that CSR can be of added value for companies and does deliver some tangible positive outcomes with regard to business performance. In a comprehensive meta study, Margolis *et al.* review existing empirical studies that address this issue and they conclude that there is a small but positive relationship between social and financial performance.[876]

7.3.3. Getting the nuclear industry on board – The Porter Hypothesis

The proposal as presented in chapter 6 puts a higher burden on the nuclear industry than is currently the case. The goals of the proposal are amongst others to achieve much higher amounts for compensation and also to terminate the subsidies to the nuclear sector in form of public funds. In general it can be said that the new proposal would lead to an increased scrutiny and responsibility to which nuclear operators would have to live up to within the European Union. Logically, these suggestions will not be welcomed by industry stakeholders, given the increased obligations and costs that would come along with these changes. It is, however, crucial for the success of the proposal that the industry shows genuine commitment to accept the proposal and also to comply with the stricter regulation of the new European regime. The Porter Hypothesis claims that stricter regulation can provide comparative advantages to industries complying with it compared to others not subject to it. The following sections will discuss this hypothesis and the extent to which it could contribute to convincing the nuclear industry as an important stakeholder to accept the proposal of chapter 6. There is ample literature about the Porter hypothesis and the following sections do not claim to provide an exhaustive analysis of it merits and theoretical foundations. Papers referenced are only used as an illustration of the different aspects of the Porter Hypothesis and the author does not aim to assess the methodology used in the respective papers. Rather there will be an attempt to deduce some core elements from the discussion that has been going on in the last years to analyse the potential of the Porter Hypothesis to increase support for the proposal as presented in chapter 6 amongst stakeholders in the nuclear industry.

7.3.2.1. Foundations of the Porter Hypothesis

In 1990, Michael Porter presented in his article on 'The Competitive Advantage of Nations' the idea that 'strict government regulations can promote competitive advantage by stimulating and upgrading domestic demand.'[877] In a short essay one year later he gave the examples of air pollution control in Germany and regulation against pesticides

875 *Ibid.*, p. 27.
876 Margolis *et al.* 2007, p. 22.
877 Porter 1990, p. 88.

and environmental damage in the US to show that in areas with very strict regulations these two countries were leading in terms of innovation.[878]

In a joint article with Claas van der Linde, we can find some more detailed explanation of the Porter Hypothesis. The argument that was made in that article is that an increased competitiveness can be the result of strict environmental regulations. These 'innovation offsets' would not only reduce the financial burden that results from compliance with such regulation, but could even outweigh these costs by being translated into an advantage compared with competing firms.[879] As an explanation for this phenomenon the authors explained that companies would not always by themselves make the best decisions. The authors presented a selection of case studies which supported their claims. They emphasised that 'the actual process of dynamic competition is characterised by changing technological opportunities coupled with highly incomplete information, organisational inertia and control problems reflecting the difficulty of aligning individual, group and corporate incentives.'[880] This can be overcome by suitably designed environmental regulation, which can lead to some advantages amongst which are raising awareness of resource inefficiencies, increasing certainty for investments and creating further pressure to enhance dynamic efficiency.[881] With regard to the question of what properly designed regulation looks like, Porter and van der Linde bring forward three main aspects: First of all, in the choice of regulatory instruments, as much flexibility as possible should be left with the industry in their choice of how to achieve innovation.[882] This goes together with another pre-requisite mentioned by Porter already in the early 1990's, that regulation should be outcome-based.[883] Next to this, continuous improvement should be aimed at, rather than prescribing a regulatory status quo which would hinder further innovation. Set goals need furthermore to be clearly defined and there should be as little uncertainty as possible during the regulatory process.[884] Complying with the principles laid out in their article would then allow them to overcome the environmental protection and industrial performance dichotomy by promoting both factors at the same time.[885]

7.3.2.2. Reception of the Porter Hypothesis

One of the most considered criticisms against the Porter hypothesis was brought forward by Palmer, Oates and Portney.[886] As a general point they criticise that the empirical evidence that has been brought forward to support the Porter Hypothesis is not really

878 Porter 1991.
879 Porter and van der Linde 1995, p. 98.
880 *Ibid.*, p. 99.
881 *Ibid.*, p. 99 + 100.
882 *Ibid.*, p. 110.
883 Porter 1991.
884 Porter and van der Linde 1995, p. 110.
885 Porter and van der Linde 1995, p. 116.
886 Palmer, Oates and Portney 1995.

convincing. Given the multitude of firms which are subject to environmental regulation, they state that it is not of any surprise to find examples amongst these firms where strict environmental regulation had its advantages.[887]

Further they question the view of Porter and van der Linde that companies would in a systematic way ignore possibilities for enhancing innovations, and they question whether government regulation is indeed needed to help firms overcome the 'organisational inertia' referred to by Porter and van der Linde.[888] This is also supported by Xepapadeas and de Zeeuw who do not see the need for environmental policy to stimulate innovation because firms would recognise this potential by themselves.[889]

Defusing some of the above-mentioned criticism, Ambec and Lanoie point out that studies which had been made to reject the Porter Hypothesis did not allow the dynamic dimension of the Porter Hypothesisto be taken into account. Further, they recall that one underlying aspect of the Porter Hypothesis is that the applied regulatory strategy does not rely on prescriptive regulation. Many of the studies criticising the Porter Hypothesis, however, did look at situations in which command and control regulation was used.[890] In their paper they conclude that better environmental performance can indeed be beneficial for firms.[891]

Referring to Palmer, Oates and Portney[892] as the main critics against the Porter Hypothesis, that only accept it in situations affecting the strategic behaviour of firms and in case companies do indeed overlook possible profits, Mohr and Saha provide some support for the Porter Hypothesis by stating that this view is too narrow.[893] They criticise studies which were used to disprove the Porter Hypothesis, as being were based on too simple assumptions, as for example perfect competition which cannot be taken as granted, and further do not take into account possible social benefits.[894]

7.3.2.3. Three versions of the Porter Hypothesis

The Porter Hypothesis has led considerable debate in the last decades. Policy makers were often in favour of it, whilst economists mostly heavily criticised it.[895] However, amongst authors that have been very critical with the Porter Hypothesis at least partial support can be identified, for example for the preference for incentivising regulation.[896] It seems that

887 *Ibid.*, p. 120.
888 *Ibid.*, p. 121+122.
889 Xepapadeas and de Zeeuw 1999, p. 166.
890 Ambec and Lanoie 2008, p. 53.
891 *Ibid.*, p. 57.
892 Palmer, Oates and Portney 1995.
893 Mohr and Saha 2008, p. 698.
894 *Ibid.*, p. 689 + 698.
895 See Ambec and Barla 2002, p. 355.
896 Palmer, Oates and Portney 1995, p. 120.

a more nuanced approach is needed and neither an unconditional adherence to, nor an outright rejection of, the Porter Hypothesis is of much added value for the further debate.

Jaffe and Palmer[897] pointed out that the Porter Hypothesis can be separated into three versions: A narrow one, a weak one and a strong one. The first considers that regulatory intervention can be more incentivising for firms to innovate if based on flexible instruments and standards. With regard to this version it can be said that this idea basically picks up the general notion of the better regulation movement with its call for more flexible regulatory instruments. The second version states that firms facing environmental regulation will invest resources in finding ways to fulfil the regulatory requirements at lower costs. Thereby the regulation will stimulate some environmental innovations. And lastly, the strong version claims that regulation will lead to innovation which outweighs the costs of complying with the regulation.[898] As implicitly already discussed above, the strong version of the Porter Hypothesis has been heavily attacked in literature.[899] However, more recent papers also find support for it.[900] Ambec et al. also present a mixed picture with regard to the strong version of the Porter Hypothesis.[901] Referring to older studies they point out that the strong version is not fully backed by empirical evidence.[902] However, they also establish that more recent studies provide more support for the strong version of the Porter Hypothesis.[903] Brännlund and Lundgren present a very comprehensive overview of empirical studies that do not give a clear picture either. Evidence presented shows that only the more recent studies provide some backing for the strong version of the Porter Hypothesis, while older studies cannot show a positive relation between environmental regulation and gains in productivity, some even revealed a negative correlation.[904]

Contrary to the divided opinions and studies on the strong version of the Porter Hypothesis, the soft version of the Porter Hypothesis finds more universal support in academic literature and can be regarded as widely accepted.[905] Ambec *et al.* refer to a multitude of studies that support the soft version by showing a positive relationship between environmental regulation and successful patent applications in the environmental field.[906] Esty and Porter show a positive correlation between a nation's competitiveness and a strict and well-structured environmental regulatory regime. Whilst they admit that correlation does not automatically prove causation, they emphasise that this finding strongly supports the weak version of the Porter Hypothesis.[907]

897 Jaffe and Palmer 1997.
898 *Ibid.*, p. 610.
899 See for example Palmer, Oates and Portney 1995.
900 See for example Berman and Bui 2001; Alpay *et al.* 2002.
901 Ambec *et al.* 2013.
902 *Ibid.*, p. 9; see also Jaffe *et al.* 1995.
903 Ambec *et al.* 2013, p. 15.
904 Brännlund and Lundgren 2009.
905 See for example Lanoie *et al.* 2011; Ambec *et al.* 2013.
906 Ambec *et al.* 2013, p. 8.
907 Esty and Porter 2005, p. 421.

7.3.2.4. Relevance of the Porter Hypothesis in the nuclear sector

The analysis of the Porter Hypothesis started with the aim to identify possibilities for how it could be used to convince industry stakeholders in the nuclear sector to accept the proposal as presented in chapter 6, laying down stricter rules and putting higher burdens on nuclear operators. The discussion in the sections above have shown that the strongest claim of the Porter Hypothesis that stricter regulation will lead to increased profits cannot be generally accepted. Therefore the stricter proposal of chapter 6 cannot be simply presented as a win-win scenario to the nuclear industry. However, the discussion in the previous sections has revealed some interesting aspects that can be of relevance to convince the nuclear industry to accept a reform of existing principles, even if they lead to increased scrutiny and higher burdens on the side of the operators. Jaffe and Palmer point out that stringent regulation can lead to a certain shock effect which can stimulate reconsideration of an industry's practices.[908] Such a questioning of existing principles is of special need in the nuclear sector. This statement has to be seen against the historical background of nuclear energy and its regulation within the European Union. When the European Atomic Energy Community was created, nuclear energy and the nuclear industry was regarded as a necessity to enhance living standards within the European Union. Article 1 of the Euratom Treaty states

> *'It shall be the task of the Community to contribute to the raising of the standard of living in the Member States and to the development of relations with the other countries by creating the conditions necessary for the speedy establishment and growth of nuclear industries.'*

This article stems from 1957 and has not been changed since then. It is doubtful that such a strong statement can still be upheld in the European Union of today, given viable alternatives to nuclear power generation. The reliance and hope that was put into nuclear energy is also nicely mirrored in an article by Weinberg in which he states that

> *'The society must then make the choice, and this is a choice that we nuclear people cannot dictate. We can only participate in making it. Is mankind prepared to exert the eternal vigilance needed to ensure proper and safe operation of its nuclear energy system? This admittedly is a significant commitment that we ask society. What we offer in return, an all but infinite source of relatively cheap and clean energy, seems to me to be well worth the price.'*[909]

The proposal can be seen as a step towards living up to the responsibility of 'eternal vigilance' and giving the nuclear industry the opportunity to take on the prime responsibility for nuclear power generation. In this light, the Porter Hypothesis and the discussion of its different versions is of relevance because it can provide flexible tools and it can also serve as a new impetus to rethink current principles. A differentiation at this point has to be made between the aspects of strengthened safety regulation and aspects

[908] Jaffe and Palmer 1997, p. 610.
[909] Weinberg 1972, p. 34.

of liability. A link between the arguments presented so far and stricter safety regulation is more obvious than linking it with aspects of liability. This difference will be discussed in the sections below.

7.3.2.4.1. Nuclear safety

The soft version of the Porter Hypothesis holds that stricter environmental regulation will lead to innovation. The reason for this being that once companies are facing stricter regulatory requirements, they are challenged to come up with new methods for complying with the regulation.[910] Using pollution abatement costs as a proxy for regulatory strictness and successful application of environmental patents as a proxy for innovation, Brunnermeier and Cohen show that a positive correlation exists between the two.[911] The value of intangible assets of a firm, consisting of, for example, patents and trademarks, increases with good environmental performance.[912] The nuclear industry can benefit from this in two ways. Increased innovation leading to a higher amount of successful patent applications also means opening new markets. If for example stricter regulation leads to the development of safer plant designs or other technical advancements in the nuclear sector, this creates market opportunities and can generate an additional source of income. Another aspect is that already existing markets reward companies for showing commitment to good environmental performance according to Konar and Cohen.[913] If nuclear operators manage to distinguish themselves from other nuclear operators, or from operators in other electricity sectors by stricter and safer regulation, this can increase their position on the market. It has to be admitted that his reasoning does not find universal support in the literature. Kitzmueller and Shimshack warn that often one cannot prove a link between environmental performance and increased innovation, eventually leading also to more financial gains.[914] However, they point at another interesting aspect of (over)complying with stricter regulation. A pro-active attitude of operators towards safety regulation can improve the relationship with regulators.[915]

In summary, it can be said that the Porter Hypothesis, and related literature, show that compliance with stricter regulatory standards can provide a number of advantages for nuclear operators. Be it better relations with the regulators or additional business opportunities and possibly enhanced profits. It also allows an assessment of regulatory strategies and how nuclear operators should face challenges posed by stricter regulation. This argument has to be seen together with a point made by Arjaliès and Ponssard who emphasise that stricter environmental regulation, and the reaction of firms to it, will only be financially beneficial if changes have been integrated into the internal processes

910 Brunnermeier and Cohen 2003, p. 279.
911 Brunnermeier and Cohen 2003.
912 Konar and Cohen 2001, p. 281+282.
913 *Ibid.*, p. 289.
914 Kitzmueller and Shimshack 2012, p. 70.
915 *Ibid.*, p. 76; see also Innes and Sam 2008.

of companies.[916] If this was the case, this argument could also encourage a good safety culture amongst workers in a nuclear power plant, a point that is of special importance in the nuclear sector, as also highlighted by the Nuclear Safety Directive.[917]

7.3.2.4.2. Nuclear liability

Linking the Porter Hypothesis to issues of liability is not very straightforward. The effect that was described in the previous section of stricter conditions leading to innovation is obviously not as such available when speaking about an increase of liability limits. However, if we look at further challenges that would arise from increasing liability limits, an argument in line with the soft version of the Porter Hypothesis can still be made. If higher liability limits lead to new markets for example for new insurance solutions to cover the higher amounts, this would also mean a form of innovation. However, profits made from this market will most probably not be reaped by the nuclear operators, but rather by the insurance industry. It can consequently be said, with regard to increasing the chances that nuclear operators would also be in favour of the proposal as presented in chapter 6, that the literature discussed in the previous sections does not provide immediate support. However, if higher liability limits are regarded as taking more responsibility, an increase of the limits can arguably have an effect on how nuclear operators are valued by consumers.[918] It can thereby also have an effect on the public acceptance of nuclear energy which would again benefit the nuclear industry.

7.3.4. An independent European Nuclear Agency

In times of EU scepticism and different challenges that the European Union is facing, not only in terms of legitimacy but also concerning the economic situation and social cohesion, the question has to be asked about how far the leading role of the Commission, or more generally the European Union is still desirable. Given the high standing of environmental issues amongst the population, however, it is exactly this field where the EU should strive for taking a leading role. Not only the Commission vis-à-vis the individual Member States, but also the EU as a whole on the international landscape. Picking up the issue of implementation and compliance, it has to be recalled that 'to be effective, a legal mandate must be well publicised, must be supported by an administrative structure able to detect most violations, an enforcement structure able to successfully prosecute most violations, and a range of sanctions sufficient to deter these violations.'[919] To achieve this within the nuclear sector, a strong authority is needed that can perform the role of a watchdog. This leads to the question of which agency or authority would be suited to play such a role in the EU with regard to nuclear safety and CSR as a tool to

[916] Arjaliès and Ponssard 2010, p. 4.
[917] Recital 19 Directive 2009/71/Euratom establishing a Community framework for the nuclear safety of nuclear installations.
[918] Kitzmueller and Shimshack draw this analogy more generally for the case of good CSR records, see Kitzmueller and Shimshack 2012, p. 74.
[919] Miller and Justice 2011, p. 177.

enhance nuclear safety as described in this chapter so far. For a watchdog to be effective, sufficient resources and competences are needed.[920] The Commission, *prima facie,* seems to be the best institution to do this. It is interesting to see that under the proposal for an amended Safety Directive the Commission indeed would have been empowered further than was the case until then, but this was heavily criticised by the industry questioning whether the Commission could legally play the role of a watch dog at all in light of the subsidiarity principle.[921] Such a statement is especially remarkable recalling article 258 TFEU which confers indeed a role as a watch dog upon the Commission.[922] Nevertheless the final amendment to the Safety Directive foresees a weaker role for the Commission.[923]

As a new impetus for an additional layer of checks and balances, the final suggestion that could enhance the chances of the proposal becoming reality in the European Union is therefore the creation of a new agency. Such an agency could on the one hand facilitate the functioning of a European system because certain aspects of the proposal from chapter 6 require an external body in order to function. This refers here more specifically to the issue of a European pooling system. An independent expert body could increase the chances that classifications into different risks were accepted. Such an agency could also be in charge of striving towards more uniform safety standards, another pre-requisite for a European pooling system to work.[924] In other high risk sectors there are agencies at the European level. In the oil and maritime sector there is for example the European Maritime Safety Agency or in the chemical sector the European Chemical Agency. The lack of an independent European agency in the area of nuclear safety is a flaw that needs to be remedied to accommodate the different interests at stake and to 'Europeanise' a solution for a European problem of potential transboundary pollution of nuclear accidents within the European Union.

7.3.4.1. Potential and limits of European agencies

In the literature, agencies are said to have some advantages within the institutional set up of the European Union. Agencies for example can take over some of the administrative tasks which would allow the Commission to play a more active role in the political agenda-setting and giving political guidance.[925] On the other hand, it has also been argued that handing over tasks to agencies can also lead to more fragmentation, which would come along with weakened accountability due to a more complex institutional structure by introducing agencies as another regulatory level. Furthermore, if agencies

920 Fanto 2010, p. 51.

921 FORATOM Position on the Commission's draft proposal to amend the Nuclear Safety Directive, p. 5.

922 Article 258 TFEU allows the Commission to initiate infringement proceedings against Member States in case of non-compliance with their obligations under the Treaties.

923 Compare article 8(e) as foreseen in the Draft Proposal COM(2013) 343 final with the final article 8(e) of the Council Directive 2014/87/EURATOM amending Directive 2009/71/Euratom establishing a Community framework for the nuclear safety of nuclear installations.

924 See section 6.5.3.

925 Vos 2000, p. 3.

are given too many political tasks this can raise concerns with regard to the legitimacy and legality of the agency.[926] However, a strict separation between managerial and scientific tasks on the one hand and political decisions on the other hand is untenable, especially in the area of environmental regulation given the sensitive nature of such regulation.[927] This observation certainly also holds true for the nuclear sector. The creation of a European Nuclear Agency would therefore need to be able to accommodate these tensions.

With regard to the limits of the mandate that an agency in the nuclear sector could have, the *Meroni*[928] case law is still the decisive authority. In that case it was held that powers that can be delegated to agencies have to remain under the supervision of the Commission and can only be 'clearly defined executive powers'. Discretionary powers would be outside of the scope set by the *Meroni* case law.[929] This limitation raises questions with regard to the extent to which a European Nuclear Agency could indeed be of added value and live up to the tasks as suggested above. Does the monitoring of safety levels of different nuclear powers plants and the classification of different power plants into different risk categories imply a certain margin of discretion, or can these tasks be said to be clearly defined and of an executive nature? The exact powers of a European Nuclear agency would need to be set against this background. It has, however, also been argued in the literature that the restrictive *Meroni* standard is not applied in its utmost severity anymore.[930] This would also provide some more leeway for the design of a European Nuclear Agency.

If an agency in the nuclear sector was created with clearly defined tasks, this could also have a positive effect on accountability, transparency and independence, compared to a situation in which the Commission, or committees of the Commission, will perform the task whilst it is not entirely clear what the respective tasks are and who is in charge of the process.[931] However, such advantages have to be balanced against concerns of legitimacy. Establishing a new agency automatically leads to the question of which position such an agency would take within the institutional structure of a regulatory system based on the separation of powers?[932]

Creating agencies also brings a danger common to any system that involves regulators, namely the issue of regulatory capture. This problem, however, should not be tackled by removing powers from agencies or making them less independent. Rather it has to be assured that there will be 'mechanisms ensuring transparency, political supervision and

926 *Ibid.*, p. 6.
927 *Ibid.*, p. 19.
928 Case 9/56 *Meroni & Co., Industrie Metallurgiche S.p.A.* v. *High Authority of the European Coal and Steal Community* [1958] and Case 10/56 *Meroni & Co., Industrie Metallurgiche S.p.A.* v. *High Authority of the European Coal and Steal Community* [1958].
929 Vos 2000, p. 9.
930 Vos 2000, p. 10.
931 Vos 2006, p. 120.
932 *Ibid.*, p. 121.

deliberative interaction with civil society'.[933] An increased use of agencies logically has to come along with functioning mechanisms of control and accountability.[934] The following section will therefore first discuss generally some aspects of accountability, and turn then to the question of how a European Nuclear Agency could function in order to strengthen a system of multi-level governance, thereby making the link to the more general discussion on strengthening multilevel governance as presented above in section 7.3.1, as another tool to enhance the chances of acceptance of the proposal.

7.3.4.2. A European Nuclear Agency and multi-level governance

When analysing multi-layered systems of governance, the accountability of the actors involved is of crucial importance. In the framework of the European Union for example it is continuously claimed in literature that deficits in accountability are the main reasons for the legitimacy problems the Union is faced with.[935] In the case of governance involving supranational authorities, accountability of these authorities is crucial in a democracy.[936] These concerns are of equal applicability in relation to the regulation of ultra-hazardous activities and even more generally whenever regulation is involved.[937] Multiple actors are involved and both regulators as well as regulated entities have to be accountable to another entity to increase the acceptability and functionality of a system regulating hazardous activities. This is in line with Bovens' definition of accountability as 'a relationship between an actor and a forum, in which the actor has an obligation to explain and to justify his or her conduct, the forum can pose questions and pass judgement, and the actor may face consequences.'[938] This definition follows a narrow approach of accountability. Descriptions of accountability as a broader concept can also be found in literature. Koppell for example describes accountability as a complex and multifaceted concept and identifies five dimensions of accountability: Transparency, liability, controllability, responsibility and responsiveness.[939] These dimensions have been criticised for being 'umbrella concepts themselves'[940] and therefore leading to the difficulty of how to empirically test whether an actor or institution is indeed subject to accountability. This elusive notion of accountability is also emphasised by Curtin, referring to it as being used as a container concept, fit to tackle different challenges and legitimacy concerns, but remaining relatively vaguely defined.[941] Even if a certain form of accountability is there, its effect is lost if it is not put into practice in a structured and visible way.[942]

933 Vos 2000, p. 11.
934 Vos 2006, p. 125.
935 For example Arnull and Wincott 2002 and Scharpf 1999.
936 Grant and Keohane 2005, p. 29.
937 Majone 1994, p. 212.
938 Bovens 2007, p. 450.
939 Koppell 2005, p. 95–99.
940 Bovens 2007, p. 450.
941 Curtin 2006, p. 246.
942 Curtin 2007, p. 540.

As Vos points out, a central part of accountability is transparency.[943] Allowing access to relevant documents will be necessary for accountability mechanisms to work properly. Nevertheless, merely the access to documents, and providing information, is as such not sufficient and cannot be regarded as living up to the requirement of accountability.[944] There also needs to be the possibility to debate important issues. This is a crucial factor to fill transparency and publicity with a real meaning.[945] Stakeholders must have the opportunity for complaints to enhance accountability. Mere information and participation will not be enough.[946] A European Nuclear Agency would present an opportunity to accommodate these challenges, taking on a form of a pioneering role, potentially strengthening multi-level governance in the European Union as a whole. This is in line with a view presented by Curtin according to which existing agencies on the European level can be regarded as 'breeding grounds and learning sites for state-of-the-art participatory practices that ultimately may be generalised across the wider spectrum of EU administration'.[947]

Agencies can also serve as a platform for the uniform application and interpretation of European law in a certain sector.[948] Thus, once a European system along the lines of the proposal of chapter 6 is accepted, a European Nuclear Agency could also play an important role in advancing expertise and providing legal certainty in the nuclear sector. If such an agency was designed in a way that it was more accessible than formal courts for the different actors at stake, it could also bridge the different levels in a multi-level governance setting by providing a centre for dialogue.[949] Thus a European Nuclear Agency could increase not only the chances of realisation of the proposal as presented in chapter 6 but it could also play its role in the process of implementation of a European system for nuclear liability.

943 Vos 2006, p. 129.
944 Curtin 2006, p. 256.
945 *Ibid.*, p. 258+259.
946 Curtin and Senden 2011, p. 185+186.
947 Curtin 2005 p. 113.
948 Vos 2006, p. 121.
949 Vos 2000, p. 20.

CONCLUSION

'The chances of an accident on [...] a [big] scale are exceedingly remote, as indeed are the chances of any nuclear accident of significance. It is highly unlikely that an accident would occur causing damage exceeding even the compulsory £5 million cover of the operator.'[950] These words of Lord Stonham, taken from the written proceedings of a reading on the Nuclear Installation Bill in the UK in 1969, mirrors very well the confidence and optimism that was put into nuclear energy production. Whilst the past decades have shown that indeed accidents of much larger scales are possible in the nuclear sector, the regulatory environment did not entirely keep pace with this realisation. Within the European Union the nuclear sector still remains to be regulated according to a Treaty that remained basically unchanged since its foundation in the 1950's and the international responses to the Fukushima accident did not seem to suggest major reforms either. Without claiming to provide an exhaustive analysis of the multitude of challenges that one can be faced with when dealing with the regulation of the nuclear sector, this PhD thesis therefore is intended to highlight some current shortcomings in this sector and present possible tools and suggestions for reform.

Research questions and summary of findings

At the beginning of this thesis, three main research questions were given, divided into several sub-questions. Before answering these questions, they are reproduced below:

Question 1: *Is the nuclear sector within the European Union currently regulated in a way that guarantees effective liability regimes for nuclear accidents?*

> Question 1a: *According to which core paradigms should ultra-hazardous activities be regulated* and *to what extent are the oil, chemical and nuclear sectors regulated in accordance with such paradigms*?

950 Lord Stonham, Reading on the Nuclear Installation Bill, 1969, http://hansard.millbanksystems.com/lords/1969/apr/21/nuclear-installations-bill#column_342 (last accessed on 21 August 2015).

Question 2: ***If question 1 has to be answered negatively, is the European legislator in a position to remedy these shortcomings by providing an improved European regime for nuclear liability?***

Question 2a: *Which lessons can be learned from the general principles of European law and experiences of national systems for the design of a European regime for nuclear liability?*

Question 2b: *Is there a sufficient legal basis providing the opportunity for a better and more coherent regulation of the nuclear sector?*

Question 2c: *Is a centralised or a decentralised regulation of nuclear safety and liability to be preferred within the European Union?*

Question 3: ***What should a European regime for nuclear liability look like and how can the relevant stakeholders be convinced of its necessity?***

Question 3a: *According to which major principles should nuclear liability be regulated?*

Question 3b: *How can a liability system enhance its inclusiveness and provide for a mutually reinforcing role of ex ante regulation and ex post liability?*

Question 3c: *How can the feasibility and implementation of a new European regime for nuclear liability, as suggested in this thesis, be enhanced?*

The following parts will provide answers to these research questions, divided into the respective parts of this thesis. For the main research questions 1 and 2 I will first answer the sub-questions before coming back to the main questions. With regard to question 3 the answer is sufficiently given by answering the sub-questions and will not be addressed separately to avoid repetition.

Part I

Question 1a: According to which core paradigms should ultra-hazardous activities be regulated and to what extent are the oil, chemical and nuclear sectors regulated in accordance with such paradigms?

It was shown that the regulation of ultra-hazardous activities can benefit from a joint use of safety regulation and liability rules. A comparison of different modes of regulation led to the conclusion that hybrid forms of regulations that allow for a certain degree of flexibility whilst minimising the risks of too loosely defined self-regulation should be preferred. With regard to the regulatory process this process should be as inclusive as possible because public participation does not only enhance its acceptance but can also enhance the quality of regulation. Dialectic processes should be preferred and an adversarial style of regulation was shown to be more in line with principles of openness and transparency than a consensual style of regulation. The oil and the chemical sector were identified as more responsive and adaptive to changing circumstances than the nuclear sector. With regard to the nuclear sector it was shown that its regulation stays isolated from more general developments of risk regulation as they can be identified in the other high risk sectors. It is less inclusive and a certain lack of transparency and public participation was identified.

Question 1: ***Is the nuclear sector within the European Union currently regulated in a way that guarantees effective liability regimes for nuclear accidents?***

The theoretical framework for the regulation of ultra-hazardous activities and a comparison of the nuclear sector with the oil and the chemical sector revealed that currently regulation of the nuclear sector does not guarantee effective liability regimes. The structure of the nuclear sector makes it particularly prone to rent seeking behaviour and due to a lack of a countervailing power, industry seems to succeed in pushing for lenient regulation. Liability limits are much too low and there is no meaningful interplay of *ex ante* and *ex post* incentives.

Part II

Question 2a: Which lessons can be learned from general principles of European law and experiences of national systems for the design of a European regime for nuclear liability?

The comparative analysis showed that limitation of liability is a common feature in national laws of states that do rely on nuclear energy, such as France and the UK. However, the example of Germany also showed that the introduction of unlimited liability can be a workable option, and the *Solidarvereinbarung* in Germany between the different nuclear operators could serve as an inspiration for a European pooling scheme.

To be in full compliance with the Polluter Pays Principle a preference should be given to unlimited liability and it was also shown that the Polluter Pays Principle can justify a broader definition of damages that would need to be covered by a European regime for nuclear liability. With regard to the Precautionary Principle the analysis showed that it can inspire a precautionary approach which justifies a stricter scrutiny and places higher burdens on the operators of nuclear power plants. It also has the potential to enhance the role of the general public because the Precautionary Principle highlights the multi-dimensional aspect of risk.

Question 2b: Is there a sufficient legal basis providing the opportunity for a better and more coherent regulation of the nuclear sector?

With regard to a suitable legal basis it was argued that the TFEU provides a sufficient legal basis for the establishment of a liability regime for nuclear accidents. Basing such a regime upon a dual legal basis of article 114 TFEU and 192 TFEU would enable a more comprehensive regulation of the nuclear sector, facilitating the transition from an industry that is regulated according to a treaty that is still based upon the conviction that nuclear energy needs to be promoted, towards a regulation based upon a more restrictive and controlling treaty. Such a shift would also live up to changed societal expectations and could close the gap between nuclear energy and environmental protection.

Question 2c: Is a centralised or a decentralised regulation of nuclear safety and liability to be preferred within the European Union?

Political drag and the risk of regulatory chill were brought forward as arguments to support the harmonisation of nuclear safety. An even stronger argument for harmonisation in that area is the need for economies of scale. The latter argument can also justify the harmonisation of nuclear liability in the European Union because this would enable a more efficient risk management of transboundary nuclear damage. The strongest argument for centralised regulation of nuclear liability in the European Union, however, was found in the risk that an externalisation of harm takes place.

Question 2: Is the European legislator in a position to remedy existing shortcomings by providing an improved European regime for nuclear liability?

It was shown that the European legislator is in a position to remedy some of the existing shortcomings. From an institutional law point of view the European Commission possesses sufficient competences to become active in the area of nuclear liability. Basing a European liability regime on the TFEU and thereby removing it from the ambits of the promotional Euratom Treaty would furthermore increase the leeway that the Commission would have to re-think the existing principles.

Part III

Question 3: What should a European regime for nuclear liability look like and how can the relevant stakeholders be convinced of its necessity?

Question 3a: According to which major principles should nuclear liability be regulated?

Liability of the nuclear operator should be strict. To further increase the deterrent effect of a liability regime there should be the possibility of introducing criminal sanctions if it can be shown that safety regulation has been violated. Operators should have a right of recourse if the damage that resulted from a nuclear accident was caused negligently by an act or omission against the person that was negligently acting or omitting to act. The liability of the operator should in principle be unlimited. If liability is limited, this right to limitation shall be linked to specific safety requirements and can be lost under certain circumstances specified in advance. The highest amounts of available funds should be guaranteed by using a multi-layered system relying on insurance and pooling solutions.

State intervention should only take place in a facilitative manner and subject to a premium to be charged for this intervention.

Question 3b: How can a liability system enhance its inclusiveness and provide for a mutually reinforcing role of ex ante regulation and ex post liability?

Regulation and liability can work as interdependent supplements if a meaningful interplay between these two mechanisms is found. The right to limit liability, if such a right exists, can for example be made dependent on the use of specific design standards. Furthermore a breach of safety regulation could break the right to limitation of liability. Another tool that would at the same time also enhance the regime's inclusiveness could be to allow that the disregard of public opinion can lead to or facilitate the establishment of liability in the case of an accident. If for example concerns that were raised during the licensing procedure either by experts or by the public in the course of a consultation were not taken into account but could have prevented or mitigated an accident, the right to limit liability could also be lost. With regard to the inclusiveness of a liability regime it furthermore has to be stressed that public participation should be facilitated as far as possible.

Question 3c: How can the feasibility and implementation of a new European regime for nuclear liability, as suggested in this thesis, be enhanced?

Following an economic analysis of federalism it was shown that there are arguments that can be used to convince Member States to strive for more centralised regulation. With regard to the European institutions as drivers for legislative change it was shown that an empowerment of environmental and other interest groups that do not pursue the interests of the nuclear industry could establish countervailing powers which could enable a more balanced regulation of the nuclear sector in line with the stricter requirements as proposed in this thesis. Furthermore, Corporate Social Responsibility could increase the costs of rent-seeking behaviour by putting more emphasis on transparency. An analysis of the Porter Hypothesis showed that the nuclear industry could also be convinced to support a stricter regulation of the nuclear sector if it realises the chances for more innovative efficiency resulting from this. Lastly an administrative tool could enhance the chances that the suggested changes would become reality. A European Nuclear Agency could facilitate the creation of a European nuclear liability regime by acting as an independent actor advancing expertise and providing legal certainty in the nuclear sector. An accessible agency could also counter-balance current shortcomings with regard to the inclusiveness of the nuclear sector and would present an opportunity to bridge the different levels in a multi-level governance setting by providing a centre for dialogue.

Policy recommendations

A number of policy recommendations are already apparent in the previous section dealing with the summary of the main findings of this thesis. In addition to these specific recommendations this section will also provide recommendations of a more general nature.

The analysis throughout this thesis has shown that a more active role of the European Union in the area of nuclear liability would be desirable. The international systems have been evolving very slowly and experiences in the oil sector, for example, have shown how an active Commission can press for far reaching changes in international conventions. If the Commission were to become more active in this field another recommendation would be to remain very critical towards the existing international principles in the area of nuclear liability. This thesis has criticised some of these fundamental principles and has shown their inefficiency. To remedy these inefficiencies, a European initiative in the area of nuclear liability should in particular pay special attention to two aspects: The introduction of unlimited liability and a reconsideration of the principle of legal channelling. If liability limits continue in use, the right to limitation of liability should be linked to specified criteria to allow the breaking of the limits in case of, for example, violation of safety regulation. Concerning the principle of legal channelling an automatic right of recourse for nuclear operators should be considered in the light of the inefficient incentives that legal channelling provides to designers and suppliers if applied in its current form as laid down in the international conventions.

It is furthermore of crucial importance that the available funds are significantly increased. In doing so a shift is necessary from public funding to more private funding. Government intervention should be the exception and *ad hoc* solutions should be avoided. If it takes place it should take place according to economic criteria and always in a facilitative manner. If risk-based premiums are charged for such intervention it could play a supplementary role in enhancing the available amounts of compensation.

Lastly it has to be stressed that Member States relying on nuclear energy have to live up to their responsibility towards other Member States, particularly Member States that decided against the use of nuclear power generation. Nuclear energy has a role to play in the European energy mix and the nuclear industry has to realise the potential that lies in a stricter regulation of the nuclear sector. If the nuclear industry takes its obligations seriously this will also have an effect of the public acceptance of nuclear energy.

Limits and future research

The first limitation concerns the methodology used in his research because it did not rely on empirics. An empirical part could have provided different or more insights into the problems at stake and could have provided a more practical approach. The current analysis relies mostly on theoretical considerations. With regard to the role of the different actors at stake, for example interviews with some of the important stakeholders involved could have provided a deeper insight into the problems at stake and could be a topic of future research. A possible difficulty with such an approach, however, could be the accessibility of relevant stakeholders.

Excluded from the scope of this PhD are issues dealing with nuclear waste and the challenges to find a long term or final repository. Whilst these considerations are also of crucial importance they were not included in the analysis of this thesis. How these aspects could have an influence on the existence of the nuclear sector as a whole, together with the Precautionary Principle that arguably finds a stronger application in this area, certainly merits further research.

Another point for further research is whether the different liability regimes that currently exist in the European Union raise problems with regard to the principle of equal treatment. The Gomez Acebo Study for example observed that no action at European level might even lead to claims based on the principle of non-discrimination, having in mind the different ways in which victims of nuclear accidents would be treated at the moment due to the non-harmonised liability regime.[951] Recalling, however, that such differences can also be regarded as the result of differences in national preferences as for example discussed by Hofstede,[952] such a statement cannot be accepted right away and further research could show whether indeed this angle would provide additional justification for a more active role of the Commission in the area of nuclear liability.

A final point for further research follows directly from one part of the analysis of this thesis. Concerning the search for an appropriate legal basis for a nuclear liability regime a dual legal basis of article 114 TFEU and 192 TFEU was suggested. A point for future research would be to assess whether a dual legal basis would also be possible between the TFEU and the Euratom Treaty and what effects such a dual legal basis would have on the delineation of competences between these two treaties.

Lastly I want to stress that from the very outset of this project it faced one particular limit and this was that the research of this PhD thesis was very ambitious and very modest at the same time. The ambition was to capture core aspects of the nuclear sector and its regulation and to criticise the current regimes whilst at the same time also wanting to present solutions for how to make it better. This necessitated a broad approach, covering a multitude of issues. A general limitation of this work is therefore that several aspects could have been evaluated in much further detail but a choice had been made to strive for such a holistic overview, sometimes even willing to sacrifice a certain amount of depth in analysis for this. That aspect constitutes the modesty of the research presented in his thesis. It is, however, the author's conviction that only this approach can enable the reader to understand the underlying difficulties that one is faced with in the nuclear sector and which need to be tackled when rethinking its regulation.

951 Legal Study for the Accession of Euratom to the Paris Convention on Third Party Liability in the Field of Nuclear Energy, TREN/CC/01-2005, p. 61.

952 Hofstede 2001.

POLICY DOCUMENTS, GUIDELINES, REPORTS

Ameye 2014
Ameye, E., 'United States and India: two nuclear states with legislation that truly holds responsible parties liable in case of a nuclear accident', *Journal of Risk Research*, 2014.

Arjaliès and Ponssard 2010
Arjaliès, D.-L. and Ponssard, J.-P., 'A Managerial Perspective on the Porter Hypothesis: The Case of CO2 Emissions', *Cahier de recherche 2010-02*, 2010.

A7-0017/2013
Report on Corporate Social Responsibility: accountable, transparent and responsible business behaviour and sustainable growth

A7-0023/2013
Report on Corporate Social Responsibility: promoting society's interest and a route to sustainable and inclusive recovery

Black and Jacobzone 2009
Black, J. and Jacobzone, S., 'Tools for Regulatory Quality and Financial Sector Regulation: A Cross-Country Perspective', *OECD Working Papers on Public Governance*, No. 16, OECD Publishing, 2009.

CEO report 2012
Nuclear Contamination: A year after Fukushima, why does Brussels still back nuclear power?, *Corporate Europe Observatory*, 2012.

COM (2003) 624 final
Proposal for a Directive of the European Parliament and of the Council on access to justice in environmental matters

COM(2013) 343 final
Draft Proposal for a Council Directive amending Directive 2009/71/EURATOM establishing a Community framework for the nuclear safety of nuclear installations

Danzi 2009
Danzi, E., 'Some Reflections on the Exclusion of Nuclear Damage from the Scope of Application of the Environmental Liability Directive', *Regional Conference 2009 of the German Branch of AIDN/INLA*, 2009.

De Witte *et al.* 2010
De Witte, B. *et al.*, 'Legislating after Lisbon: New Opportunities for the European Parliament', *Robert Schuman Centre for Advanced Studies*, 2010.

Emmerechts 2010
Emmerechts, S., 'Environmental Protection under Nuclear Law: Still a Long Way to go', *International Nuclear Law: History, Evolution and Outlook*, OECD, 2010.

Froggatt and Carroll 2010
Froggatt, A. and Carroll, S., 'Third Party Insurance: The Nuclear Sector's "Silent" Subsidy in Europe', in: Sokolski, H. (ed.), *Nuclear Power's Global Expansion: Weighing Its Costs and Risks*, The Strategic Studies Institute Publications Office, 2010.

Herlin-Karnell 2008
Herlin-Karnell, E., 'The Lisbon Treaty and the Area of Criminal Law and Justice', 2008(3) *Swedish Institue for European Policy Studies*, 2008.

Kohlemainen 1999
Kohlemainen, H., 'The Modernisation of the International Nuclear Third Party Liability Regime – Does Exclusive Liability still make Sense?', *Reform of Civil Nuclear Liability, International Symposium Budapest*, OECD NEA, 1999.

Margolis *et al.* 2007
Margolis, J.D. *et al.*, 'Does it Pay to be Good? A Meta-Analysis and Redirection of Research on the Relationship between Corporate Social and Financial Performance', 2007.

Pelzer 1999
Pelzer, N., 'Focus on the Future of Nuclear Liability Law', *Reform of Civil Nuclear Liability, International Symposium Budapest*, OECD NEA, 1999.

Pelzer 2013
Pelzer, N., 'Operators' pooling arrangement: a national and international perspective', *OECD/NEA Wokshop*, 2013.

Rehbinder 2010
Rehbinder, E., 'Liability for Nuclear Harm under the German Atomic Energy Act', 2010.

Schwartz 2006
Schwartz, J., 'International Nuclear Third Party Liability Law: The Response to Chernobyl', *International Nuclear Law in the Post-Chernobyl Period,* OECD, 2006.

Smrkolj 2008
Smrkolj, M., 'The Use of the "Disconnection Clause" in International Treaties: What does it tell us about the EC/EU as an Actor in the Sphere of Public International Law?' *Garnet Conference*, 2008.

Von Busekist 2006
Von Busekist, O., 'A Bridge Between Two Conventions on Civil Liability for Nuclear Damage: the Joint Protocol Relating to the Application of the Vienna Convention and the Paris Convention', OECD, 2006.

Vogel 2001
Vogel, D., 'The New Politics of Risk Regulation in Europe', *London School of Economics and Political Science*, 2001.

Vos 2000
Vos, E., 'European Administrative Reform and Agencies', *EUI Working Papers*, 2000.

LEGISLATION

International Conventions

Paris Convention on Third Party Liability in the Field of Nuclear Energy as amended by the Additional Protocol of 28 January 1964 and by the Protocol of 16 November 1982, and by the Protocol of 12 February 2004.
Vienna Convention as Amended by the Protocol of 12 September 1997 to Amend the Vienna Convention on Civil Liability for Nuclear Damage.
International Convention on Civil Liability for Oil Pollution Damage, 1969.
International Convention on the Establishment of an International Fund for Compensation for Oil Pollution Damage, 1971.
International Convention for the Prevention of Pollution From Ships, 1973.
International Convention for the Safety of Life at Sea, 1974.
Joint Protocol relating to the Application of the Vienna Convention and the Paris Convention, 1988.
Convention on Environmental Impact Assessment in a Transboundary Context, 1991.
International Convention on Civil Liability for Oil Pollution Damage, 1992.
International Convention on the Establishment of an International Fund for Compensation for Oil Pollution Damage, 1992.
Lugano Convention on Civil Liability for Damage Resulting from Activities Dangerous to the Environment, 1993.
Convention on Nuclear Safety, 1994.
Convention on Access to Information, Public Participation in Decision-Making and Access to Justice in Environmental Matters, 1998.
Convention on Supplementary Compensation for Nuclear Damage, 1998.
Protocol of 2003 to the International Convention on the Establishment of an International Fund for Compensation for Oil Pollution Damage, 2003.

EU Sources

Directive 75/442/EEC of 15 July 1975 on waste.
Recommendation 75/436/Euratom, ECSC, EEC of 3 March 1975 on cost allocation and action by public authorities on environmental matters.

Directive 82/501/EEC of 24 June 1982 on the major-accident hazards of certain industrial activities.

Regulation (Euratom) No. 3954/87 of 22 December 1987 laying down maximum permitted levels of radioactive contamination of foodstuffs and of feedingstuffs following a nuclear accident or any other case of radiological emergency.

Directive 96/82/EC of 9 December 1996 on the control of major-accident hazards involving dangerous substances.

Commission Decision 1999/329/EC [1999].

Communication from the Commission of 2 February 2000 on the precautionary principle.

Communication from the Commission of 21 March 2000 to the European Parliament and the Council on the Safety of the Seaborne Oil Trading.

Communication from the Commission of 6 December 2000 to the European parliament and the Council on a Second Set of Measures on Maritime Safety following the sinking of the Oil Tanker Erika.

Regulation 44/2001 of 22 December 2000 on jurisdiction and the recognition and enforcement of judgments in civil and commercial matters.

Regulation (EC) No 1406/2002 of 27 June 2002 establishing a European Maritime Safety Agency.

Directive 2003/4/EC of 28 January 2003 on public access to environmental information and repealing Council Directive 90/313EEC.

Regulation 358/2003 of 27 February 2003 on the application of Article 81(3) of the Treaty to certain categories of agreements, decisions and concerted practices in the insurance sector.

Directive 2003/35/EC of 26 May 2003 providing for public participation in respect of the drawing up of certain plans and programmes relating to the environment and amending with regard to public participation and access to justice Council Directives 85/337EEC and 96/61/EC.

Directive 2003/105/EC of 16 December 2003 amending Council Directive 96/82/EC on the control of major-accident hazards involving dangerous substances.

Directive 2004/35/EC of 21 April 2004 on environmental liability with regard to the prevention and remedying of environmental damage.

Council Decision 2005/370/EC of 17 February 2005 on the conclusion, on behalf of the European Community, of the Convention on access to information, public participation in decision-making and access to justice in environmental matters.

Directive 2005/35/EC of 7 September 2005 on ship-source pollution and on the introduction of penalties for infringements.

Directive 2006/12/EC of 5 April 2006 on waste which was repealed by Directive 2008/98/EC of the European Parliament and of the Council of 19 November 2008 on waste and repealing certain Directives.

Recommendation 2006/851/Euratom of 24 October 2006 on the management of financial resources for the decommissioning of nuclear installations, spent fuel and radioactive waste confirms the applicability of the Polluter Pays Principle to the nuclear sector.

Regulation (EC) No 1907/2006 of 18 December 2006 concerning the the Registration, Evaluation, Authorisation and Restriction of Chemicals (REACH), establishing a European Chemicals Agency, amending Directive 1999/45/EC and repealing Council Regulation (EEC) No 793/93 and Commission Regulation (EC) No 1488/94 as well as Council Directive 76/769/EEC and Commission Directives 91/155/EEC, 93/67/EEC, 93/105/EC and 2000/21/EC.

Communication from the Commission to the Council and the European Parliament - Nuclear Illustrative Programme, presented under Article 40 of the Euratom Treaty for the opinion of the European Economic and Social Committee COM(2006) 844 final (10th of January 2007).

Council Regulation (EC) 864/2007 of 11 July 2007 on the law applicable to non-contractual obligations.

Commission Decision 2007/530 Euratom of 17 July 2007 on establishing the European High Level Group on Nuclear Safety and Waste Management.

Commission decision 2008/281/EC, [2008].

Directive 2008/56/EC of 17 June 2008 establishing a framework for Community action in the field of marine environmental policy.

Council Directive 2009/71/Euratom of 25 June 2009 establishing a Community framework for the nuclear safety of nuclear installations.

Commission Regulation 267/2010 of 24 March 2010 on the application of Article 101(3) of the Treaty on the Functioning of the European Union to certain categories of agreements, decisions and concerted practices in the insurance sector.

Council Directive 2011/70/Euratom of 19 July 2011 establishing a Community framework for the responsible and safe management of spent fuel and radioactive waste.

Communication from the Commission 25 October 2011 to the European Parliament, The Council, The European Economic and Social Committee and the Committee of the Regions - A renewed EU strategy 2011–2014 for Corporate Social Responsibility

Directive 2011/92/EU of 13 December 2011 on the assessment of the effects of certain public and private projects on the environment.

Directive 2012/18/EU of the European Parliament and of the Council of 4 July 2012 on the control of major-accident hazards involving dangerous substances, amending and subsequently repealing Council Directive 96/82/EC.

Directive 2014/87/Euratom of 8 July 2014 amending Directive 2009/71/Euratom establishing a Community framework for the nuclear safety of nuclear installations.

BIBLIOGRAPHY

Adelle and Anderson 2013
Adelle, C. and Anderson, J., 'Lobby groups', in: Jordan, A. and Adelle, C. (eds.), *Environmental Policy in the EU: Actors, Institutions and Processes*, Oxon: Routledge, 2013.

Ahner *et al.* 2012
Ahner, N. *et al.*, 'Differentiated Integration Revisited: EU Energy Policy as Experimental Ground for a Schengen Successor?', 39(2) *Legal Issues of Economic Integration*, 2012, p. 249–272.

Alpay *et al.* 2002
Alpay, E.S. *et al.*, 'Productivity Growth and Environmental Regulation in Mexican and U.S. Food Manufacturing', 84(4) *American Journal of Agricultural Economics*, 2002, p. 887–901.

Ambec *et al.* 2013
Ambec, S. *et al.*, 'The Porter Hypothesis at 20: Can Environmental Regulation Enhance Innovation and Competitiveness?', 7(1) *Review of Environmental Economics and Policy*, 2013, p. 1–21.

Ambec and Barla 2002
Ambec, S. and Barla, P., 'A theoretical foundation of the Porter hypothesis', 75(3) *Economics Letters*, 2002, p. 355–360.

Ambec and Barla 2002
Ambec, S. and Barla, P., 'Can Environmental Regulations be Good for Business? An Assessment of the Porter Hypothesis', 14(2) *Energy Studies Review*, 2006, p. 42–62.

Ambec and Lanoie 2008
Ambec, S. and Lanoie, P., 'Does it Pay to be Green? A Systematic Overview', 22(4) *Academy of Management Perspectives*, 2008, p. 45–62.

Ameye 2010
Ameye, E., 'Channelling of Nuclear Third Party Liability towards the Operator: Is it Sustainable in a Developing Nuclear World or is there a Need for Liability of Nuclear Architects and Engineers?', 19(1) *European Energy and Environmental Law Review*, 2010, p. 33–58.

Ameye and Arregui 2012
Ameye, E. and Arregui,I.I., 'National nuclear third party insurance pools revisited from a European Union competition law perspective', 30(3) *Journal of Energy & Natural Resources Law*, 2012, p. 265–300.

Applegate 2000
Applegate, J.S., 'The Precautionary Preference: An American Perspective on the Precautionary Principle', 6(3) *Human and Ecological Risk Assessment*, 2000, p. 414–443.

Arcuri 2005
Arcuri, A., *Governing the Risk of Ultra Hazardous Activities. Challenges for Contemporary Legal Systems*, dissertation, Rotterdam: Erasmus University, 2005.

Armour *et al.* 2009
Armour, J. *et al.*, 'Transactions with creditors', in: Kraakman *et al.* (eds.), *The Anatomy of Corporate Law*, Oxford: Oxford University Press, 2009.

Armstrong 2002
Armstrong, K.A., 'Mutual Recognition', in: Barnard, C. and Scott, J. (eds.) *The Law of the Single European Market*, Oxford: Hart Publishing, 2002.

Arnull and Wincott 2002
Arnull, A. and Wincott, D., *Accountability and legitimacy in the European Union*, Oxford: Oxford University Press, 2002.

Ayres and Braithwaite 1992
Ayres, I. and Braithwaite, J., *Responsive Regulation: Transcending the Regulatory Debate*, New York: Oxford University Press, 1992.

Baldwin 1997
Baldwin, R., 'Regulation: After Command and Control', in: Hawkins (ed.), *The Human Face of Law*, Oxford: Clarendon Press, 1997.

Barents 1993
Barents, R., 'The Internal Market Unlimited: Some Observations on the Legal Basis of Community Legislation', 30(1) *Common Market Law Review*, 1993, p. 85–109.

Barker *et al.* 2010
Barker *et al.*, 'Can a Participatory Approach Contribute to Food Chain Risk Analysis?', 30(5) *Risk Analysis*, 2010, p. 766–781.

Barnard 1992
Barnard, C., 'Where politicians fear to tread?, 17(2) *European Law Review*, 1992, p. 127–133.

Beck 1998
Beck, U., *World Risk Society*, Oxford: Polity Press, 1998.

Becker 1968
Becker, G.S., 'Crime and Punishment: An Economic Approach', 76(2) *Journal of Political Economy*, 1968, p. 169–217.

Becker 1983
Becker, G.S., 'A Theory of Competition Among Pressure Groups for Political Influence', 98(3) *The Quarterly Journal of Economics*, 1983, p. 371–400.

Becker 1989
Becker, G.S., 'Political Competition Among Interest Groups', in: Shogren, J.F. (ed.), *The Political Economy of Government Regulation*, Dordrecht: Kluwer Academic Publishers, 1989.

Bengtsson 2010
Bengtsson, G., 'Global Trends in Chemical Management', in: Eriksson, J., Gilek M. and Rudén, C. (eds.), *Regulating Chemical Risks*, Dordrecht: Springer, 2010.

Berman and Bui 2001
Berman, E. and Bui, L.T.M., 'Environmental Regulation and Productivity: Evidence from Oil Refineries', 83(3) *Review of Economics and Statistics*, 2001, p. 498–510.

Bhagwati and Hudec 1997
Bhagwati, J. and Hudec, R.E., *Fair trade and Harmonisation: prerequisites for free trade?*, Cambridge: MIT Press, 1997.

Birnie and Boyle 2002
Birnie, P. and Boyle, A., *International Law and the the Environment*, Oxford: Oxford University Press, 2002.

Bovens 2007
Bovens, M., 'Analysing and Assessing Accountability: A Conceptual Framework', 13(4) *European Law Journal*, 2007, p. 447–468.

Bovens 2007a
Bovens, M., 'New Forms of Accountability and EU-Governance', 5(1) *Comparative European Politics*, 2007, p. 104–120.

Bowles *et al.* 2008
Bowles *et al.*, 'The Scope of Criminal Law and Criminal Sanctions: An Economic View and Policy Implications', 35(3) *Journal of Law and Society*, 2008, p. 389–416.

Boyle 2011
Boyle, A., 'Developments in the International Law of Environmental Impact Assessments and their Relation to the Espoo Convention', 20(3) *Review of European Community & International Environmental Law*, 2011, p. 227–231.

Braithwaite 2006
Braithwaite, J., 'Responsive Regulation and Developing Economies', 34(5) *World Development*, 2006, p. 884–898.

Braithwaite and Drahos 1999
Braithwaite, J. and Drahos, P., 'Ratcheting Up and Driving Down Global Regulatory Standards', 42(4) *The Society for International Developments*, 1999, p. 109–114.

Broberg *et al.* 2013
Broberg, T. *et al.*, 'Testing the Porter Hypothesis: the effects of environmental investments on efficiency in Swedish industry', 40(1) *Journal of Productivity Analysis*, 2013, p. 43–56.

Bronckers and van Gerven 2009
Bronckers, M. and van Gerven, Y., 'Legal remedies under the EC's new Chemicals Legislation REACH: Testing a new model of European Governance', 46(6) *Common Market Law Review*, 2009, p. 1823–1871.

Brown 1998
Brown, J.M., 'Parent Corporation's Liability under CERCLA Section 107 for the Environmental Violations of Their Subsidiaries', 31(4) *Tulsa Law Review*, 1996, p. 819–850.

Bruggemann et al. 2012
Bruggemann, V. *et al.*, 'Stimulating Insurability of Catastrophic Risks by the Government', 23(1) *Duke Environmental Law & Policy Forum*, 2012, p. 185–241.

Brunnermeier and Cohen 2003
Brunnermeier, S.B. and Cohen, M.A., 'Determinants of environmental innovations in US manufacturing industries', 45(2) *Journal of Environmental Economics and Management*, 2003, p. 278–293.

Bubna-Litic 2011
Bubna-Litic, K., 'Compliance and Enforcement Related to Mandatory Corporate Reporting Requirements: Is there a Future?', in: Paddock, L. *et al.* (eds.), *Compliance and Enforcement in Environmental Law*, Cheltenham: Edward Elgar Publishing, 2011.

Buchanan 1984
Buchanan, J.M., 'Politics without Romance: A Sketch of Positive Public Choice Theory and Its Normative Implications', in: Buchanan, J.M. and Tollison, R.D. (eds.), *The Theory of Public Choice – II*, Michigan: University of Michigan Press, 1984.

Buchanan and Tullock 1965
Buchanan, J.M. and Tullock, G., *The calculus of consent*, Michigan: University of Michigan Press, 1965.

Cameron 2007
Cameron, P.D., *Competition in Energy Markets. Law and Regulation in the European Union*, New York: Oxford University Press, 2007.

Carroll 2008
Carroll, S., 'Perspective on the Pros and Cons of a Pooling-type Approach to Nuclear Third Party Liability', *Nuclear Law Bulleting*, 2008, p. 75–97.

Carroll 2009
Carroll, S., 'European Challenges to Promoting International Pooling and Compensation for Nuclear Reactor Accidents', *Social Science Research Network*, 2009, p. 1–38.

Chandler 2003
Chandler, G., 'The Curse of "Corporate Social Responsibility"', 2(1) *New Academy Review*, 2003, p. 31–34.

Cenevska 2009
Cenevska, I., 'The exercise of giving way to "giving in" – some aspects of the Member States' Euratom obligations revisited', 6(4) *Journal for European Environmental & Planning Law*, 2009, p. 481–493.

Cenevska 2010
Cenevska, I., 'The European Parliament and the European Atomic Energy Community: a legitimacy crisis?', 35(3) *European Law Review*, 2010, p. 415–424.

Chalmers 2010
Chalmers, D., *European Union law*, Cambridge: Cambridge University Press, 2010.

Chapman 2007
Chapman, A., *Democratizing Technology: Risk Responsibility and the Regulation of Chemicals*, London: Earthscan, 2007.

Coffey 1994
Coffey, M.P., 'In Defense of Limited Liability – a Reply to Hansmann and Kraakman', 1(1) *George Mason University Law Review*, 1994, p. 59–92.

Coglianese 2006
Coglianese, C., 'Citizen Participation in Rulemaking: Past, Present, and Future', 55(5) *Duke Law Journal*, 2006, p. 943–968.

Cohen and Santhakumar 2007
Cohen, M.A. and Sanhakumar, V., 'Information Disclosure as Environmental Regulation: A Theoretical Analysis', 37(3) *Environmental & Resource Economics*, 2007, p. 599–620.

Craig and de Burca 2008
Craig, P. and de Burca, G., *EU Law: Text, Cases and Materials*, Oxford: Oxford University Press, 2008

Craig and de Burca 2011
Craig, P. and de Burca, G., *EU Law: Text, Cases and Materials*, Oxford: Oxford University Press, 2011.

Currie 2008
Currie, D.E.J., 'The Problems and Gaps in the Nuclear Liability Conventions and an Analysis of How an Actual Claim would be brought under the current existing Treaty Regime in the Event of a Nuclear Accident', 35(1) *Denver Journal on International Law and Policy*, 2008, p. 85–127.

Curtin 2006
Curtin, D., 'Delegation to EU Non-Majoritarian Agencies and Emerging Practices of Public Accountability', in: Geradin *et. al.* (eds.), *Regulation through Agencies in the EU: A new Paradigm of European Governance*, Cheltenham: Edward Elgar, 2006.

Curtin 2007
Curtin, D., 'Holding (Quasi-)Autonomous EU Administrative Actors to Public Account', 13(4) *European Law Journal*, 2007, p. 523–541.

Curtin and Meijer 2006
Curtin, D. and Meijer, A.J., 'Does Transparency strengthen legitimacy?', 11(2) *Information Polity*, 2006, p. 109–122.

Curtin and Senden 2011
Curtin, D. and Senden, L., 'Public Accountability of Transnational Private Regulation: Chimera or Reality?', 38(1) *Journal of Law and Society*, 2011, p. 163–188.

Cusack 2003
Cusack, T.F., 'A Tale of two Treaties: An Assessment of the Euratom Treaty in Relation to the EC Treaty', 40(1) *Common Market Law Review*, 2003, p. 117–142.

Dawar 2010
Dawar, K., 'Disconnection Clauses: An Inevitable Symptom of Regionalism?', 2010(11) *Society of International Economic Law*, 2010, p. 1–10.

De Burca 2008
De Burca, G., 'Developing Democracy Beyond the State', 46(2) *Columbia Journal of Transnational Law*, 2008, p. 221–278.

Dearborn 2009
Dearborn, M., 'Enterprise Liability: Reviewing and Revitalizing Liability for Corporate Groups', 97(1) *California Law Review*, 2009, p. 195–262.

De Sadeleer 2002
De Sadeleer, N., *Environmental Principles: From Political Slogans to Legal Rules*, Oxford: Oxford University Press, 2002.

De Sadeleer 2012
De Sadeleer, N., 'Principle of Subsidiarity and the EU Environmental Policy', 9(1) *Journal for European Environmental Planning Law*, 2012, p. 63–70.

De Sadeleer 2012a
De Sadeleer, N., 'Environmental Governance and the Legal Bases Conundrum', 31(1) *Yearbook of European Law*, 2012, p. 373–401.

De Smedt 2009
De Smedt, K., 'Is Harmonisation Always Effective? The Implementation of the Environmental Liability Directive', 18(1) *European Energy and Environmental Law Review*, 2009, p. 2–18.

Ebbesson 2006
Ebbesson, J., 'Transboundary corporate responsibility in environmental matters: fragments and foundations for a future framework ', in: Winter, G. (ed.), *Multilevel Governance of Global Environmental Change*, Cambridge: Cambridge University Press, 2006.

Ebbesson 2010
Ebbesson, J., 'The rule of law in governance of complex socio-ecological changes', 20 *Global Envrionmental Change*, 2010, p. 414–422.

Ebbesson 2011
Ebbesson, J., 'A Modest Contribution to Environmental Democracy and Justice in Transboundary Contexts: The Combined Impact of the Espoo Convention and Aarhus Convention', 20(3) *Review of European Community & International Environmental Law*, 2011, p. 248–257.

Emiliou 1994
Emiliou, N., 'Opening Pandora's Box: the legal basis of Community measures before the Court of Justice' 19(5) *European Law Review*, 1994, p. 488–507.

Esty and Geradin 1998
Esty, D.C., and Geradin, D., 'Environmental Protection and International Competitiveness: A Conceptual Framework', 32(3) *Journal of World Trade,* 1998, p. 5–46

Esty and Geradin 2001
Esty, D.C., and Geradin, D., 'Regulatory Co-opetition', in: Esty and Geradin (eds.), *Regulatory Competition and Economic Integration,* Oxford: Oxford University Press, 2001.

Esty and Porter 2005
Esty, D.C. and Porter, M.E., 'National Environmental Performance: An Empirical Analysis of Policy Results and Determinants', 10(4) *Environment and Development Economics,* 2005, p. 391–434.

Fanto 2010
Fanto, J., 'Organizational Liability', 19 *Journal of Law & Policy,* 2010, p. 45–54.

Faure 1995
Faure, M., 'Economic Models of Compensation for damage Caused by Nuclear Accidents: Some Lessons for the Revision of the Paris and Vienna Conventions', 2(1) *European Journal of Law and Economics,* 1995, p. 21–43.

Faure 1998
Faure, M., 'Harmonisation of Environmental Law and Market Integration: Harmonising for the wrong reasons?', *European Environmental Law,* 1998, p. 169–174.

Faure 2000
Faure, M., 'The Harmonisation, Codification and Integration of Environmental Law: A Search for Definitions', *European Environmental Law,* 2000, p. 174–182.

Faure 2000a
Faure, M., 'Product Liability and Product Safety in Europe: Harmonisation or Differentiation?', 53(4) *Kyklos,* 2000, p. 467–508.

Faure 2001
Faure M., 'Regulatory Competition vs Harmonisation in EU Environmental Law', in: Esty and Geradin (eds.), *Regulatory Competition and Economic Integration,* Oxford: Oxford University Press, 2001.

Faure 2003
Faure, M., 'How Law and Economics may contribute to the Harmonisation of Tort Law in Europe', in: Zimmermann (ed.), *Grundstrukturen des Europäischen Deliktrechts,* Baden-Baden: Nomos, 2003.

Faure 2007
Faure, M., *L'analyse économique du droit de l'environnement*, Brussels: Bruylant, 2007.

Faure 2007a
Faure, M., 'Financial Compensation for Victims of Catastrophes: A Law and Economics Perspective', 29(3) *Law & Policy*, 2007, p. 339-367.

Faure 2008
Faure, M., 'Calabresi and Behavioural Tort Law and Economics', 1(4) *Erasmus Law Review*, 2008, p. 75-102.

Faure 2009
Faure, M., 'Environmental liability', in: Faure, M. (ed.), *Tort Law and Economics*, Cheltenham: Edward Elgar, 2009.

Faure 2010
Faure, M., 'Criminal Liability for Oil Pollution Damage: An Economic Analysis', in: Faure, M. *et al.* (eds.), *Maritime Pollution Liability and Policy - China, Europe and the US*, Alphen aan den Rijn: Kluwer Law International, 2010.

Faure and Betlem 2008
Faure, M. and Betlem, G., ' Applying national liability law to transboundary pollution: some lessons from Europe and the United States', in: Faure and Ying (eds.), *China and International Environmental Liability*, Cheltenham: Edward Elgar, 2008.

Faure and Fiore 2008
Faure, M. and Fiore, K., 'The Coverage of Nuclear Risk in Europe: Which Alternative?', 33(2) *The Geneva Papers on Risk and Insurance. Issues and Practice,* 2008, p. 288-322.

Faure and Fiore 2009
Faure, M. and Fiore, K., 'An Economic Analysis of the Nuclear Liability Subsidy', 26(2) *Pace Environmental law Review*, 2009, p. 419-447.

Faure and Liu 2012
Faure, M. and Liu, J., 'The Tsunami of March 2011 and the Subsequent Nuclear Incident at Fukushima: Who compensates the Victims?', 37(1) *William & Mary Environmental Law & Policy Review*, 2012, p. 129-218.

Faure and Liu 2014
Faure, M. and Liu, J., 'Compensation for Environmental Damage in China: Theory and Practice', 31(1) *Pace Environmental Law Review*, 2014, p. 226-309.

Faure and Skogh 1992
Faure, M. and Skogh, G., 'Compensation for Damages Caused by Nuclear Accidents: A Convention as Insurance', 17(65) *The Geneva Papers on Risk and Insurance*, 1992, p. 499–513.

Faure and van den Bergh 1987
Faure, M. and van den Bergh, R., 'Negligence, Strict Liability and Regulation of Safety Under Belgian Law: An Introductory Economic analysis', 12(43) *Geneva Papers on Risk and Insurance*, 1987, p. 95–114.

Faure and van den Bergh 1990
Faure, M. and van den Bergh, R., 'Liability for nuclear accidents in Belgium from an interest group perspective', 10(3) *International Review of Law and Economics*, 1990, p. 241–254.

Faure and van den Bergh 1995
Faure, M. and van den Bergh, R., 'Restrictions of competition on insurance markets and the applicability of EC antitrust', 48(1) *Kyklos*, 1995, p. 65–855.

Faure and van den Bergh 2002
Faure, M. and van den Bergh, R., Competition on the European Market for Liability Insurance and Efficient Accident Law', 9(3) *Maastricht Journal of European and Comparative Law*, 2002, p. 279–306.

Faure and vanden Borre 2008
Faure, M. and vanden Borre, T., 'Compensating Nuclear Damage: A Comparative Economic Analysis of the U.S. and International Liability Schemes', 33(1) *William & Mary Environmental Law and Policy Review*, 2008, p. 219–287.

Faure and Wang 2004
Faure, M. and Wang, H., 'Liability for oil pollution – the EU approach', *Environmental Liability*, 2004, p. 55–67.

Faure and Wang 2008
Faure, M. and Wang, H., 'Financial caps for oil pollution damage: A historical mistake?', 32(4) *Marine Policy*, 2008, p. 592–606.

Feess and Wohlschlegel 2006
Feess, E. and Wohlschlegel, A., 'Liability and Information Transmission: The Advantage of Negligence-based Rules', 92(1) *Economics Letters*, 2006, p. 63–67.

Fiore 2009
Fiore, K., 'No-fault compensation systems', in: Faure, M. (ed.), *Tort Law and Economics*, Cheltenham: Edward Elgar, 2009.

Fisher 2008
Fisher, E., 'The "perfect storm" of REACH: charting regulatory controversy in the age of information, sustainable development, and globalisation', 11(4) *Journal of Risk Research*, 2008, p. 541–563.

Foster 2011
Foster, N., 'Individual liability of company officers', in: Gobert, J. and Pascal, A.-M. (eds.), *European Developments in Corporate Criminal Liability*, Oxon: Routledge, 2011.

Getimis and Kafkalas 2002
Getimas, P. and Kafkalas, G., 'Empirical Evidence and Comparative Analysis of Policy-Making in the Pursuit of Innovation and Sustainability', in: Heinelt *et. al.* (eds.), *Participatory Governnace in Multi-Level Context*, Opladen: Leske + Budrich, 2002.

Goedde 2003
Goedde, P., 'In Search of a Civil Nuclear Liability Regime for North Korea', 27(1) *Asian Perspective*, 2003, p. 225–259.

Golay 2000
Golay, M.W., 'Improved nuclear power plant operations and safety through performance-based safety regulation', 71(1–3) *Journal of Hazardous Materials*, 2000, p. 219–237.

Goyder 1992
Goyder, D.G., *EC Competition law*, Oxford: Clarendon Press, 1992.

Grant and Keohane 2005
Grant, R.W. and Keohane, R.O., 'Accountabiliy and Abuse of Power in World Politics', 99(1) *American Political Science Review*, 2005, p. 29–43.

Gunningham and Sinclair 1998
Gunningham, N. and Sinclair, D., 'Instruments for Environmental Protection', in: Gunningham, N. and Grabosky, P. (eds.), *Smart Regulation: Designing Environmental Policy*, Oxford: Oxford University Press, 1998.

Guthrie *et al.* 2001
Guthrie, C. *et al.*, 'Inside the Judicial Mind', 86(4) *Cornell Law Review*, 2001, p. 777–830.

Hachez 2008
Hachez, N., 'Case C-308/06, International Association of Independent Tanker Owners and Others: The Requirement of Direct Effect in he Judicial Review of EU Law Against International Law', 15(1) *Columbia Journal of European Law*, 2008, p. 143–164.

Haghighi 2008
Haghighi, S.S., 'Energy Security and the Division of Competences between the European Community and its Member States', 14(4) *European Law Journal,* 2008, p. 461–482.

Haines 2009
Haines, F., 'Regulatory Failures and Regulatory Solutions: A Characteristic Analysis of the Aftermath of Disaster', 34(1) *Law & Social Inquiry,*', 2009, p. 31–60.

Hancher 1989
Hancher, L., 'Energy and the Environment: Striking a Balance?', 26(3) Common Market Law Review, 1989, p. 475–512.

Handrlica 2010
Handrlica, J., 'Euratom powers in the field of nuclear liability revisited', 3(1) *International Journal of Nuclear Law,* 2010, p. 1–18.

Hansmann and Kraakman 1991
Hansmann, H. and Kraakman, R., 'Toward Unlimited Shareholder Liability for Corporate Torts', 100(7) *The Yale Law Journal,* 1991, p. 1879–1934.

Haritz 2011
Haritz, M., *An Inconvenient Deliberation: The Precautionary Principle's Contribution to the Uncertainties Surrounding Climate Change Liability,* Alphen aan den Rijn: Kluwer Law International, 2011.

Harrington 2000
Harrington, S.E., 'Rethinking Disaster Policy', 23(1) *Regulation,* 2000, p. 40–46.

Hasnas 2009
Hasnas, J., 'The Centenary of a Mistake: One Hundred years of Corporate Criminal Liability', 46 *American Criminal Law Review,* 2009, p. 1329–1358.

Heine and Kerber 2002
Heine, K. and Kerber, W., 'European Corporate Laws, Regulatory Competition and Path Dependence', 13(1) *European Journal of Law and Economics,* 2002, p. 47–71.

Heinelt 2002
Heinelt, H., 'Achieving Sustainable and Innovative Policies through Participatory Governance in a Multi-level Context', in: Heinelt H. *et. al.* (eds.), *Participatory Governance in Multi-Level Context,* Opladen: Leske + Budrich, 2002.

Heldt 2014
Heldt, T., 'Corporate Social Responsibility (CSR) and its relevance for the nuclear sector', in: Manóvil, R.M. (ed.), *Nuclear Law in progress,* Buenos Aires: Legis, 2014.

Heyvaert 2010
Heyvaert, V., 'Regulating Chemical Risk: REACH in a Global Governance Perspective', in: Eriksson, J., Gilek M. and Rudén, C. (eds.), *Regulating Chemical Risks*, Dordrecht: Springer, 2010.

Heyvaert 2011
Heyvaert, V., 'Governing Climate Change: Towards a New Paradigm for Risk Regulation', 74(6) *The Modern Law Review*, 2011, p. 817–844.

Hinteregger 2008
Hinteregger, M., 'The new Austrian Act on Third Party Liability for Nuclear Damage', 62 *Nuclear Law Bulletin*, 1998, p. 27–34

Hirschmann 1970
Hirschmann, A.O., *Voice, Exit and Loyalty: Responses to Decline in Firms, Organizations, and States,* Cambridge, Massachuses and London: Harvard University Press, 1970.

Hofstede 2001
Hofstede, G., *Culture's Consequences,* Thousand Oaks: Sage Publications, 2001.

Innes and Sam 2008
Innes, R. and Sam, A.G., 'Voluntary Pollution Reductions and the Enforcement of Environmental Law: An Empirical Study of the 33/50 Program', 51(2) *Journal of Law and Economics*, 2008, p. 271–296.

Jacobsson 2004
Jacobsson, K., 'Soft regulation and the subtle transformation of states: the case of EU employment policy', 14(4) Journal of *European Social Policy*, 2004, p. 355–370.

Jaffe and Palmer 1997
Jaffe, A.B. and Palmer, K., 'Environmental Regulation and Innovation: A Panel Data Study', 79(4) *The Review of Economics and Statistics*, 1997, p. 610–619.

Jans and Vedder 2012
Jans, J.H. and Vedder, H.H.B., *European Environmental Law After Lisbon*, Groningen: Europa Law Publishing, 2012.

Jendróska 2012
Jrndróska, J., 'Citizen's Rights in European Environmental Law: Stock-Taking of Key Challenges and Current Developments in Relation to Public Access to Information, Participation and Access to Justice', 9(1) *Journal for European Environmental & Planning Law*, 2012, p. 71–90.

Jensen 2010
Jensen, M.C., 'Value Maximisation, Stakeholder Theory, and the Corporate Objective Function', 22(1) *Journal of Applied Corporate Finance*, 2010, p. 32–42.

Jordan and Tosun 2013
Jordan, A. and Tosun, J., 'Policy implementation', in: Jordan, A. and Adelle, C. (eds.), *Environmental Policy in the EU: Actors, Institutions and Processes*, Oxon: Routledge, 2013

Kahan *et al.* 2010
Kahan, D.M. *et al.*, 'Fear of Democracy: A Cultural Evaluaion of Sunstein on Risk', in: Slovic, P. (ed.), *The Feeling of Risk: New Perspectives of Risk Perception*, London and Washington: Earthscan, 2010.

Keenan and Rubin 1988
Keenan, D. and Rubin, P.H., 'Shadow Interest Groups and Safety Regulation', 8(1) *International Review of Law and Economics*, 1988, p. 21–36.

Kerber and van den Bergh 2008
Kerber W. and van den Bergh, R., 'Mutual Recognition Revisited: Misunderstandings, Inconsistencies and a Suggested Reinterpretation', 61(3) *Kyklos*, 2008, p. 447–465.

Kimber 1995
Kimber, C.J.M., 'A Comparison of Environmental Federalism in the United States and the European Union', 54(4) *Maryland Law Review*, 1995, p. 1658–1690.

Kiss 2006
Kiss, A., 'State Responsibility and Liability for Nuclear Damage', 35(1) *Denver Journal of International Law & Policy*, 2006, p. 67–83.

Kitzmueller and Shimshack 2012
Kitzmueller, M. and Shimshack, J., 'Economic Perspectives on Corporate Social Responsibility', 50(1) *Journal of Economic Literature*, 2012, p. 51–84

Kjaer 2010
Kjaer, P., *Between Governing and Governance*, Portland: Hart Publishing, 2010.

Klamert 2010
Klamert, M., 'Conflicts of legal basis: no legality and no basis but a bright future under the Lisbon Treaty?', 35(4) *European Law Review*, 2010, p. 497–515

Kohler-Koch 2012
Kohler-Koch, B., 'Post-Maastricht Civil Society and Participatory Democracy', 34(7) Journal of *European Integration*, 2012, p. 809–824.

Kolstad, Ulen and Johnson 1990
Kolstad, C.D., Ulen, T.S. and Johnson, G.V., 'Ex Post Liability for Harm vs. Ex Ante Safety Regulation: Substitutes or Complements?', 80(4) *The American Economic Review*, 1990, p. 888–901.

Konar and Cohen 1997
Konar, S. and Cohen, M.A., 'Information as Regulation: The Effect of Community Rights to Know Law on Toxic Emissions', 32(1) *Journal of Environmental Economics and Management*, 1997, p. 109–124.

Konar and Cohen 2001
Konar, S. and Cohen, M.A., 'Does the Market Value Environmental Performance?', 83(2) *The Review of Economics and Statistics*, 1997, p. 281–289.

Kopela 2011
Kopela, S., 'Civil and Criminal Liability as Mechanisms for the Prevention of Oil Marine Pollution: The Erika Case', 20(3) *Review of European Community and International Environmental Law*, 2011, p. 313–324.

Koppell 2005
Koppell, J., 'Pathologies of Accountability', 65(1) *Public Administration Review*, 2005, p. 94–108.

Korobkin and Ulen 2000
Korobkin, R.B. and Ulen, T.S., 'Law and Behavioral Science: Removing the Rationality Assumption from Law and Economics', 88(4) *California Law Review*, 2000, p. 1051–1144.

Krämer 2006
Krämer, L., 'The EU: a regional model?', in: Winter, G. (ed.), *Multilevel Governance of Global Environmental Change*, Cambridge: Cambridge University Press, 2006.

Krämer 2013
Krämer, L., 'The EU, access to environmental information and the open society', 14(4) *ERA Forum*, 2013, p. 463–474.

Landes and Posner 1984
Landes, W. and Posner, R., 'Tort law as a regulatory regime for catastrophic personal injuries', 13(3) *Journal of Legal Studies*, 1984, p. 417–434.

Lanoie *et al.* 2011
Lanoie, P. *et al.*, 'Environmental Policy, Innovation and Performance: New Insights on the Porter Hypothesis', 20(3) *Journal of Economics & Management Strategy*, 2011, p. 803–842.

Larsson 1999
Larsson, M.-L., 'Legal Definitions of the Environment and of Environmental Damage', in: Wahlgren, P. (ed.), *Scandinavian Studies in Law, Volume 38, Legal Issues of the Late 1990's*, Stockholm: Stockholm Institue for Scandinavian Law, 1999.

Latin 1985
Latin, H., 'Ideal v. Real Regulatory Efficiency: Implementation of uniform standards and fine tuning reforms', 37(5) *Stanford Law Review*, 1985, p. 1267–1332.

Lee 2014
Lee, M., *EU Environmental Law, Governance and Decision-Making*, Oxford: Hart Publishing, 2014.

Legrand 1997
Legrand, P., 'The Impossibility of Legal Transplants', 4 *Maastricht Journal of European & Comparative Law*, 1997, p. 11–124.

Leiter *et al.* 2011
Leiter, A.M. *et al.*, 'Environmental regulation and investment: Evidence from European industry data', 70(4) *Ecological Economics*, 2011, p. 759–770.

Lenaerts 1988
Lenaerts, K., 'Nuclear border installations: a case study', 19(3) *European Law Review*, 1988, p. 159–187.

Levi-Faur 2011
Levi-Faur, D., 'Regulation and regulatory governance', in: Levi-Faur, D. (ed.), *Handbook on the Politics of Regulation*, Cheltenham: Edward Elgar, 2011.

Liermann and Veuchelen 2006
Liermann, S. and Veuchelen, L., 'The optimisation approach of ALARA in nuclear practice: an early application of the precautionary principle? Scientific uncertainty versus legal uncertainty and its role in tort law', 15(4) *European Environmental Law Review*, 2006, p. 98–107.

List and Co 2000
List, J.A. and Co, C.Y., 'The Effects of Environmental Regulations on Foreign Direct Investment', 40(1) *Journal of Environmental Economics and Management*, 2000, p. 1–20.

List and Gerking 2000
List, J.A. and Gerking, S., 'Regulatory Federalism and Environmental Protection in the United States', 40(3) *Journal of Regional Science*, 2000, p. 453–471.

Löfstedt *et al.* 2011
Löfstedt, R. *et al.*, 'The changing nature of communication and regulation of risk in Europe', 14(4) *Journal of Risk Research*, 2011, p. 409–429.

Löfstedt and Vogel 2001
Löfstedt, R. and Vogel, D., 'The Changing Character of Regulation: A Comparison of Europe and the United States', 21(3) *Risk Analysis*, 2001, p. 399–416.

Majone 1994
Majone, G., 'The Rise of the Regulatory State in Europe', 17(3) *West European Politics*, 1994, p. 77–101.

Majone 2011
Majone, G., 'Strategic issues in risk regulation', in: Levi-Faur, D. (ed.), *Handbook on the Politics of Regulation*, Cheltenham: Edward Elgar, 2011.

Mallin 2009
Mallin, C.A., *Corporate Governance*, Oxford: Oxford University Press, 2009.

Martinico 2014
Martinico, G., 'Asymmetry and Complex Adaptive (Legal) Systems: The Case of the European Union', 21(2) *Maastricht Journal of European and Comparative Law*, 2014, p. 281–299.

May 2007
May, P.J., 'Regulatory regimes and accountability', 1(1) *Regulation & Governance*, 2007, p. 8–26.

McBarnet 2007
McBarnet, D., 'Corporate Social Responsibility beyond law, through law, for law: the new corporate accountability', in: Barnet, D. *et al.* (eds.), The New *Corporate Accountability: Corporate Social Responsibility and the Law*, Cambridge: Cambridge University Press, 2007.

McBarnet and Kurkchiyan 2007
McBarnet, D. and Kurkchiyan, M., 'Corporate Social Responsibility through contractual control? Global supply chains and "other regulation"', in: Barnet, D. *et al.* (eds.), The New *Corporate Accountability: Corporate Social Responsibility and the Law*, Cambridge: Cambridge University Press, 2007.

McRae 1998
McRae, B., 'The Compensation Convention: Path to a Global Regime for Dealing with Legal Liability and Compensation for Nuclear Damage', 61(1) *Nuclear Law Bulletin*, 1998, p. 25–38.

Miller 1985
Miller, J.C., 'The FTC and voluntary standards: Maximizing the net benefits of self-regulation', 4(3) *Cato Journal*, 1985, p. 897–904.

Miller and Justice 2011
Miller, J.G. and Justice, C., 'Organizational Liability for Environmental Crimes in Civil and Common Law Systems', in: Paddock, L. *et al.* (eds.), *Compliance and Enforcement in Environmental Law*, Cheltenham: Edward Elgar Publishing, 2011.

Mitchell 2007
Mitchell, L.E., 'The board as a path toward corporate social responsibility', in: Barnet, D. *et al.* (eds.), The New *Corporate Accountability: Corporate Social Responsibility and the Law*, Cambridge: Cambridge University Press, 2007.

Mohr and Saha 2008
Mohr, R.D. and Saha, S., 'Distribution of Environmental Costs and Benefits, Additional Distortions, and the Porter Hypothesis', 84(4) *Land Economics*, 2008, p. 689–700.

Montjoie 2012
Montjoie, M., 'Les relations entre le Traité Euratom et le TFUE en matière de protection de l'environnement', 560 *Revue de L'Union Européenne*, 2012, p. 471–483.

Nanda and van Dyke 2006
Nanda, V.E. and van Dyke, J.M., 'International Nuclear Law: An Introduction', 35(1) *Denver Journal of International Law & Policy*, 2006, 1–12.

Nießen 2010
Nießen, D., 'Prospects of a Nuclear Liability Regime in the Framework of the European Union', 4(1) *Zeitschrift für Europäisches Umwelt- und Planungsrecht*, 2010, p. 187–191.

Nollkaemper 1998
Nollkaemper, A., 'How public international (environmental) law can furnish a rule of decision in Civil Litigation', 12(1) *Tijdschrift voor Milieuaansprakelijkheid*, 1998, p. 3–11.

Oates and Schwab 1988
Oates, W.E. and Schwab, R.M., 'Economic Competition among Jurisdictions: Efficiency enhancing or Distortion inducing?', 35 *Journal of Public Economics*, 1988, p. 333–354.

Ogus 1994
Ogus, A., *Regulation: Legal Form and Economic Theory*, Oxford: Clarendon Press, 1994.

Ogus 1999
Ogus, A., 'Competition between National Legal Systems: A Contribution of Economic Analysis to Comparative Law', 48(2) *The International and Comparative Law Quarterly*, 1999, p. 405–418.

Ogus 2007
Ogus, A., 'Better Regulation – Better Enforcement', in: Weatherill, S. (ed.), *Better Regulation*, Oxford: Hart Publishing, 2007.

Ogus and Zhang 2005
Ogus, A. and Zhang, Q., 'Licensing Regimes East and West', 25(1) *International Review of Law and Economics*, 2005, p. 124–142.

Okpara and Idowu 2013
Okpara, J.O. and Idowu, S.O., 'Corporate Social Responsibility: A Review of the Concept and Analysis of the Business Case for Corporate Social Responsibility in the Twenty-First Century', in: Okpara, J.O. and Idowo, S.O. (eds.), *Corporate Social Responsibility: Challenges, Opportunities and Strategies for 21st Century Leaders*, Berlin and Heidelberg: Spinger, 2013.

Olson 1965
Olson, M., *The Logic of Collective Action: Public Goods and the Theory of Groups*, Cambridge: Harvard University Press, 1965.

Palmer, Oates and Portney 1995
Palmer, K., Oates, W.E. and Portney, P.R., 'Tightening Environmental Standards: The Benefit-Cost or the No-Cost Paradigm?', 9(4) *Journal of Economic Perspectives*, 1995, p. 119–132.

Peers 2008
Peers, S., 'EU Criminal Law and the Treaty of Lisbon', 33(4) *European Law Review*, 2008, p. 507–529.

Pelzer 2007
Pelzer, N., 'International Pooling of Operators' funds: An Option to Increase the Amount of Financial Security to Cover Nuclear Liability?', 3(1) *Nuclear Law Bulletin*, 2007, p. 37–55.

Pelzer 2008
Pelzer, N., 'On Global Treaty Relations – Hurdles on the Way towards a Universal Civil Nuclear Liability Regime', 6(1) *Zeitschrift für Europäisches Umwelt- und Planungsrecht*, 2008, p. 268–280.

Pelzer 2010
Pelzer, N., 'Deliberations on Compensation and Remediation of Nuclear Damage to the Environment', 2010(2) *Nuclear Law Bulletin*, 2010, p. 49–57.

Pereira 2008
Pereira, R., 'On the Legality of the Ship-Source Pollution 2005/35/EC Directive – The Intertanko Case and Selected Others', 17(6) *European Energy and Environmental Law Review*, 2008, p. 372–383.

Pesendorfer 2006
Pesendorfer, D., 'EU Environmental Policy under Pressure: Chemical Policy Change between Antagonistic Goals?', 15(1) *Environmental Politics*, 2006, p. 95–114.

Pesendorfer 2011
Pesendorfer, D., 'Risk regulation and precaution', in: Levi-Faur, D. (ed.), *Handbook on the Politics of Regulation*, Cheltenham: Edward Elgar, 2011.

Philipsen 2003
Philipsen, N., *Regulation of and by Pharmacists in the Netherlands and Belgium. An Economic Approach*, Antwerpen and Groningen: Intersentia, 2003.

Philipsen 2008
Philipsen, N., 'Regulation of professions: a European perspective', in: Faure, M. and Stephen, F. (eds.), *Essays in the Law and Economics of Regulation*, Antwerp: Intersentia, 2008.

Popelier 2014
Popelier, P., 'Europe Clauses and Constitutional Strategies in the Face of Multi-Level Governance', 21(2) *Maastricht Journal of European and Comparative Law*, 2014, p. 300–319.

Popelier and Vandenbruwaene 2014
Popelier, P. and Vandenbruwaene, W., 'The Constitutional Adulthood of Multi-Level Governance', 21(2) *Maastricht Journal of European and Comparative Law*, 2014, p. 225–228.

Porter 1990
Porter, M.E., 'The Competitive Advantage of Nations', March/April *Harvard Business Review*, 1990, p. 73–91.

Porter 1991
Porter, M.E., 'America's green strategy', April *Scientific American*, 1991, p. 168.

Porter and van der Linde 1995
Porter, M.E. and van der Linde, C., 'Toward a New Conception of the Environment-Competitiveness Relationship', 9(4) *Journal of Economic Perspectives*, 1995, p. 97–118.

Preston and Hanson 2013
Preston, B. and Hanson, C., 'The Globalisation and Harmonisation of Environmental Law: An Australian Perspective', 16(1) *Asia Pacific Journal of Environmental Law*, 2013, p. 1–36.

Rahim and Nasrullah 2013
Rahim, M.M. and Nasrullah, N.M., 'Corporate Social Responsibility Implementation in the EU and USA: The Trend and the Way Forwards', in: Okpara, J.O. and Idowo, S.O. (eds.), *Corporate Social Responsibility: Challenges, Opportunities and Strategies for 21st Century Leaders*, Berlin and Heidelberg: Spinger, 2013.

Ramseyer 2012
Ramseyer, J.M., 'Why Nuclear Power Companies Build Nuclear Reactors on Fault Lines: The Case of Japan', 13(2) *Theoretical Inquiries in Law*, 2012, p. 457–485.

Rashbrooke 2004
Rashbrooke, G., 'Clarification or Complication? The New Energy Title in the Draft Constitution for Europe', 22(3) *Journal of Energy & Natural Resources Law*, 2004, p. 373–387.

Renn and Klinke 2001
Renn, O. and Klinke, A., 'Public Participation across Borders', in: Linneroth-Bayer, J *et al.* (eds.), *Transboundary Risk Management*, London: Earthscan, 2001.

Rest 1997
Rest, A., 'International Environmental Liability Law before German Courts', 11(5) *Tijdschrift voor Milieuaansprakelijkheid*, 1997, p. 116–122.

Revesz 1992
Revesz, R.L., 'Rehabilitating Interstate Competition: Rethinking the "Race-to-the-bottom" Rationale for Federal Environmental Regulation', 67 *New York University Law Review*, 1992, p. 1210–1254.

Revesz 1997/1998
Revesz, R.L., 'The Race to the Bottom and Federal Environmental Regulation: A Response to Critics', 82 *Minnesota Law Review*, 1997/1998, p. 535–564.

Revesz 2001
Revesz, R.L., 'Federalism and Regulation: Some Generalizations', in: Esty and Geradin (eds.), *Regulatory Competition and Economic Integration*, Oxford: Oxford University Press, 2001.

Rexhäuser and Rammer 2014
Rexhäuser, S. and Rammer, C., 'Environmental Innovations and Firm Profitability: Unmasking the Porter Hypothesis', 57(1) *Environmental and Resource Economics*, 2014, p. 145–167.

Ritter and Braun 2005
Ritter, L. and Braun, W.D., *European Competition Law: A practitioner's guide*, The Hague: Kluwer Law International, 2005

Robinson 1992
Robinson, J., 'The Legal Basis of EC Environmental Law', 4(1) *Journal of Environmental Law*, 1992, p. 109–120.

Rosas 2011
Rosas, A., 'The Staus in EU Law of International Agreements Concluded by EU Member States', 34(5) *Fordham International Law Journal*, 2011, p. 1304–1345.

Rowe and Frewer 2000
Rowe, G. and Frewer, L.J., 'Public Participation Methods: A Framework for Evaluation', 25(1) *Science, Technology & Human Values*, 2000, p. 3–29.

Salles 2011
Salles, D., 'Responsibility based environmental governance', 4(1) *Surveys and Perspectives Integrating Environment & Society*, 2011, p. 1–7.

Sambeth 1983
Sambeth, J., 'The Seveso accident', 12(4–5) *Chemosphere*, 1983, p. 681–686.

Schaefer and Mueller-Langer 2009
Schaefer, H.-B. and Mueller-Langer, F., 'Strict liability versus negligence', in: Faure, M. (ed.), *Tort Law and Economics*, Cheltenham: Edward Elgar, 2009.

Scharpf 1999
Scharpf, F.W., *Governing in Europe: Effective and democratic?*, Oxford: Oxford University Press, 1999.

Schmalz-Bruns 2002
Schmalz-Bruns, R., 'The Normative Desirability of Participatory Governance', in: Heinelt *et al.* (eds.), *Participatory Governnace in Multi-Level Context,* Opladen: Leske + Budrich, 2002.

Schmidpeter 2013
Schmidpeter, R., 'Corporate Social Responsibility: A New Management Paradigm?', in: Okpara, J.O. and Idowo, S.O. (eds.), *Corporate Social Responsibility: Challenges, Opportunities and Strategies for 21st Century Leaders,* Berlin and Heidelberg: Spinger, 2013.

Scott 2009
Scott, C., 'Governing Without Law or Governing Without Government? New-ish Governance and the Legitimacy of the EU', 15(2) *European Law Journal*, 2009, p. 160–173.

Selin 2007
Selin, H., 'Coalition Politics and Chemicals Management in a Regulatory Ambitious Europe', 7(3) *Global Environmental Politics*, 2007, p. 63–93.

Shavell 1979
Shavell, S., 'On Moral Hazard and Insurance', 93(4) *The Quarterly Journal of Economics*, 1979, p. 541–562.

Shavell 1980
Shavell, S., 'Strict liability versus negligence', 9(1) *The Journal of Legal Studies*, 1980, p. 1–25.

Shavell 1984a
Shavell, S., 'Liability for Harm versus Regulation of Safety', 13(2) *Journal of Legal Studies*, 1984, p. 357–374.

Shavell 1984 b
Shavell, S., 'A model of the optimal use of liability and safety regulation', 15(2) *Rand Journal of Economics*, 1984, p. 271–280.

Shavell 2004
Shavell, S., *Foundations of Economic Analysis,* Cambridge: Belknap Press of Harvard University Press, 2004.

Simoncini 2014
Simoncini, A., 'The European Union as a 3-D Constitutional Space', 21(2) *Maastricht Journal of European and Comparative Law*, 2014, p. 243–264.

Sinclair 1997
Sinclair, D., 'Self-Regulation versus Command and Control? Beyong False Dichotomies', 19(4) *Law & Policy*, 1997, p. 529–559.

Sitnikov 2013
Sitnikov, C., 'CSR Life-Cycle Exploration', in: Okpara, J.O. and Idowo, S.O. (eds.), *Corporate Social Responsibility: Challenges, Opportunities and Strategies for 21st Century Leaders*, Berlin and Heidelberg: Spinger, 2013.

Skogh 1998
Skogh, G., 'Development Risks, Strict Liability and the Insurability of Industrial Hazards', 23(2) *Geneva Papers on Risk and Insurance*, 1998, p. 247–264.

Slovic 2000
Slovic, P., *The Perception of Risk*, London and Sterling: Earthscan, 2000.

Slovic *et al.* 1982
Slovic, P. *et al.*, 'Why Study Risk Perception?', 2(2) *Risk Analysis*, 1982, p. 83–93.

Slovic *et al.* 2004
Slovic, P. *et al.*, 'Risk as Analysis and Risk as Feelings: Some Thoughts about Affects, Reason, Risk, and Rationality', 24(2) *Risk Analysis*, 2004, p. 1–12.

Smith 2014
Smith, T., 'Nuclear Licensing in the United States: enhancing public confidence in the regulatory process', *Journal of Risks Research*, 2014, p. 1–14.

Soljan 2000
Soljan, V., 'The New Definition of Nuclear Damage in the 1997 Protocol to Amend the 1963 Vienna Convention On Civil Liability for Nuclear Damage', in: Reyners, P. (ed.), *Reform of Civil Nuclear Liability*, Paris: OECD, 2000.

Spier 2013
Spier, J., 'The need for breaking new ground in the realm of climate change', in: Faure, M. and Wibisana, A. (eds.), *Regulating Disasters, Climate Change and Environmental Harm – Lessons from the Indonesion Experience*, Cheltenham: Edward Elgar, 2013.

Stanic 2010
Stanic, A., 'EU Law on Nuclear Safety', 28(1) *Journal of Energy & Natural Resources Law*, 2010, p. 145–158.

Stavang 2010
Stavang, E., 'Two Challenges for the ECJ when examining the Environmental Liability Directive', 18(5) *Environmental Liability*, 2010, p. 198–201.

Steele 2004
Steele, J., *Risk and Legal Theory*, Oxford: Hart Publishing, 2004.

Stout 2012
Stout, L.A., 'The Problem of Corporate Purpose', 48 *Issues in Governance Studies*, 2012, p. 1–14.

Svendsen 1998
Svendsen, G.T., *Public Choice and Environmental Regulation*, Cheltenham: Edward Elgar, 1998.

Tetley 2006
Tetley, M., 'Revised Paris and Vienna Nuclear Liability Conventions – Challenges for Insurers', 77(1) *Nuclear Law Bulletin*, 2006, p. 27–39.

Teubner 1983
Teubner, G., 'Substantive and Reflexive Elements in Modern Law', 17(2) *Law & Society Review*, 1983, p. 239–285.

Thomas and Heffron 2012
Thomas, A. and Heffron, R.J.A., *Third Party Nuclear Liability: The Case of a Supplier in the United Kingdom*, Cambridge: Electricity Policy Research Group, 2012.

Tiebout 1956
Tiebout, C.M., 'A Pure Theory of Legal Expenditures', 64(5) *Journal of Political Economy*, 1956, p. 416–424.

Trebilcock and Winter 1997
Trebilcock, M. and Winter, R.A., 'The Economics of Nuclear Accident Law', 17(2) *International Review of Law and Economics*, 1997, p. 215–243.

Treib, Bähr and Falkner 2007
Treib, O., Bähr, H. and Falkner, G., 'Modes of governance: towards a conceptual clarification', 14(1) *Journal of European Public Policy*, 2007, p. 1–20.

True 2003
True, C., 'Legislative competences of Euratom and the European Community in the energy sector: the Nuclear Package of the Commission', 28(5) *European Law Review*, 2003, p. 664–685.

Tyran and Zweifel 1993
Tyran, J.-R. and Zweifel, P., 'Environmental risk internalisation through capital markets (Ericam): The case of nuclear power', 13(4) *International Review of Law and Economics*, 1993, p. 431–444.

Van Boom 2009
van Boom, W.H., 'Harmonizing Tort Law: A Comparative Tort Law and Economics Analysis', in: Faure (ed.), *Tort Law and Economics*, Cheltenham: Edward Elgar, 2009.

Van Dam 2006
Van Dam, C., *European Tort Law,* Oxford: Oxford University Press, 2006.

Van Dam 2009
Van Dam, C., 'Who is Afraid of Diversity? Cultural Diversity, European Co-operation, and European Tort Law', 20(2) *King's Law Journal*, 2009, p. 281–308.

Vandenbergh 2013
Vandenbergh, M.P., 'The Implications of Private Environmental Governance', 99(1) *Cornell Law Review,* 2013, p. 117–139.

Van den Bergh 1994
Van den Bergh, R., 'The Subsidiarity Principle in European Community Law: Some Insights from Law and Economics', 1 *Maastricht Journal of European & Comparative Law,* 1994, p. 337–366.

Van den Bergh 2000
Van den Bergh, R., 'Towards an Institutional Legal Framework for Regulatory Competition in Europe' 53, 2000, p. 435–465.

Van den Bergh 2004
Van den Bergh, R., 'Towards Efficient Self-Regulation in Markets for Professional Services', in: Ehlermann, C.-D. and Atanasiu, I. (eds.), *European Competition Law Annual 2004: The Relationship between Competition Law and (Liberal) Professions,* Oxford/Portland Oregon: Hart Publishing, 2004.

Vanden Borre 2007
vanden Borre, T., 'Shifts in Governance in Compensation for Nuclear Damage, 20 Years after Chernobyl', in: Faure, M. and Verheij, A. (eds.), *Shifts in Compensation for Environmental Damage,* Wien and New York: Springer, 2007.

Vanden Borre 2010
vanden Borre, T., 'Nuclear Liability: An anachronism in EU Energy Policy?', in: Roggenkamp, M. and Hammer, U. (eds.), *European Energy Law Report VII,* Antwerp: Intersentia, 2010.

Van Dyke 2006
van Dyke, J.M., 'Liability and Compensation for Harm Caused by Nuclear Activities', 35(1) *Denver Journal of International Law & Policy,* 2006, p. 13–46.

Van Gerven 1996
Van Gerven, W., 'Bridging the Unbridgeable: Community and National Tort Laws after Francovich and Brasserie', 45(3) *International and Comparative Law Quarterly,* 1996, p. 507–544.

Van Rossem 2009
van Rossem, J.W., 'Interaction between EU Law and International Law in the Light of *Intertanko* and *Kadi*: The Dilemma of Norms Binding the Member States but not the Community', 40 *Netherlands Yearbook of International Law*, 2009, p. 183–227.

Vedder 2008
Vedder, H., 'The Treaty of Lisbon and European Environmental Policy', *Social Science Research Network*, 2008.

Verdejo 2001
Verdejo, C.G., 'International Conventions and EU Law on the Illegal Trafficking of Cultural Goods: Complementarity and Conflicts', in: Kronenberger, V., *The European Union and the International Legal Order: Discord or Harmony?*, The Hague: Asser Press, 2001.

Veuchelen 2009
Veuchelen, L., 'The Legal Value of General Principles, Technical Norms and Standards in European Nuclear Safety Law: The Imbalance Between Soft and Hard Law and the Need for Global Regulatory Governance', 18(4) *European Energy and Environmental Law Review*, 2009, p. 215–228.

Vogel 2001a
Vogel, D., 'Environmental Regulation and Economic Integration', in: Esty and Geradin (eds.), *Regulatory Competition and Economic Integration*, Oxford: Oxford University Press, 2001.

Vos 2006
Vos, E., 'Independence, Accountability and Transparency of European Regulatory Agencies', in: Geradin *et al.* (eds.), *Regulation through Agencies in the EU: A new Paradigm of European Governance*, Cheltenham: Edward Elgar, 2006.

Waite 2005
Waite, A., 'The quest for environmental law equilibrium', 7(1) *Environmental Law Review*, 2005, p. 34–62.

Walker 1983
Walker, J.L., 'The Origins and Maintenance of Interest Groups in America', 77(2) *The American Political Science Review*, 1983, p. 390–406.

Wang 2007
Wang, H., 'Shifts in Governance in the International Regime of Marine Oil Pollution Compensation: A Legal History Perspective', in: Faure, M. and Verheij, A. (eds.), *Shifts in Compensation for Environmental Damage*, Wien and New York: Springer, 2007

Wang 2011

Wang, H., *Civil liability for marine oil pollution damage: a comparative and economic study of the international, US and the Chinese compensation regime,* Alphen aan den Rijn: Kluwer Law International, 2011.

Wates 2005

Wates, J., 'The Aarhus Convention: a Driving Force for Environmental Democracy', 2(1) *Journal for European Environmental & Planning Law,* 2005, p. 2–11.

Weinberg 1976

Weinberg, A., 'The Maturity and Future of Nuclear Energy', 64(1) *American Scientist,* 1976, p. 16–21.

Wesley *et al.* 2013

Wesley A. *et al.*, 'Corporate Social Responsibility: A Governable Space', in: Okpara, J.O. and Idowo, S.O. (eds.), *Corporate Social Responsibility: Challenges, Opportunities and Strategies for 21st Century Leaders,* Berlin and Heidelberg: Spinger, 2013.

Wettig *et al.*

Wettig, J. *et al.* 'Major industrial accident regulation in the European Union', 65(1–2) *Journal of Loss Prevention in the Process Industries,* 1999, p. 19–28.

Wibisana 2008

Wibisana, M.R.A.G., *Law and Economic Analysis of the Precautionary Principle,* Maastricht, 2010.

Wibisana 2011

Wibisana, M.R.A.G., 'The Development of the Precautionary Principle in International and Indonesian Environmental Law', 14(1&2) *Asia Pacific Journal of Environmental Law,* 2011, p. 169–202.

Wiener 2011

Wiener, J.B., 'The Real Pattern of Precaution', in: Wiener, J. *et al.* (eds.) *The Reality of Precaution,* Washington: RFF Press, 2011.

Wiener *et al.* 2011

Wiener, J.B. *et al., The Reality of Precaution,* Washington: RFF Press, 2011.

Winter 2006

Winter, G., 'The legal nature of environmental principles in international, EU, and exemplary national law', in: Winter, G. (ed.), *Multilevel Governance of Global Environmental Change,* Cambridge: Cambridge University Press, 2006.

Winter *et al.* 2008

Winter, G. *et al.*, 'Weighing up the EC Environmental Liability Directive', 20(2) *Journal of Environmental Law,* 2008, p. 163–191.

Wolf 2011
Wolf, S., 'Euratom, the European Court of Justice, and the Limits of Nuclear Integration in Europe', 12(8) *German Law Journal*, 2011, p. 1637–1658.

Woodliffe 1989
Woodliffe, J., 'Making sense of article 37 of the Euratom Treaty', 14(2) *European Law Review*, 1989, p. 101–105.

Xepapadeas and de Zeeuw 1999
Xepapadeas, A. and de Zeeuw, A., 'Environmental Policy and Competitiveness: The Porter Hypothesis and the Composition of Capital', 37(2) *Journal of Environmental Economics and Management*, 1999, p. 165–182.

Xing and Kolstadt 2002
Xing, Y. and Kolstadt, C.D., 'Do Lax Environmental Regulations Attract Foreign Investment?', 21(1) *Environmental and Resource Economics*, 2002, p. 1–22.

Zandvliet 2011
Zandvliet, R., 'Corporate Social Responsibility Reporting in the European Union: Towards a More Univocal Framework', 18(38) *Columbia Journal of European Law Online*, 2011.

Zerk 2006
Zerk, J.A., *Multinationals and Corporate Social Responsibility*, Cambridge: Cambridge University Press, 2006.

VALORISATION ADDENDUM

1. Relevance: What is the social and/or economic relevance of the research results?

Although the role of nuclear energy is arguably decreasing within the European Union, developments in some Member States clearly show that nuclear energy will remain an important part of the European energy mix. This makes it even more crucial that a robust regulation of the nuclear sector is guaranteed within the European Union. In case of a nuclear accident the effects will be felt throughout the entire European Union. Not only with regard to the effect it will have on the choice of a Member States' energy source but also with regard to its effect on the environment and society as a whole. Thus, the proposal, as presented in chapter 6 of this thesis, to rethink the way in which nuclear liability is currently regulated is both of economic and social relevance. Stricter regulation of the nuclear sector and an increased responsibility of the nuclear industry has the potential to increase the public acceptance of nuclear energy as part of the European energy mix. The social relevance of this research is most prominent in two aspects. Firstly, given the huge impact that a nuclear accident within the European Union would have on the European citizens, it is of crucial importance that civil society is educated in and informed about the core aspects of nuclear liability. The approach chosen in this research enables civil society to get a better grasp of the regulation of the nuclear sector and its shortcomings. Secondly, this research calls for a stronger role of civil society in the regulation of the nuclear sector which also shows the social relevance of this thesis.

2. Target groups: To whom, in addition to the academic community, are the research results of interest and why?

The broad scope of this thesis makes it accessible to a wide audience. The area of nuclear law is still an area that only a few experts know and is still seen as separate from other areas of law. This book makes the bridge between nuclear law and other fields of law and presents it more as an inherent part of European law. Readers of this book will get a good insight into the major issues that one is faced with in the nuclear sector. It thus provides civil society an opportunity to educate itself in the regulation of nuclear energy and pressing legal questions accompanied with the commercial exploitation thereof. Equally, this book is of relevance for governments and policy advisers because it provides not only a description of the currently existing systems but also highlights shortcomings and suggests alternatives. It thereby can serve as a guide for different stakeholders to allow a better educated and more nuanced discussion of the regulation of the nuclear sector and nuclear liability within the European Union.

3. Activities/Products: Into which concrete products, services, processes, activities or commercial activities can the results be translated and shaped?

The results of this research are presented as clear and concrete policy proposals that could lead to a rethinking of the regulation of the nuclear sector. These proposals could be picked up by governments, policy makers or interest groups and serve as arguments for a reform of the nuclear sector. This is of special relevance because recently also the European Union is considering to become more active in the area of nuclear liability. It is possible that in the future the Commission would come up with a Directive tackling the issue of nuclear liability. The results of this research could inspire the policy debates that would occur on the European and national levels in the course of such legislative action.

Next to this, the results of this research also present a further opportunity of valorisation. A central claim made throughout this thesis is that there is a need for higher liability limits, or possibly even no limits at all. To be able to cover such higher limits new ways of financing will need to be addressed. Thus the results of this research also provide a possible impetus to the financial and insurance markets to get more involved in the area of nuclear liability and insurance of nuclear operators.

4. Innovation: To what degree can the results be called innovative in respect to the existing range of products, services, processes, activities and commercial activities?

From an institutional law point of view, this research presents a refocusing and shifts the attention in the nuclear sector from the Euratom Treaty towards the TFEU. The results show that a liability regime for nuclear accidents could also be accommodated under the TFEU. This aspect and the results thereof have not been properly addressed in the literature so far. The proposal as presented in chapter 6 calls for a rethinking of some of the major principles of nuclear liability that currently exist. Following these proposals would significantly alter the regulatory landscape in the nuclear sector.

5. Schedule & implementation: How can these plans for valorisation be shaped?

Speaking at conferences and keeping liaisons with not only the environmental but also the nuclear community will be of crucial importance to convince the respective stakeholders of the added value of the suggested plans. The chances for successful implementation will, however, also strongly depend on the political will of the Member States to strive for changes within the nuclear sector. The main thing that can be done to stimulate this will be the continuous dissemination of this research. Some parts of this book have already been published and this book can be regarded as the next step towards reaching an increased audience. Currently also other publications are under development to further enhance the reach of this research.

CURRICULUM VITAE

Tobias Heldt was born in 1986 in Bergisch-Gladbach, Germany. In 2010 he graduated as a Bachelor of Laws from Maastricht University. Afterwards he stayed at Maastricht University to follow the Master Program of Globalisation and Law with a specialisation in Corporate and Commercial Law. He graduated *cum laude* in 2011 and joined the Maastricht Institute for Transnational Legal Research (METRO) in October of that year to conduct his doctoral research. Next to his work at Maastricht University he was also working as a Legal Adviser for the Nuclear Research Center (SCK•CEN) in Mol, Belgium.

IUS COMMUNE EUROPAEUM

A peer-reviewed book series in which the common foundations of the legal systems of the Member States of the European Union are the central focus.

The *Ius Commune Europaeum* series includes horizontal comparative legal studies as well as studies on the effect of treaties within the national legal systems. All the classic fields of law are covered. The books are published in various European languages under the auspices of METRO, the Institute for Transnational Legal Research at Maastricht University.

Editorial Board: Prof. Dr. J. Smits (chair), Prof. Dr. M. Faure, Prof. Dr. Chr. Joerges, Prof. Dr. J. du Plessis and Prof. Dr. E. Vos.

Recently published:
Volume 129: *Nobody's Perfect. Comparative Essays on Appeals and Other Means of Recourse Against Judicial Decisions in Civil matters*, A. Uzelac and C.H. van Rhee (eds.)
Volume 130: *Legal Aid in the Low Countries*, B. Hubeau and A. Terlouw (eds.)
Volume 131: *State Aid and Public Procurement in the European Union*, S. Schoenmaekers, W. Devroe and N. Philipsen (eds.)
Volume 132: *Property Law Perspectives III*, A. Apers, S. Bouly et al. (eds.)
Volume 133: *Multi-Party Redress Mechanisms in Europe: Squeaking Mice?*, V. Harsági and C.H. van Rhee (eds.)
Volume 134: *Europe at the Edge of Pluralism*, D. Gozdecka and M. Kmak
Volume 135: *Cooperative Agreements between Public Authorities. The Influence of CJEU Case Law on National Legal Systems*, K. Wauters
Volume 136: *Common Core, PECL and DCFR: Could They Change Shipping and Transport Law?*, W. Verheyen, F.G.M. Smeele and M.A.I.H. Hoeks
Volume 137: *Who does What? On the Allocation of Competences in European Private Law*, B. Akkermans, J. Hage, N. Kornet and J.M. Smits
Volume 138: *The Nature of Mutual Recognition in European Law.* W. van Ballegooij
Volume 139: *Evidence in Contemporary Civil Procedure. Fundamental Issues in a Comparative Perspective*, C.H. van Rhee and A. Uzelac (eds.)
Volume 140: *The effect of D&O insurance on managerial risk taking*, Max Gaber
Volume 141: *Information and Notification Duties*, Ilse Samoy and Marco B. Loos
Volume 142: *The Application of the Theory of Efficient Breach in Contract Law. A Comparative Law and Economics Perspective*, Wenqing Liao

www.ingramcontent.com/pod-product-compliance
Ingram Content Group UK Ltd.
Pitfield, Milton Keynes, MK11 3LW, UK
UKHW051927100926
8556IPUK00022B/1406

9 781780 683553